First published 2023
by The Musical Times Publications Limited
22 Gibson Square, London N1 0RD

Second impression, with minor corrections, 2026

Printed in Great Britain by
The Print Centre, Berkhamsted, Herts.

ISBN 978-0-9545777-3-5

PETER PHILLIPS

THE BLUE FRENCH

AUTHOR'S NOTE TO THE SECOND (2026) IMPRESSION

The most trenchant comment about the first impression (2023) of this book came from a distinguished novelist, who wished I had told more about what my characters did when they finally got to their respective bedrooms. Apparently, this reticence indicated that I was an inexperienced writer. I replied that I did not have the words for it. Love, and even desire, I can do, but not actual sex. So I must report that this printing is, apart from minor corrections, exactly the same as the first.

CONTENTS

Chapters	1	TUESDAY, 4 JUNE 2019	11
	2	WEDNESDAY, 5 JUNE 2019	63
	3	THURSDAY, 6 JUNE 2019	109
	4	FRIDAY, 7 JUNE 2019	151
	5	SATURDAY, 8 JUNE 2019	201

AUTHOR'S NOTE

Although this story is based on a real event, and much of it revolves around the daily experiences of The Tallis Scholars on tour, only two of the characters described here – Anton and Lotte – come close to representing living people. All the others have either been invented from scratch or have been put together piecemeal.

I am indebted to François Truffaut's *La Nuit Américaine*, John Steinbeck's *Cannery Row* and *Tortilla Flat*, Tony Leung Ka-fai's *Midnight Diner*, and Evelyn Waugh's society novels for inspiration.

I would like to thank Madeleine Collinge, Caroline Trevor, Harriet Pilcher, Jane Armstrong, Benjamin Sullivan, Fátima Mendes and Gazimba Simão for help in bringing the book to publication.

DRAMATIS PERSONAE

The staff and habitués of The Blue French restaurant

Ahmed, *owner and head waiter*

Eugene, *waiter*

Bob and Sally Gallagher, *regular diners*

Elderly Mrs Pritchard, *the same*

Those associated with The Gamut Range and The Regis Quartet

Anton Wellbrooke and Lotte Bailey, *husband and wife, respectively director and erstwhile contralto*

Caduta Massi, *a Sicilian soprano, living in London*

Joe Farrant, *student conductor*

Chrissy Peacock, Robin West, Fran Moody, Angela *sopranos*

Jonathan Williams, Nancy Silver, Judith Brook *altos*

Alastair White *tenor*

Stewart Hammond, Ben Causton, Fred II *basses*

(Other singers unnamed)

Those associated with Voces Civitatis

Steve Taylor, *entrepreneurial conductor of amateur choirs, also responsible for the Whyte Chorale*

Jeremy Cartright, *apparently a sober buffoon*

Christy Benningham, *secretary to the group and soprano*

Singers introduced to Joe by Christy: Jim Pistols, Fred Fellony, Alan Coppice, Oliver Moth-Comet, Jane Spring, Kathy Whitener, Alex Stout, Terri Thomas, Nicola Roebuck, Dave Acolyte, Vinny Coste, Malcolm Sargent

Becky Cavanagh, *youthful contralto, and her family*

Caius ffrench Beytagh, *hanger-on*

Bob Parsons, *singer and Inspector of public safety*
Martin Clark, *singer and businessman*

Those associated with The Whyte Chorale

Brian Wiggins, *fan of The Gamut Range*
Polly, *a member of the Chorale*
Johnny Tissot, *rehearsal pianist*
Darren and Penny, *Highbury's representatives*
Jeff, *photographer*

Those associated with the BBC

Barbara Prentice, *interviewer*
Rustin Samson, *producer*
Three unnamed technicians

Other players

Tom Morris, *academic*
Francis Quirk, *critic*
Araminta Flatt, *formerly a soprano*
Leonid Moudrich, *Russian bass*
Divieto di Sosta, *friend of Caduta's*
Passo Carrabile, *friend of Caduta's*
Claudia, *waitress in Cremona*

There are two ways to convene a vocal ensemble: you pay the singers, or they pay you.

Chapter 1

TUESDAY, 4 JUNE 2019

AHMED stood in the doorway of the restaurant, looking up Tippett Avenue. It was a long street, bordered by tall houses built in the 1830s, with lines of perspective running as far as the eye could see, which pleased him. If he looked all the way to the end these lines would slope gently up from the pavement, and down from the roof tops, until, apparently, they almost met. At least the eye wanted them to meet. Ahmed had long wondered how such a thing could be rendered on paper, as a drawing, since he knew the lines were not in reality like that. This illusion had obsessed him for as long as he had been able to stand in that doorway, twelve years now. The obsession had extended to listening to his customers talking around the subject of how the music they performed was put together. He had heard them speak of lines.

In his restaurant, known universally as The Blue French, Ahmed's customers were essentially of two kinds: local people, often retired, looking for an inexpensive meal which carried an undemanding hint of the exotic; and musicians, mostly starting out on their careers, who had come to rehearse in a red-brick Victorian facility positioned opposite his street door, known as The Bunker. Surprisingly, since musicians love to gather, The Bunker lacked a canteen. Ahmed was soon found to be close at hand.

The previous day, a Monday and therefore usually quiet, Ahmed had been struck by the level of excited conversation generated by the musicians from over the road. Through overhearing this conversation both he and the clientele who lived locally had learned that there was to be a concert at the end of the week, in Marlowe Wharf, which would involve whole armies of singers, stretched to the limit of human competence and endurance, by daring to perform the most difficult piece of music ever written for voices – Thomas Tallis's 40-part motet *Spem in alium*. They learned from the hubbub that this piece was so demanding that performances, even at a professional level, were extremely rare; and that even the most highly-paid choirs were known to have broken down before reaching the end. They had further gathered that three choirs were to approach this colossus, rehearsing separately and together. These three choirs would include a professional ensemble, a noted amateur group based in the City, and a random selection of employees from a supermarket chain.

Ahmed had smiled and braced himself. He already knew many of the people who would surely pass through his door during such a week. Many were old customers of long standing, the longest probably Anton Wellbrooke and his wife Lotte Bailey, who lived just up the road and were bound to be taking a leading role in the promised concert. He smiled some more, acknowledging that his role would be to stay in the restaurant. He had never been to one of their concerts, nor even entered The Bunker, just endlessly heard about them. And that was enough.

The weather forecast was for a heat wave, tempered by storms. He knew that singing made people thirsty. It also made them noisy. His small hostelry was not ideally equipped to refresh large numbers of people all at once, but he relished the challenge nonetheless. He loved these musicians as if they were his children, as the ones who were regular visitors loved him. This was his world, precariously pieced together some years previously, about to go about its business.

The name of Ahmed's restaurant – The Blue French – was more of a nickname than a formal title, its component parts paying tribute both to the colour of the paint on the exterior woodwork and to the past orientation of its cuisine. There had been a restaurant of some kind in this building since the '60s, originally Italian, with the paintwork green, and then, in an attempt to go upmarket, French. The proper name which Ahmed had inherited was *Le Sacré Coeur*, but since he couldn't reliably pronounce or spell it he had immediately looked for something less difficult. He had welcomed the suggestion of 'The Blue French' from one of his customers early on, finding it agreeably easy-going, and changed the sign outside. He felt he could run a place with such a name and found he hadn't lost customers over it: no one minded the change, nor cared that the paint was no longer very blue nor the cuisine any longer very French. As it turned out, changing the interior decoration was more of an issue.

AHMED TURNED AWAY and surveyed the scene inside. Everything was familiar, from long experience. The seventeen tables, with their blue-and-white chequered oilcloth coverings, were disposed about the available space so that they could all seat four people without inconvenience, and yet be easily rearranged to facilitate larger gatherings. The far end of the room, furthest from the door where he was now standing, was given over to a miniscule kitchen, concealed from the diners by a flimsy partition and sporting a narrow entrance guarded by a hanging curtain of beads. And there, deep inside this constricted area, were the chefs, of indefinite number, busily scraping and chopping. No one ever saw these people; but it was apparent that they were there because whenever Ahmed called out an order the whole apparatus

– partition, curtain and surrounding masonry – would let out a hum which rose and fell as the cooking went forward. At busy times this hum would become a vibration, a hidden engine, felt at all the tables, bringing hope.

The intention of Ahmed's predecessors at the restaurant had been to evoke the ambience of a typical Parisian brasserie. To this end its walls were covered in posters, as was, unfortunately for Ahmed who liked to keep them up-to-date, the ceiling. Certainly this had not been his idea; but he had inherited the principle with the posters, originally a motley collection of advertisements for yesteryear spectaculars, and although his customers didn't mind if the name changed, he was surprised to find that they expected the ambience they were used to maintained. So once a year he would climb a step-ladder and scrape the current incumbents off, replacing them with new ones that he hoped he could bear to look at for the next twelve months.

He had also inherited, on the long interior wall of the restaurant, a set of framed prints of leading French chefs – Escoffier, Bocuse, Robuchon and Ducasse amongst others, fattened up and looking immensely pleased with themselves – no doubt originally placed there *pour encourager les autres*, but a further imposition on Ahmed, who was slim and wiry, and had never been formally trained in the finer ways of French cooking. He cared for this room, though, as he would have cared for a family if he had had one, watching over every tiny detail. He often repeated to himself the comment, made by Anton Wellbrooke, that this interior made one want to experience it in all weathers – warm inside with a blizzard raging against the windows; sitting at a table just inside, protected from driving, warm-weather rain; sitting half in shade, half outside in early-evening summer sunshine, cocktail in hand and not a cloud in the sky. It led him to think that a restaurant which a *bon vivant* such as Anton wanted to enter at any time, had passed the first and most basic test of welcome.

And Ahmed was indeed always unfailingly glad to see his customers, greeting them with an alert eye, a half-smile, the word 'welcome' on his lips, his hands resting on the waist-band of his scrupulously white apron, fingers splayed forwards, thumbs to the rear. This was his characteristic pose, the cut-out that all his clients instantly recognised, the caricature that did the rounds of the musicians in the rehearsal building on the other side of the street. At 45, Ahmed's compact, grizzled look lent itself well to caricature, his unfailing good nature somehow always implied. This stance created the best possible impression of the fare on offer.

It was true that he had not received any formal training as a chef. But as a boy in Jerusalem, where he had been born and spent his early years, he had had the good fortune to hang around the kitchen of his grandmother and absorb the traditions of Arabic cooking that went on there. At the time he hadn't seemed to pay any attention to the techniques on display, and his relatives didn't seem to take much notice of him, alongside his numerous siblings and cousins, but he soon needed no instruction in how best to prepare *ful* or *manakish*. When the time came for him to make a living he proved to be a natural.

When he took over The Blue French he was able to keep the French reference alive by playing on the history of neighbouring Lebanon, the country closest to his heart. He presented its Arabic-sounding dishes and French-sounding wines as an exercise in fusion. As time went by, however, and despite the sudden popularity of fusion cooking, he lost interest in the subterfuge. He had long specialised in making the simplest ingredients of his homeland varied and interesting: *fava* and *garbanzo* beans, different ways of making flatbread, how best to use the everyday herbs and spices of the countryside – cumin, za'atar, sumac, oregano; and eventually decided to keep to that.

As a result his *mezze* soon became as widely famed as his knowledge of Lebanese wines, though with these he could make use of the French reference without subterfuge, since the French had set up the leading vineyards in the first place – Chateaux Musar, Kefraya, Ksara, with their ever-increasing spin-offs and imitators. His choice of every-day drinking from these vineyards – Hochar from Musar, Reserve du Couvent from Ksara and Blanc de Blancs from Kefraya – became so renowned in diplomatic circles that early in his time in London he was made a Knight of the Order of the Cedar (fifth grade) *in absentia*. At that time his personal story – why he was in London at all - was still unknown; and he was not the type to encourage confidences. He was the type who said little, observed a lot, and gave the impression, just by the way he stood, of being sympathetic. His English was not perfect, but the things in it that were imperfect, and the accent he delivered these imperfections in, were well received.

He reflected how lucky he was that the two elements in his clientele – locals and musicians – had come together in a mutually sustainable pact: food and drink would be served to the musicians breaking between sessions as needed, so he didn't close mid-afternoon, while these snacks were of sufficient pedigree to act as starters for the more expensive needs of his general public. In fact the two groups came to support each other very willingly. The people of the area, most of them looking back on lives spent sitting in offices, were well programmed to want to rub shoulders with artists of any description; and the musicians didn't mind a little attention, which on occasion could lead to extra audience members at their concerts. Under Ahmed's benign regime new connections were made.

As midday came and went, Ahmed turned back to the street, wondering who would be his first customers. It was his boast that The Blue French was open 'twelve to twelve', a precise schedule he found easy to keep since he lived upstairs, above it. As he waited he thought further about what he had overheard the previous day. There were to be several overlapping rehearsals to the end of the week in The Bunker, involving amateur singers as well as professional ones, a congress which tended to intensify the atmosphere around his tables, and not always in the most fluent way. He had learnt that, although they always showed instinctive respect for each other, most things in the reactions of these singers were at variance, at least when they were in their social groups: culinary and alcoholic needs, expectations of what a rehearsal should consist of, whether to talk about music at all. Someone from outside the world of English ensemble singing might have supposed that there wouldn't be much to set these two categories of musicians apart. Experience had told Ahmed otherwise.

Finally he observed three people approaching, dressed for the warm weather, proceeding slowly. These were Joe Farrant, a student conductor known, inaccurately, to everyone as 'the intern', who was slated to help out wherever he might be needed with the choirs about to descend; and Bob and Sally Gallagher, elderly habitués from a few doors away. They spotted Joe and Ahmed at the same moment.

'Fancy seeing you here, hohoho', Bob called out indiscriminately.

'Welcome', said Ahmed, hands resting on his hips above his white apron, conveying a kind of approachable strength.

They entered the restaurant and sat down at separate tables, close to each other. None of them consulted the menu, but ordered from memory. 'Oh, Ahmed, I'm on at one. I'd love a bowl of *baba ganoush* and some olives?' said Joe.

'Coming up', said Ahmed, a phrase he had learnt early on, delivered with a flourish. He conveyed the order to the kitchen and waited for the Gallaghers.

'That delicious *siyadieh* I had the other day', Bob said proudly. '*Tabbouleh* for me,' said Sally, 'and two glasses of Blanc de Blancs.'

'What are you doing at one? Bob asked Joe.

'Well, I'm sort of sitting in on a rehearsal for the concert on Saturday?' said Joe, who was in the habit of watching Australian sitcoms online and had adopted their speech patterns without noticing. 'It's part of my conducting course at the Academy, but anyway I help putting the music out, sometimes giving notes on the piano, sometimes even singing when a part is missing. Getting to know everyone.'

'Aha. What sort of concert is it?'

'It's a kind of choral concert, all of choral music, in one of the old wharf buildings down in Deptford. Not a million miles from the Greenwich Observatory. Marlowe Wharf. You should come?'

'Who is taking part?' asked Sally.

'It's going to be a real mix – the famous professional ensemble, The Gamut Range; the not so famous amateur choir, Voces Civitatis; and the more-genuinely-community choir, called The Whyte Chorale, based round here, so there is local interest; and some others whose names I can't remember. Every group gets to do a slot. And then they all come together at the end to sing a really special piece by Tallis.' He rushed on with unstoppable enthusiasm. 'The problem will be whether the amateurs will be able to sing alongside the professionals and make this piece work, and whether we will have enough time this week to rehearse it? It's going to be like one of those action movies where you don't know until the last second whether it's all worked out', he finished, wide-eyed.

Sally thought for a moment, resisting the eyes and the rush. 'Did you say one of the groups was a local choir called the white something?'

'Yes', said Joe, very quickly.

'Is that an entirely appropriate name for a community activity these days?'

Joe looked away. 'Whyte is usually spelt with a "y"?' he offered. 'At least it was in the Tudor period', he added, squeezing out a laugh.

'So is lynch,' said Sally, sniffing. 'Whose clever idea was that?'

'Named after the Tudor composer Robert Whyte?' Joe went on. 'It was Steve's idea, the founder and conductor.'

Sally decided to let it go. 'Will they sing some of this composer?'

'To be honest with you, I hope not,' said Joe, 'his music is rather difficult.' But before he could explain further there was a brief commotion at the door, and Steve himself walked in.

'Welcome', said Ahmed, 'I suppose you also must leave at one? What would you like?'

'Is that tower of decimated aubergine, bits of courgette, pepper of uncertain colour and halloumi, drowned in olive oil speedily available?' he asked, reinterpreting an item on the menu with an ironical flourish. 'And a mug of your most fragrant tea? A bloke requires taste with practicality before going to work', and he flipped a smile about the room.

'Coming up', said Ahmed, maintaining a level tone.

Steve Taylor was also slated to play a part in the concert at the end of the week, though his part was bound to be more essential than Joe's, since he was the stand-by rehearser of both The Gamut

Range and Voces Civitatis, as well as the founder and sustainer of The Whyte Chorale. His expertise and reliably friendly manner to amateur singers, no matter how uncertain they might be, or unsatisfactory the results they might deliver, had made him an invaluable co-worker in situations like these.

He sat down easily at Joe's table. 'Well, young Joe', he said, 'what are we up to this afternoon?' the word 'afternoon' losing some of its consonants.

'I'm putting out the music and chairs for your rehearsal this evening, and you're thanking me by taking me through *Spem in alium*?'

'Ah, and why have we arrived here hours before the off with the singers?' he asked, though he knew the answer.

'Because we are going down to the library to do some sorting? And the librarian is going to meet us there at 2.30?'

Steve enjoyed talking to Joe. He was a fresh-faced lad, well-spoken and polite, yet clearly from the kind of background that put Steve at his ease. Joe's enthusiasm for every type of choral music was without irony, his excitable pronouncements striking the ear differently from the warier endorsements which tended to come out of the full-time members of the profession. He was also useful about the place, able to help with the manual stuff, but also to think ahead about practical rehearsal problems and ask the right questions of the management. As a talented conducting student he could help out in this department too, though he was careful never to over-press his claims.

Ahmed reappeared bearing plates and cups, and set them down.

'If you don't mind my asking, what happens when you are taken through that Latin-sounding thingy?' asked Bob genially from the next-door table.

'Well you see, in Saturday's concert I shall have to play the keyboard for one of the choirs, which is a monster mouthful of notes,' Joe giggled at the concept. 'There are so many voices that I need help in deciding which ones to bring out? I know Steve has done this a million times, and knows the pitfalls.'

'The real problem, sport,' said Steve firmly, wishing Joe had identified a less cloying speech-pattern, 'is that Tallis wrote the music in separate parts. This means that some poor modern bugger has had to collate them all, and produce a piano reduction. Since this is basically an impossible task, this someone has to decide what to leave out. But,' he added, letting irritation at all the elementary misunderstandings and stupidities lying scattered about this path, which other "experts" had failed to grasp, get the better of him, 'this being speculative, you as accompanist are going to have to be part of the process of collation.'

'Is that what you call interpretation?' asked Sally, sensing that the detail on offer was about to become too specific for her in the context of her *tabbouleh* salad.

'Not exactly, but,' said Joe, carefully broadening the topic, 'you can never exactly predict, when amateur singers sit down, tired but keen to do some singing, what answers they will demand of the guy out front, in a split second, right off the bat. They actually need to be told everything, yet they need to be told it in a way which shows they knew it, really, all along. The conductor's job is to reassure them. With amateurs like those in Voces Civitatis, who spend their professional lives 24/7 being super-confident know-alls, this is a very delicate balance to strike. With the Whyte Chorale the dynamic is bound to be a bit different.' Steve looked at Joe, wondering how one so young could possibly know so much about his job. Joe returned his respectful gaze and laughed. 'I have been watching you, you know.' They laughed together.

'Ah', said Sally, who felt she and her husband had delved deeply enough for one encounter; and the two tables fell quiet. Steve and

Joe ate their meals, soon taking themselves off to The Bunker, to prepare one of the rehearsal rooms and to wield a pencil over Tallis's giant score.

Ahmed had kept a watchful eye on Joe and Steve's table, aware that they were going to bear the brunt of whatever would transpire later that afternoon and evening in The Bunker. He wondered if Mr Wellbrooke would join them. More pressingly he looked about for his wayward server, Eugene, who was due to start work at midday, but never did. However, despite being unreliable, Eugene was a fixture at The Blue French, a figure of mystery to everyone who knew him, even of fascination.

To distract himself from his anxiety, and for the umpteenth time, Ahmed rehearsed in his mind what he imagined his customers might think of Eugene, testing the fabric of his reasoning as if to find the holes which would reveal that his helper was actively putting people off. On the plus side he didn't think anyone minded that Eugene's origins were as uncertain and as unspecified as his own. Nor that, although Eugene actually said very little, what he did say came over in a strange and unplaceable accent. They were both effectively in the same position. For all he knew the customers found it charming that Eugene's English seemed so vulnerable they often hastened to fill in with the right word, though if they had just waited a second longer they would have discovered this was unnecessary.

But then it was unclear what Eugene's mother tongue really was. The only language, apart from English, he was asked to speak in public was French. Ahmed had asked him repeatedly to drop in the odd French tag to maintain the original pretence of his restaurant, but Eugene's 'Bonn hap-titt' was so rank that Ahmed came to think it would be best to discontinue the effort, given that some of his customers could do a lot better themselves, and no one cared. This failure was held to have put an end to any further pretence that this was a French establishment. Eugene didn't speak Arabic, as Ahmed did. All that anyone ever noticed was that when Italian could be heard he became uncharacteristically alert, hanging around the table in question, pretending not to be there, listening. This was the only clue anyone had ever had as to his background. Ahmed's thoughts were interrupted by a group of musicians who had entered the restaurant and were disposing themselves around several of the tables.

Not long after he had taken their order, and more with relief than irritation, Ahmed finally saw Eugene rounding the corner. He was intrigued to see a group of young female singers walking a careful distance behind him, talking in lowered voices.

'It beats me why Ahmed keeps him on,' said a young alto named Nancy Silver. 'He seems disinclined to do anything much, like clearing plates away, or setting tables. You'd have thought Ahmed would want that done, at least.'

'He is quite decorative,' said Robin West, a soprano. 'Perhaps Ahmed appreciates this', a remark followed by suppressed laughter.

'They can hardly be lovers,' said Judith Brook, another alto. 'Ahmed seems a very private person to me. Almost sexless.'

'Perhaps he's a love-child', said Nancy, looking at her fellow singers for corroboration, eyes brimming.

'Of course he isn't,' replied Judith. 'Are you blind? Eugene has damask skin, blue eyes, a head topped with prematurely white hair, and a face as smooth as alabaster, unlined by hard work, exposure to the sun or anything else that might distort its pleasing impact. Ahmed has dark skin, brown eyes, close-cropped brown hair and a face well-lined by hard work. Go figure.'

Stung by this summary rejection of her prurience, Nancy made a dismissive noise with her tongue and led the group into the restaurant, where they joined their colleagues already installed; and Eugene did his best to vanish. Nonetheless the question of his origins was kept open. They recognised that despite his insouciance, he was popular with them and the clientele. They liked the way his manner beckoned more than it teased or repelled, drawing people towards him with few words. If a customer wanted him to do something, he would monitor the need with a little pout, shimmy between the tables, look away, and say 'yes?' This monosyllable was always delivered in the same off-hand style, yet it rarely provoked a hostile reaction. He had somehow charmed the regulars, who were careful never to repeat the error of a recent new-comer who, on failing to receive total server satisfaction, said in a loud voice: 'Why don't you pull your fucking finger out?' It was never forgotten how Eugene stood to his full not inconsiderable height, as frail as a bean-pole, and quavered 'because I've never been given the opportunity to stick it in', at which he wiped his beautiful eyes, averted his gaze, and shimmied away again. He was consoled by every sentient person in the room, leaving the boor to reflect on his manners.

In fact the incident had a happy ending. The transgressor, who turned out to be a leading music critic for a major broadsheet, was taken aside by Ahmed and asked if there was anything he could do to make amends for the unsatisfactory service. This man, who had begun to notice that the room was full of musicians he might do well to get along with, had become emollient and apologised unreservedly. Having passed the initiation test the hard way, he came to feel as much at home between those four walls as any of its easier-going visitors, and returned often. Eugene treated him in exactly the same way as he had done the first time, careful not to smile.

BY 1.30 AHMED'S DOMAIN not only contained Eugene, but was dotted about with musicians, coming in to rehearse for a variety of different engagements with different types of accompaniment. Most were singers rather than instrumentalists, since the social scene with the players was more diffuse and more international, making it less likely that they would come together in the same local hostelry. It was astonishing, on the other hand, how the singers all knew each other – from being child choristers together, from school, from being choral scholars in the Oxford and Cambridge chapel choirs and lay clerks in the cathedrals, from social contacts which multiplied like something contagious.

And it was well recognised that this social cohesion helped the disciplines of small ensemble singing. They were like a small army unit, drilled in the same basic procedures and expectations from a very young age in many cases, using identical terms, the same nods to tradition and the same lingual jokes – not just the same language, but the same argot within it. This familiarity made it possible for British groups to function more quickly, more expertly and in a sense more ruthlessly when the chips were down, than their multinational competitors on the continent. The classic situation, often referenced, was a live television job, on the other side of the world, on the day of arrival after countless hours of flying, of music that had only been sung through once in prior rehearsal. It wasn't just a question of how good a voice you had. Pride works in diverse ways. Pride would prevent a serious-minded non-British singer from compromising his or her art by getting in front of a camera in unpropitious circumstances; a British singer lives for those challenges, and expects to meet them.

Ahmed was used to weekday lunches like this one. When the singers were preparing for work which would tax them, as now, they would eat together or apart, as convenience rather than socialising dictated, sober and self-contained. Only the regular members of the public who happened to be there might jolt the atmosphere. On this Tuesday, unfortunately, one of the members of the public was Araminta Flatt, a noisy woman who had done some singing 'in her day', and loved to chat to her 'progeny'. She had never sung prominently enough for any evidence of it to be current, but to judge from the number of stories she had of famous practitioners she had known personally, she had certainly done the rounds. She was well known to everybody, even accepted, later in the day, for her good stories. But at lunchtime she was anathema.

'Oh hello,' she said, espying a well-established soprano, called Chrissy Peacock, and settling herself down at her table 'My dear, what are you in for today?'

It was one of those unspoken codes of conduct that singers of Chrissy's type would never say 'Would you mind most awfully – I'm preparing for a rather taxing afternoon?' Or even, if such circumlocution might be in danger of missing the mark, a more demotic 'Oh do piss off, I'm trying to prepare myself.' Singers of Chrissy's type were unalterably modest in manner to outsiders. So it was that confrontation was avoided, and a conversation of sorts went forward.

'Oh hello Araminta,' said Chrissy, eyeing her hand-made *manakish*. 'Two things for me this afternoon: Haydn's "Nelson" Mass, for Thursday next week in the Barbican. I've been literally called in to deck out the orchestral rehearsal – the conductor is young and nervous, poor thing. And then a note-bashing session with The Regis Quartet. I fear this may be a rather gruelling...'

'Oh, lucky old you. Such wonderful music in front of you this afternoon, as no doubt every afternoon.' A sigh and a pause alerted

Chrissy to what was likely to follow. 'I must have told you of the time in '62 when I had to step up and sing the big solo in the "Nelson" Mass? We were recording it for Argo in King's Chapel – Sir David was conducting, though Sir Neville was there to do the concert preview. I was barely 20 years old, but still the leading soprano in the chorus – just a handful of us, very few for the standards of those days, and Sylvia Stahlman – you know the American soprano who tried to trick her way onto the Italian stage by calling herself Giulia Bardi – pulled up lame right that very afternoon. No, wait a minute, wasn't it April Cantelope, who we used to all Capril Antelope (haha)? No, that must have been on the "Creation" Mass recording, when darling Bob was singing, and something similar happened – I'll tell you in a moment. No, it must have been the *soi-disant* Bardi: I can hear her dixieland inflections in the Latin to this day – she came from Nashville you know. Anyway she started coughing and generally acting up, at which Sir David, rubbing his cheek in a gesture we all found adorable, looked at us and said would anyone like to stand in. It was all quite informal and friendly really. Naturally, being the youngest and, how can I put it, freshest of the sopranos there, I was pushed forward by my colleagues – I would never have dared to suggest such a thing myself – and duly sang the aria with the London Symphony Orchestra as my accompaniment. Sir David was enraptured; and Sir Neville came running up and said I must do it in the concert later that day, since the Bardi would never be well enough. So I did. I remember the dress...'

'Did you do the recording as well?' asked Chrissy, wondering how to escape.

'Very nearly, sweetheart. But by the next day, which was the recording day, Sylvia had disposed of her cough sufficiently for the niceties to be observed, though everyone expressed regret that such a young talent as mine would not yet have the platform it deserved. But wonderful things came from this once-in-a-lifetime chance. I was going to tell you about how Bob Tear...'

A gentle redistribution of the phlegm in Ahmed's throat – an activity in which he was linguistically expert – positioned nearby, caused a diversion. 'Excuse me, Madame Flatt, but Mr Quirk just heard you speak of someone he said was a famous soprano, and asked me if you would mind telling him more. He says he is working on a survey of operas for the BBC radio, and is sure that personal memories from you would help him very much to go forward.'

Francis Quirk, the critic who had previously been brusque with Eugene, was now confident enough of his rehabilitation in The Blue French to ask Ahmed for little favours. In the wider world he was anyway respected. In late middle-age he was a member of the small and dwindling band of classical music reviewers who were admired for sticking to their guns and only reviewing 'elitist' endeavours. His appearance, which detractors called oxymoronic, suggested he wanted to keep in touch with both the old and the young, an understandable policy for someone who wrote across the classical board. The lower half of him was clearly designed to appeal to the more traditional among his readers – hand-made shoes and flannel trousers of scrupulous cut, from the old-established shops on the High Street in Oxford. His upper half, with diminishing coherence, moved through a floppy jacket and tee-shirt to a scrubby beard topped by a baseball cap. It was not surprising that people looked at him twice before speaking, a caution that he welcomed.

He had noticed the trial which Chrissy was undergoing, and had caught Ahmed's receptive eye. In an undertone they had hit upon a course of action, which doubly pleased Mr Quirk. He could enter an inner sanctum; and he could find out from an eye witness what La Stahlman had really been like. And he was a beginner with Araminta's stories. Araminta made her apologies to Chrissy, and was swiftly repositioned by Ahmed at Francis's table.

Gingerly at first, Chrissy looked about her. Her eyes focused on a table on the other side of the restaurant, where three singers she knew well were smiling at her and beckoning. These were the other members of The Regis Quartet – a countertenor, tenor and bass – stocking up before attending the rehearsal Chrissy had outlined to Araminta Flatt. Managing her facial expression with care, Chrissy took up her food – Eugene arriving just too late to help her – and joined them. Two coffees and two teas were procured. Two plates of *baklava* and *meghli* were also ordered, since the countertenor and tenor would have to wait while Chrissy and Stewart, the bass, went over the road to rehearse their arias. The other two were not needed for the Haydn, but had come in early to discuss tactics for the future of their group, which had only just formed.

The rationale behind the founding of The Regis Quartet was to sing medieval polyphony, as opposed to renaissance, with the upcoming concert in Marlowe Wharf on Saturday as the opportunity to launch it. While they would all inevitably be caught up in the performance of *Spem in alium*, the event had also been planned as a showcase, in which different groups could choose their repertoires and have a slot to themselves before the Tallis. It was assumed that there would be plenty of music from the Renaissance period in the concert, so a little medieval music was welcomed by the organisers; and once Chrissy had agreed to become in effect the lead singer, the debut of this ensemble seemed set fair. She duly invited three other singers, all friends not at all averse to a little more exposure, and all in their first year as professional singers, having just graduated. In addition to herself (who preferred the lower end of the accepted soprano spectrum), there was Stewart Hammond, a bass of impressive height and build who also specialised in lower notes; Jonathan Williams, a high countertenor with fragile nerves; and Alastair White, a tenor, known for his hours-long visits to the gym and running marathons. When he wasn't monitoring his appearance in something reflective he might be heard insisting that he, too, preferred the lower notes of the customary tenor range. Jonathan, by contrast, had no low notes at all, able to sing soprano with greater ease than traditional alto.

'What are we going to sing on Saturday that will show us off in the best light?' asked Chrissy, looking round at her colleagues for some kind of consensus, aware that the line-up of voices she had sanctioned for the group was not entirely suited to the repertoire she had also sanctioned.

'Well, we've named ourselves like after Regis, perhaps we should introduce ourselves to the world by singing some of his music', said Stewart.

'Do you know any?' asked Alastair, instinctively feeling his biceps while adopting a no-nonsense tone of voice.

'No,' replied Stewart, 'but Chrissy seemed sure it would like suit us, and that it's worth doing, didn't you, Chrissy?'

'Yes,' she replied cautiously. 'Just in case, I've brought a set of copies along of his *Salve sponsa*, so you can see what you think – it says on the tin that it is scored just right for us – soprano, alto, tenor, bass. I'll leave two copies for you to look over while we go and sing some Haydn. See you over there in 45?' And with that she and Stewart left for The Bunker.

BY 4PM THE CUSTOMARY afternoon torpor had set in at The Blue French, a change-over time when the regular customers at lunch had paid up and gone home, leaving the tables to the musicians as they came and went from rehearsal. It was a hot day outside, the shutters to the main street were drawn back, and Eugene had disappeared again. Jonathan and Alastair had left to join the other two in The Bunker. Nonetheless Ahmed knew he couldn't go upstairs to his flat, much as he longed to, because he offered food through the afternoon and prided himself on adapting to the needs of itinerant musicians, as long as this was between 'twelve and twelve'. He realised that what some of them also wanted was an all-night service, for when they had landed at Heathrow late, after a day of travel back from a gig the previous evening, caught the last tube, were hungry, didn't feel like going to bed yet, and were prepared to float home at the end of it all. But he drew the line at this. He had had experience of 24-hour restaurants, when no one came in at four in the morning except down-and-outs, or at best people with early flights, disinclined to pay for a short night in a hotel and looking for somewhere to doss. All they wanted was a cup of coffee, as cheap as possible. Anyway he wasn't prepared to do the cooking, should anyone actually want a meal, nor were any of the kitchen staff. He couldn't pay them enough, and he wouldn't earn much from the passing trade. He did feel the romance of having a meal at 2am, and of giving clients the opportunity to walk slowly home, tired but happy. But 12 hours on his feet was enough.

He resisted the lure of a chair, and waited. Two elderly smokers were standing outside the door, deep in conversation. Eventually the four members of The Regis Quartet could be seen leaving The Bunker, looking sweaty and dissatisfied. They greeted Ahmed and sat down heavily. 'Welcome,' said Ahmed with his characteristic half-smile, 'what would you like?' Iced lemonade was ordered all round.

'Oh Ahmed,' said Jonathan 'you have no idea what we've just been through. How on earth are we supposed to sing THAT?' Jonathan pointed at the copy he was carrying. 'It wanders on, has no shape, no sonority. The parts are written out in the wrong clefs, and the bass has a different key signature from the other voices. And anyway I can only sing one note in ten. I ought to be singing Chrissy's part.' His strong features went flabby as he pouted.

Jonathan had long had a problem with his vocal range, for all that it was perfectly employable in the right context. This was an issue associated with deciding to sing falsetto in the first place. He was a well-built man, not as tall as Stewart but bearded and thickly haired, with an imposing stage presence. Such a figure, flipping and looping around the highest notes it is possible for an uncastrated male to sing had been known to raise some eyebrows to the point of ridicule on the faces of his listeners in the audience. Jonathan was sensitive to this reaction and, if sufficiently provoked, could start to malfunction. His secret weapon was the gear change every falsettist has between their head-voice and their chest-voice, which in his case was pronounced and, if the spirit took him, could be exaggerated. He would fix the smirkers with a steady stare, swoop down from his soprano-range coloratura to hit the change full-force, emitting noises likened to *Concorde* going through the sound-barrier; after which, like *Concorde* and with the sweetest expression, he would fly skywards again, resuming his role of caresser and seducer, as if nothing had happened.

'At least my part needs to be written out in the right clef for a tenor,' said Alastair, testily. 'I'm not a bloody baritone. And I refuse to transpose from these copies', he added, fearing one of the others would try to solve their problems by demanding a different pitch, less convenient for him.

Ahmed gave them a shrewd look. They were young. They were starting out. He wanted to give them good, fatherly advice.

'Well, I'm not expert, sure, but there is much beautiful music. Do you have to sing this piece?'

'Well, Chrissy?' said Jonathan.

Chrissy nodded wearily. She realised she had made a mistake in choosing an alto who effectively had the same range as her; and she had made a mistake in choosing the kind of music which only ever has one, low top part, with a clutch of lower parts beneath it. The alto needed to join the clutch, not sing soprano. She had taken the requests of the organisers of the Saturday concert too literally, and got carried away on too little information. Few people knew about the minutiae of medieval music, and Chrissy wasn't one of the few. However she knew enough to know that if Regis's music was like this, there would be plenty more like it from his coevals – maybe it was all like this. She thought it very unlikely she was going to find one single piece with two equal-range top parts. She was beginning to think that renaissance polyphony, after all, would be their only hope. They would need a new name. The nod was followed by a deep sigh.

At this juncture, and fortuitously in a way, Tom Morris walked through the door. At 44 he was an academic who had travelled a bit, everywhere admired for his quick mind. His modest tweed jacket, college tie and sleeveless knitwear cardigan had a habit of making a good impression in places where he was a stranger, which, surprisingly given how many of the regulars he knew there, had until recently included Ahmed's restaurant. There was a skip in his step today and, on catching sight of Ahmed he decided to take a punt, greeting him in time-honoured fashion with '*as-salam ealaykum*'. Ahmed, beaming from ear to ear, immediately replied '*ealaykum as-salam*'. However, not yet a regular, Tom parried the question of what to order and skimmed the proffered menu. Having grasped it in a few seconds he ordered a plate of *ful medames.* He immediately recognised the singers sitting further into the room, two of whom he knew well, having examined them for their degrees at UCL. By profession, however, he was an academic, much resorted to at times of crisis, a man of such steady and reliable judgement that people referred to him as god. Weeks later Ahmed, who by then had got to know him, would put a characteristic finger on it, observing that Tom 'knew many things, but knew them gently'.

He walked over to the singers' table.

'I suppose I don't need to ask what you are all doing here', he said.

'What on earth are you doing here? This isn't one of your usual haunts, is it?' asked Alastair.

'I've been summoned, you know, to adjudicate at the *Spem* rehearsal this evening.'

'Good Lord, I knew there were like several groups taking part, but I didn't realise it would be a competition. Anyway how does one group outdo another in *Spem*?', asked Stewart, absent-mindedly vocalising a bottom something.

'Ah no. I'm expected to pontificate on the notes themselves. And in The Gamut Range rehearsal as well, not only in *Spem*. Apparently they are using some dodgy editions of music by Byrd. I have the printed sources lined up on my laptop here in case of doubt.' He patted his shoulder-bag and paused, sensing the air of crisis. He noticed the copies which the singers had brought back from their rehearsal, lying on the table.

'What's that?' he asked, 'It looks a bit of a mess.' He became aware that four young, fragile egos were laid out on the table with the copies, before him. Chrissy explained the problem.

'So, you want a piece of medieval music that has two high top parts, one lowish tenor part, and one Russian-style bass part?' They nodded in unison. 'Someone is going to have to write it for you,' he chuckled, 'because you sure aren't going to find anything, you know, from the period. How far have you got with it?' he continued. 'Let me see.' Chrissy offered her copy for inspection.

'Johannes Regis,' said Tom. '*Salve sponsa tui genitrix*. Where did you find it?'

'Literally in the Complete Edition of Regis,' said Chrissy. 'We were asked to do some medieval music and I thought I would take a risk, with a composer I'd actually heard of, God help me.'

'Ah. I fear you could have chosen better, though nothing is going to solve your immediate problem of the voice ranges. One issue here is that there's a voice-part missing. This was a five-part piece, which surely must have been unknown to the scholars who put this volume together, or they would never have published it like this, you know. So many pitfalls in this repertoire! It is remarkable how much this music was behind Renaissance music in development, and how quickly things changed after 1500. I'm not sure what to advise you to do. I'll give it some thought.'

NOT TOO MANY MINUTES LATER the bustle of the evening began to be felt, as several ensembles collected to prepare for the concert on the coming Saturday. While the two amateur ensembles would need to focus all their attention on the parts assigned them in *Spem in alium* – and the more practice they had at this the better – the members of The Gamut Range wouldn't look at the scores for another three days if they could possibly help it. Unfortunately for them they couldn't help it. Assembling now to rehearse a different programme, they would be obliged to join the others towards 10pm for a complete run-through of the big Tallis.

Ahmed, who was following this ebb and flow for the umpteenth time, reflected that the dramatic difference in necessary rehearsal time for the different groups was one of the tell-tale signs that distinguished the amateur world from the professional. He had also noticed how variously the call-time of 7pm was interpreted by the many singers taking part. He knew that the out-and-out professionals would not only all be in the rehearsal room by 6.55pm, but that they would all have left his restaurant some time before that. With the local society choir – Voces Civitatis – he knew that a start-time was a more speculative statement, one that Steve Taylor would insist on time and again, but which never quite galvanised the singers as was hoped. Counter-intuitively the more Steve said it, the vaguer became the response, as if the responsibility had been taken on the chin at the moment of delivery, somehow creating more wiggle-room thereafter.

However Ahmed knew that although the professionals always started on time, they also always finished on time, or if possible early. He knew this because his restaurant would then suddenly fill with them, as regular as clockwork. With The Gamut Range he would expect to welcome the whole ensemble with very few absentees, members whose last thought or desire was to sing one note more than they had to. The amateurs, on the other hand, once finally gathered together, would be quite happy to carry on past the official finishing time, assuming they didn't have other responsibilities at home; indeed most of them simply wanted to keep singing, easily able to continue for another half an hour and more. These singers would never repair to the restaurant before the stipulated finishing time. And when they did it wasn't the whole group.

Nonetheless this was how Ahmed liked it, a restaurant full of singers, their work done for the day. It was true that the different groups kept to themselves, rarely intermingling, but even if they said nothing to each other, there was a palpable sense of fellow-feeling and respect. Ahmed was fascinated how this was possible when everyone seemed too shy to approach those they didn't know and introduce themselves, but he recognised it was part of the territory, being British and being a singer. Even talking about music seemed to be frowned upon by some, where in other places it might have brought performers closer together.

This was what he could look forward to on this Tuesday evening. And he did look forward to it – the personalities, the conversations, old customers and new, brought together under his auspices with music and hospitality as the common factors. Even the non-musicians who were his regular customers were there for the musical ambience, their numbers gently increasing month by month and year by year, as it became known they could join this rather exclusive club.

The only person who seemed not to relish all this was Eugene, not obviously unhappy, but aloof. He didn't seem to care what people thought of him, yet perhaps it was this very reason, and for something vulnerable in his expression, that made him sympathetic. Robin West, the soprano who had found him decorative, was not alone in this opinion, though she now felt embarrassed at having expressed it. Blessed with a quiet manner, big eyes and a high vocal range, she rarely allowed herself to make an outstanding remark. She seemed timid, a result of being the youngest of a large Catholic family. Underneath, however, there was evidence of a core of steel, having got herself to London without any money behind her, where she quickly established herself in the bear-pit of the London professional singers' market. Nonetheless her upbringing with eleven older siblings had taught her to be cautious in all sorts of ways, not least when entering a room. She would still approach a door hesitantly, gauging the atmosphere on the other side, before sliding into the room as unobtrusively as possible, hoping not to be noticed. She had trouble saying anything which would draw attention to her, always introducing her answers to direct questions with phrases like 'provided that' or 'as long as'. If pressed on a topic she would habitually start with 'What worries me about this is...' and never with 'What thrills me is...' Yet, when it came to singing, she was the most unflappable and reliable colleague anyone could think of singing next to, the very definition of professional, and exceptionally popular with her fellow-workers. She never sang a wrong note, never lost her voice, and was keen to take on a big solo when one was on offer.

Eugene somehow picked up on the gentleness in this young woman and, despite himself, found he would look for her in the crowd. Of course it took them an age to say anything to each other. For weeks he would glide up to her table, say 'yes?' and then stop just a fraction longer for the reply than was at all normal for him. At first she just looked up at him, surprised. But after a little time she gave him the beginnings of a smile which, after a little more time, delayed him longer. He began to think he would like to sit down at her table, but knew this was impossible. Anyway what would he say? What was it in this gentleness that struck a chord in him? All his sexual experiences to date had been with men, none of them lasting. He didn't fancy her exactly, just felt warmed by her.

Steve Taylor and Joe Farrant came back from visiting the library.

'Well, matey, that was a step in the wrong direction,' said Steve. 'All that dust, and illegible oldness. How were we supposed to decide which copies were priceless, and which long past their sell-by date, just like that?'

'And which photocopies would not fall foul of the copyright police, if they should be recognised on stage?' said Joe.

They were tired and sweaty from having had to make these decisions in an airless store-room, and had agreed that a beer at Ahmed's was an irresistible idea. However, since they were both about to take a rehearsal, this posed a ticklish problem of etiquette, especially at Ahmed's, where they knew they would be surrounded by colleagues. They knew they would be perfectly capable of doing a good job on a beer, but it looked bad. The acceptable procedure was that singers and their staff could get hammered at the end of the day, but not any earlier.

They looked at each other as Ahmed welcomed them back, his half-smile just a little broader as he registered their predicament.

'Two lemonades please, Ahmed', said Steve, in a brisk tone of voice.

'Coming up', said Ahmed.

Eugene took this opportunity to melt back into the restaurant, as if he had never left it. As he did so he caught Ahmed's eye, at which the casual observer might have expected to see a beam of reproach from employer to employee. Instead those quick onto the plot saw an almost indescribable look – of love and patience and concern – that didn't seem to answer the case at all. If they weren't in love, what were they? They made such an unlikely pair.

The four members of The Regis Quartet were soon joined by other members of The Gamut Range, who were assembling for a three-hour session. The plan was that these singers would rehearse for a concert they were giving in Cremona on Thursday, and then join the other choirs for the run-through of *Spem in alium*. Their appearance was necessary because Tallis had conceived his music for eight separate choirs of five voice-parts each. How he had done this without the aid of a computer was one of the more certain talking-points on the few occasions when these professionals actually talked about music. But however much they admired Tallis's handiwork they were disinclined to rehearse it, especially on a day like this, when the very mixed bag of amateurs fielding the other five choirs would be unlikely to sing straight through without mishap. This would inevitably result in them having to go over and over something they could do at first sight, to the detriment of their voices. So they took comfort in the fact that they had a rehearsal of their own to manage, unable to arrive at the general rehearsal before about 9.40. To sing it once through took ten minutes.

BY 6.15 THE RESTAURANT WAS LOUD with singers of every kind greeting each other. Just like teenagers they eyed those they didn't know with circumspection, and kept to the people they did know. All fifteen professionals of The Gamut Range were there, some of them 'grabbing' a quick 'bite' before going to work, generating a bubble of contented conversation. The amateurs of Voces Civitatis, many of them fresh from their excellent jobs in the City where they had been working all day, self-consciously laid themselves back, and were rather less scrupulous about being sober. Steve, whose job it would be to rehearse them this evening, looked about him. As with every good amateur choir they had a totally reliable secretary who also sang a bit. This was Christy Benningham, Steve's right-hand, a woman of lists and timings. She surveyed the swelling crowd.

'I've received messages from Anne, Anna, Sarah, Emma, Fred I and Andy to say they can't make it this evening', she informed him, wishing she could take the blame and so dilute the moment.

'Jesus H – in a choir of 24 people that is an unhealthy percentage,' said Steve, visibly annoyed. 'How are we going to fulfil our part in *Spem*? We need at least 20 singers.'

'Fulfil our parts, plural, would be a more accurate way of putting it, bro', quipped Fred II, a young bass standing within earshot, who had little desire to look up to his elders. Steve eyed him with distaste.

Christy hastened to explain. 'Yes, well you see, it's very unfortunate. Anna's mum is not feeling well, and as you know she lives alone. Anna felt she had to go and look after her, but couldn't find a baby-sitter and couldn't take the children for fear of infection. Emma offered to stand in, and Andy is, well, fond of Emma. Sarah never comes to weekday rehearsals, as you know, and the other two have work that they have to do this evening. They all really promised they would be here on Friday, though.'

'You think I know a lot of things I don't know,' snapped Steve. 'Why do we have these endless rehearsals, if the singers can't be bothered to turn up? They are not for my benefit.'

'They do all love singing, and they are thrilled to be in this choir, I promise you', said Christy, desperate to pacify.

She looked nervously at him, having learnt long ago that his smile, so encouraging in some situations, could prove misleading. He could be friendly and edgy without warning. He was clearly not the product of the much-referenced English public-school system, nor of any of the universities which traditionally proceed from those schools. He had been to a local comprehensive, left as early as he could, dossed around for a bit, before finally going to a music academy. Music had gripped him, despite himself, and especially choral music. He found he had a talent for encouraging non-specialists to sing in choirs, and soon started his own groups around town, as well as picking up existing ensembles as their conductors moved on. By the age of 35 he had put together an impressive portfolio of groups, each with a small stipend – the singers paid to be in them – taken together amounting to a living wage. His manner, of necessity, had to be smiling and encouraging at all times, giving the impression to his charges that they were standardly within an ace of a magical performance, requiring just one more massive push. Over the years this manner, and his legendary patience, had created quite a reputation. His other responsiblity this week, The Whyte Chorale, was the product of a television station inviting him to go into ordinary workplaces and encourage the staff to form a choir. In this case it had been the offices of a supermarket chain in Finsbury. The invitation to conduct Voces Civitatis, on the other hand, had come through artistically inclined businessmen who knew his reputation.

Working with these two groups came easily to him. The real challenge was when he had to deal with the professionals. Those singers, and their conductor, could not only do everything at sight that he and his amateur singers took weeks to manage, he also felt they looked down on him. Whether this was true or not, he had a chip on his shoulder which pride encouraged him to exaggerate. His speech was artificially cockneyfied; his conversation was deliberately kept working-man's direct, every remark only one remove away from being introduced with the phrase 'Jesus, get a life, mate'; while his appearance had avoided anything which could be said to have a distinctive style for so long that he had ceased to notice what a mess he was, and had certainly ceased to care.

When the professionals left together at 6.45 those members of Voces Civitatis who were there – about ten of the expected 24 – followed, not least because Christy was telling them to. However, they all knew that some members wouldn't have arrived yet, and now knew that several wouldn't come at all. They could look forward to a pregnant pause around 7pm in the rehearsal venue, and more strong words from Steve. Ahmed watched the procession leave. He also watched a stream of cars drive up and park in the street outside, for the next 25 minutes.

One car in particular caught his attention – a Maserati. The owner, as he got out and locked it up, behaved as though he owned not only the car, but the street, The Bunker and most of the surrounding real estate. This man regretted being 20 minutes late for a rehearsal, but thought everyone would understand that they were lucky a busy man like him came at all. Besides he was an ex-choral scholar of King's College Cambridge, which put him in a very special category, he thought. Ahmed turned to Eugene, who had an eye for glamour, and asked him who this person was, since he had never seen him in his restaurant. Eugene cleared his throat. 'Jerry someone,' he replied with his usual brevity. Then, suddenly taking wing added: 'If it's the same Jerry they talk about, the singers think he's an idiot.'

'That car costs a year's income for some of our customers,' said Ahmed, 'yet they are all singing in the same concert.' He scratched his stubbly face, wondering how this was possible.

Eugene made indistinct noises and attempted to clear away some of the plates that the recent exodus had left behind. Ahmed turned to serve the four or five tables occupied by his more regular clientele.

'Where have all those young people gone?' asked elderly Mrs Pritchard, skewering Ahmed's take on small, battered and deep-fried fish with a vigorous fork and cramming as many of them as she could manage into her mouth. This left some to stick out sideways awaiting a second swallow, recalling the feeding method of puffins on the surface of the sea. Eugene, who had caught sight of this from the far end of the room, began to giggle. Ahmed composed himself.

'They are all singers, making ready for rehearsal in that big brick building opposite. They have a concert on Saturday in Wharf building.'

'How lovely,' said Mrs Pritchard, who in her time had been a senior civil servant in the Department of Trade and Industry where, over a long career, she had been able to form firm ideas of what she liked. One of the things she found she disliked, as it turned out, was Mr Pritchard, at an early stage her boss. 'I wonder who will provide the music.'

Ahmed looked confused. 'Well, they will.'

'But you said they were singers. Which orchestra will accompany them?'

'No orchestra. They are quite alone.'

'Oh', said Mrs Pritchard, and tightened the fabric of her summer shawl more tightly about her, as if she had just felt a blast of cold air.

OVER THE ROAD three rehearsals were getting under way. The Whyte Chorale was under the direction of Joe on this occasion, since Steve could not be in two places at once, leaving him free to take Voces Civitatis. The Gamut Range was in the smallest available room, being the least numerous of the three, rehearsing under their founder and conductor, Anton Wellbrooke, generally known to his colleagues, but behind his back, as HRH, though Steve Taylor was in the habit of embellishing this. He, along with every member of the Whyte Chorale, had failed to make it to Ahmed's in advance of 7pm; and neither he nor the members of The Whyte Chorale would go back there after the singing was done, though for differing reasons. The supermarket trainees were of widely differing ages and backgrounds, unused to socialising together, but they shared the common problem that they needed a job, and the money. They had no experience and little stomach for the gatherings of singers of any kind, and very little cash to spend on restaurant-grade refreshments. Only about half of the 70 or so who had signed up for this project had actually arrived at The Bunker, and it didn't take them long to feel like fish out of water. The more timid other half of the signees had felt like fish out of water even earlier in the process, at the first rehearsal, and could not be counted on to appear again. Anton, on the other hand, loved The Blue French with all his soul; but this evening an interview he had recorded on BBC Radio Three was due to be broadcast at 10.15, and he was determined not to miss it. He would be back, probably tomorrow.

By about 7.30 all the expected members of Voces Civitatis had found their seats, the friendly waves and mouthed 'How are you's' to and from the latecomers finally over. At last Steve could now set to work on the problems of nailing Choirs 4, 5, 6 and 7 of *Spem*: five voice-parts in each choir, making therefore 20 parts to be mastered. This would have been a tall order at the best of times, but it was made immeasurably more difficult by the fact that Choirs 1, 2 and 3 were missing (eventually to be sung by The Gamut Range), as was Choir 8 (the province of The Whyte Chorale).

Johnny Tissot, the group's rehearsal pianist, had to cobble together the missing 20 parts, as Joe had explained to the Gallaghers. At the very beginning, where few voices were singing, this was relatively easy; but by the time Choir 4 was due to start, in bar 16, there was already a great deal missing. No one could be blamed, but the challenge thus presented to the altos of Choir 4, who led their group in, became twofold: vagueness in what was going on around them in the other choirs as represented by Johnny's mock-up on the piano of 15 voice-parts; and the look of expectation on Steve's face, which by then had become unbearable to behold.

He had been calling out the beats in a loud voice up to that point, but as the altos' deadline approached he increasingly pointed and gestured in such a way that everyone was certain they were going to go wrong, or were already wrong even though they hadn't started, and now didn't dare to. With the kind of patience Steve was famous for he approached the lead time and again, building up knowledge and confidence, until at last Choir 4 knew where to begin; and 5, 6 and 7 could take their cue from them.

A choir like Voces Civitatis was stronger when there were only a few voice-parts to be sung – preferably four – and all the 'sopranos' could sing soprano, the 'altos' alto, and so on. Then there could be leaders and followers in each section, and the end result could be solid. *Spem in alium* not only required every singer present to sing unusually tricky lines by themselves or, just possibly, with one other, but they had to do this while surrounded by unconfident colleagues on the neighbouring lines. Fortunately for the reputation of this group, they were also down to sing other pieces in the Saturday concert, which were destined to suit them better. These included Byrd's famous *Ave verum* and *Laudibus in sanctis*.

After an hour of slipping and sliding with *Spem*, morale was so low at Steve's rehearsal that he thought it would be politic to regroup and sing some Byrd. Nonetheless, still annoyed by how late the rehearsal had started, he refused to sanction a coffee break, and went straight on with *Laudibus in sanctis*. This turned out to be a tactical error. To his surprise one of the tenors was so tired from his day's work in the office, and dispirited with his own singing, that he decided to become argumentative.

Up went his hand.

'Steve, could you remind us of your *ficta* policy in bar 36?'

Steve looked up warily, as he clocked that this was one of his least favourite questions, bound to lead to argument and time-wasting, asked by one of his least favourite members. He might allow himself on occasion to don the proverbial anorak and bang on about academic musical procedures, but he didn't expect his rank and file to do this. And certainly not in open rehearsal. He attempted an expression which would convey scrupulousness with rugged determination. He was aware that one of his little fetishes – not always treated with the respect he thought it deserved – was to have become a self-appointed expert in the history and transmission of Renaissance music in general, and Tudor music in particular. He knew very well that people like HRH, with his posh education, had been more or less obliged to study these things from an academic standpoint to get a degree, by teachers in whose interests it lay to make the standpoint seem as complicated as possible. He had never had this opportunity, but had come to rely on his own experiences with the music to find good answers to questions like this one. Such insights, however, could make him quarrelsome with Anton and his Ilk when performance practice came into the conversation, making it a topic they tried to avoid when he was around.

'Yes,' he said. 'Only at perfect cadences – and not always then.'

'Ah. Well. What should we do here, since this cadence also comes at bar 8 and 20? The copy I have in front of me suggests a C♯ in the earlier instances, but not here.'

'Exactly,' came a voice from the basses. 'We have the same problem in bar 50. You can't really claim that this is not a perfectly perfect cadence, can you?' Giggles and general relaxation followed this observation, from quite a popular young man.

Steve tried again: 'Don't be bloody dense. Obviously the editor has not been entirely consistent about this. Bar 36, for example, is an interrupted cadence and therefore doesn't qualify for a *ficta* sharp.'

A murmur could be heard about the room.

'Why has he made us use a crap edition, then?'

'What are we supposed to do in bar 64?'

'This is no policy at all. All the important theorists agree on this.'

'Not to use *ficta* sharps makes the whole thing sound like a weak revival of the Arts and Crafts movement.'

Laughter followed the murmurs, leavened by some soprano-pitch squawking and a sharp thud from the bass section. Jerry had been trying to imitate the singing of a perfect cadence with added *ficta*, at soprano pitch. This effort caused him to fall off his chair, grinning from ear to ear and looking around for sympathetic admiration. Steve was left feeling isolated. He dug deep, remembering his training on the council estate where he was brought up.

'Look, people,' he said, his accent becoming harsher with every syllable. 'We have very little time to get all this right. There's only one more rehearsal before the day. I expect you all to practise your parts at home until you're note perfect. Don't forget that this is a big opportunity for us. We are in very distinguished company, with important critics coming to review us.'

'Perfect', came another carefully timed interjection from the back of the room. 'We'll cover ourselves in glory then.'

The rehearsal continued, the tenors and basses now slightly less inclined to do what was asked of them; the sopranos and altos as ready as ever to be offended, but in the same moment keener than ever to give Steve their unswerving loyalty.

If Steve felt pressured, it was nothing to what Joe was experiencing downstairs with the 35 members of The Whyte Chorale who had decided to give singing a try. It was not that they were all clueless. Some of them had good voices, but none had learnt to read music. They could have sung a single melody together with some spirit, and in fact would do so, but Choir 8 of *Spem in alium* was so far beyond them that Joe could only marvel at the wishful thinking on someone's part in expecting them to try. A big, friendly sing-along, with all the participants having a place in the final concert, was a lovely idea, provided there was at least a piano to keep the less experienced in the right place. Unfortunately Tallis had known nothing of pianos, which didn't prevent Joe from making use of one now. Since some of the lines repeat the same snippets of music, he had all 35 of them sing each of the lines for as long as there was a perceptible tune, playing them over first. This went down well, and in its own terms was quite successful, though only a fraction of the music was covered.

After a while, the novelty having worn off, Joe decided to concentrate on the two items the group was down to sing by themselves: *Greensleeves* and *Strawberry Fair*. Here a piano would be no problem. The singers began to enjoy themselves.

The Gamut Range were expected to bear the brunt of the Saturday programme, which was to include Allegri's bums-on-seats *Miserere*. This historic confection had long attracted popular interest, underpinned by a number of good stories, but the abiding interest still lay in one particular note, a high C which the soprano soloist is required to sing five times. This remarkable feat of technique and endurance has been known, for generations now, to send music-lovers into raptures not easily conjured up by any other means. The only proviso is that it should be sung very well. Not every voice is made for it, and The Gamut Range had decided to invite a specialist high soprano on this occasion, a Sicilian singer called Caduta Massi. She was not a regular member of the group, and so was not due to take part in the concert in Cremona on Thursday. She was therefore not present at this rehearsal, which involved music for a number of future events. Anton, the founder and conductor, organised the three hours available like a military exercise, beginning at 7pm with the break coming exactly as laid down by the unions after 80 minutes, and lasting exactly 15 minutes. The only downer was that they couldn't end early on this occasion, since they had to join the others at 9.40pm. By 9.20pm they had rehearsed nearly two hours of repertoire to their satisfaction, at which they fell into congenial conversation. Eventually they went downstairs.

There they found Anton already in position, alongside two pianos and a host of singers. No one knew where to stand, and Anton, realising that half the people present were singing in Choir 8 only, closed his eyes and pretended to be doing something important with the huge score in front of him.

It was in Christy Benningham's nature to come to the fore in moments like this, though she had no particular love of doing so: she just couldn't bear the mess. In a way she was making life more pleasant for herself by taking over. In short order she got the members of The Whyte Chorale to stand in formation at the extreme right-hand side of the rehearsal space. She briskly informed the members of The Gamut Range to stand to the extreme left, and divide into the three choirs they were to sing, leaving them to it. With her own people she was sharp, discouraging chit-chat. Nonetheless she had to face up to questions like 'Should I stand here like next to Greg?' and 'If I stand behind Nicola I won't be able to see the beat' and 'It is such a crush that I'll have to hold my copy above my head' and so on, in a constant barrage. But she was good at this sort of management, and in a remarkably short time all eight of Tallis's choirs were in some sort of position. Anton decided his vast score would now not fall backwards off the stand, and called everyone to silence. He counted Choir 1 in.

It has been insightfully said that the effect of 40 voices wandering about inside the cathedral-like space Tallis created for them in *Spem in alium*, can resemble the sound of a vacuum cleaner: a pitchless hum of gently undulating sound. This truism was diluted now by having two pianos underpinning the texture – Johnny accompanying Choirs 4 to 7, Joe Choir 8.

With this scaffolding in place the appointed ten minutes for singing it through was not exceeded, and, on the dot of 10pm, the professionals left the room and headed for Ahmed's. The members of The Whyte Chorale, looking confused, melted away; the members of Voces Civitatis bethought themselves of their domestic situations and largely decided to 'go for a quick one'. Ahmed's beer supply was about to be put to the test, which, reliable professional that he was, he had seen coming. A special shipment of Timmy Taylor's *Landlord*, chosen under instruction from one of the basses in The Gamut Range, had been procured for the evening. The bottles were now lined up on one of the tables near the door to the street.

GROUPS LARGE AND SMALL, leaving The Bunker, scattered about the neighbourhood. Anton strode off alone, his house being nearby, in order to catch his broadcast. 'Where are you going?' Alastair White called after him. 'I was going to suggest a beaker'. 'I have a broadcast at 10.15', Anton called back. 'Oh,' said Alastair, instantly losing interest. 'Good luck anyhow', said Ahmed, gently, at his retreating form.

It was a rule of The Blue French that at times like these the tables remained where they were, and no more than four people could sit at them, for fear that the locals would be disturbed mid-meal. Christy arrived with a small cohort of amateurs, at the same time as Joe. They distributed themselves tactfully around three tables at the street end of the room, having asked Ahmed for their favoured dish or glass as they came in. This had resulted in a flurry of announcements in the direction of the kitchen, causing the little restaurant to bulge with activity. Joe, keen to meet everybody, started to ask the names of those he didn't recognise.

'Let me make the introductions,' said Christy. 'This is Jim Pistols.'

'Hi, Jim', said Joe beaming.

'Fred Fellony and Alan Coppice', said Christy.

'Funny names', said Joe, laughing.

'And there's Oliver Moth-Comet, a baritenor. Very useful.'

'Call me Mozzy', hailed Oliver, allowing himself a stage wink.

Joe stopped laughing.

'You've met Johnny, our accompanist. Next to him is our young hope for the future of soprano-land, Jane Spring; and on her right Kathy Whitener.'

'Hi', said Joe, beginning to feel that a joke he couldn't immediately identify was being played on him.

'Alex Stout is our tenor soloist whenever possible. Then two splendid mezzo-sopranos, Terri Thomas and young Nicola

Roebuck. With Dave Acolyte and Vinny Coste, stalwart basses both, gossiping away behind those pint pots.'

'Ah?,' said Joe, by now feeling distinctly uneasy. Shifting in his chair, he espied another young man looking for somewhere to perch. 'What is your name?' he said with uncharacteristic hesitation.

'Malcolm Sargent.'

'You don't say,' said Joe, his discomfort rising to the surface. 'Not Sir Malcolm Sargent, I suppose?'

'Well, of course not', said Malcolm.

'Were your parents music-lovers when young?' asked Joe.

'You must be effing joking', said Malcolm, unimpressed with the line of questioning. Deciding that the company at one of the other tables would suit him better, he walked off.

Christy had followed this exchange with increasing alarm, wanting everyone to be friends and not understanding what had gone wrong. 'Who was Malcolm Sargent?' she asked the table at large.

'He was the bravest, loveliest man you could ever hope to meet,' projected Araminta Flatt from some distance down the room, motivated by the general shaking of heads. 'I shall never forget that day he came on to the stage of the Royal Albert Hall in 1967 – I had been nominated lead soprano in the symphony chorus – it was the Last Night of course – to say goodbye to the thousands and thousands of fans packed in there, the BBC Symphony Orchestra behind him banging their desks, everyone clapping and cheering as if the world had gone mad. He died two weeks later of cancer: everyone knew this was it. They called him "Flash Harry", but I can tell you from personal experience that he was a gorgeous man to work for. The perfect musician, and the perfect gentleman. You see he took over the Proms from Henry Wood himself... in 1948 I think it was. When he asked me...'

At one of the nearer tables Tom Morris, the musicologist who had been asked to help with dodgy notes in the foregoing rehearsals, sat quietly with a glass of white Ksara and a plate of *moutabel*. He had not been referred to once earlier in the evening, except to be asked whether he would like to sing in Choir 8, an honour he had declined. So he had dotted between the three rehearsal rooms, wanting to be helpful, but managing to be in the wrong room at every call, failing to help Steve with his *ficta* interrogation. Now he allowed the atmosphere of the restaurant, calming and energising all at once, to refresh him.

Eugene, noticing Tom was on his own, thought he looked approachable. As a means to an end, he began to describe ever decreasing circles around his table, until he finally came to rest, gossamer-light, at Tom's side.

'Can I get you anything?' he said, elliptically.

'That's very kind,' said Tom, intrigued by this person he hadn't met before and uncertain as to his status in the restaurant. 'You must work here.' He smiled.

'Yes', said Eugene, and smiled back. There was a silence.

'I'm an academic, you know,' Tom offered. 'I've researched some of the music they were singing this evening.'

'Oh', said Eugene. Now he had dipped his toe in the dangerous waters of conversation, he took heart and looked around for Robin. She was sitting at a table with three other people. 'Excuse me', he said and went to stand as if he wasn't there, in another part of the room.

Seeing him leave, Christy, who had invited Tom to come along that evening in the first place and was feeling guilty that he had had nothing to do, sat down opposite him.

'Mind if I join you?' she asked. 'I won't stay long. Have to get on home.'

'Not at all', said Tom.

'As a matter of interest, have you heard of Malcolm Sargent?'

'Yes, indeed,' he replied, 'though I'm now, you know, more knowledgeable than I was', and he nodded in the direction of Araminta, who had finally fallen silent.

'She is quite a character, isn't she?' Christy said. 'I wonder what she really did in her career.'

Tom shook his head. 'I fear she dabbled. She comes from a wealthy family, you know' – he paused to find the most fitting words – 'who had artistic leanings. As in the old days, when the second son went into the army, and the third became a clergyman, in her family I suspect the oldest daughter got on with the breeding and the others, you know, flirted with the arts.'

'You seem to know a lot about her', said Christy, impressed.

'Her father was a prominent diplomat who gave some money to my college. Very helpful it was too, in establishing a chapel choir. Can I get you a drink?'

'No thanks, I must go and make sure everything is well at home', and she was just in the process of collecting herself and her lists together when Chrissy Peacock came by.

'May I sit down?' Chrissy said. 'I don't want to talk about sodding Regis, incidentally.'

'No one is forcing anyone to talk about Regis, sodding or otherwise', laughed Tom.

'Please sit down, and let me get you a drink,' said Chrissy to Christy. 'What's your name?'

'Christy', said Christy to Chrissy.

'You don't say,' said Chrissy, affecting a jocular tone. 'Mine's Chrissy.'

They looked at each other with obvious pleasure. 'I thought the way you marshalled the troops in that *Spem* rehearsal was just perfect,' said Chrissy. 'I wish I could deal with a crowd of disorganised no-hopers like that. You saved everyone a lot of trouble. HRH was poised to be completely useless, as usual.'

'Who is HRH?' asked Christy, allowing herself to feel that maybe her household could do without her for a few minutes more.

'Anton, our conductor. He gets all hopeless and flustered when confronted by people he doesn't know very well. And to be honest Choir 8 was a bit of a trial. Whose bright idea was that, I wonder?' and she looked round for Eugene.

'Steve's,' said Christy, recalling that it had also been his idea to name the Chorale after Robert Whyte. 'He's so hopeless', and she sighed with affection.

'Yes?' said Eugene, gliding up.

'A bottle of whatever Tom has in his glass, and a plate of olives please'

'Oh, I don't think I'm going to be able to stay long enough to join in with a bottle of wine,' said Christy, all anxiety. 'I'm expected at home.'

'For Christ's sake stay a moment longer,' said Chrissy, hoping she might be able to get this 30-something housewife to relax a little. 'I'm going to call you "T" ', she added, giggling in an adult way.

They studied each other more closely. Christy looked old for her age, as though she had let daily stress get the better of her. Having admitted it into her home life, she went on to expect it in what was meant to be her down time – singing, and organising singers. Steve had quickly made the most of this opportunity she so obviously presented, without much thought for what it might mean for her, gladly heaping administrative burdens on her. He squared what little conscience he had about making use of this unpaid help with the thought that she wasn't a very good singer, and was lucky to be in such a good choir. All this put together had made Christy unnaturally thin and drawn, wearing expensive clothes which didn't suit her, bought with her husband's money.

Chrissy, on the other hand, wore inexpensive clothes to advantage. She, nearer 40 than Christy was, had no partner and had never had a long-term relationship. She preferred women to men, but would have taken up either in a partner if the right person had come along. She lived for singing, which made her an inward-looking person and, given the necessary determination needed to survive in the singing world, a tough nut to crack. She had made herself one of the most useful sopranos on the market, able to sing anything from medieval isorhythmic motets to baroque arias. Like Robin West she was never ill, never made a mistake, and always delivered. Unlike Robin, however, Chrissy would walk straight into a room, looking straight ahead and usually without smiling, ready in advance to take on whatever difficulty there might be lurking. She assumed everyone else in the groups she had decided to sing in were as competent as she was, and if they turned out not to be she had little sympathy for them.

She was, then, both popular and unpopular with her colleagues. But with Christy she realised immediately she was dealing with something unfamiliar: someone as tough and no-nonsense as she was, but in a quite different way. Perhaps the whole difference in the end was that she, Chrissy, was dealing with professionals every day of her life, and Christy was dealing with children (of which she had four), a husband who paid her little attention, and amateur singers who liked to behave like children once away from the office. To cope in these contrasting spheres required different kinds of toughness. Chrissy had seen all this at the rehearsal earlier, and been fascinated. She longed to draw Christy out.

Eugene flickered up, carrying a bottle, three small plates and some olives. With one graceful movement he fetched a corkscrew from his apron, exposed the cork and removed it.

'Wow. You did that well,' said Tom, smiling. 'I've passed many years practising, but you know never got it to such a degree of refinement.'

Eugene imperceptibly raised his chin. 'Yes', he said, and floated off, nimbly sidestepping a projectile which had been announced by a loud pop from afar, and now could be felt parting the air. It ended up crashing into the wall behind them. Apparently Jerry had bought a bottle of Ahmed's best champagne, shaken it up, and released the cork under pressure. The pop was followed by much laughter and guffawing from the singers gathered round. Ahmed said nothing, but folded his arms. The professionals looked at each other. There was something about Jerry which didn't fit in a community like this – he was too rich, too loud, somehow too threatening.

'Oh God, he's so hopeless', groaned Christy, fearing negative comment from those who didn't know him.

'That fool,' said Chrissy. 'What a pimple. Does anyone know how he's made his money?'

'Yes', said Tom and Christy together. But before they could say more, there was another pop, followed by a bang and further laughter. Ahmed was now having a quiet word.

'Besides,' said Chrissy, 'he is going to have to drive that appalling car home at the end of the evening, and God help anyone who comes near it.'

'I doubt he has actually had a single mouthful of that fizz,' said Tom. 'He often plays much drunker than he is. He just enjoys the camaraderie.'

'Anyway "T", tell me a bit about yourself – the interesting bits', said Chrissy, tiring of Jerry and his antics. Christy began to unwind.

THE CIRCLE AROUND JERRY at the front of the restaurant consisted of most of the men from Voces Civitatis who had come on to the restaurant, and one of the women – Terri Thomas. They had opted to stand in a group, rather than sit, which Ahmed had judged, wrongly as it tuned out, to be sufficiently far from the other diners not to disturb them. Jerry formed the centre, seeming to act as a magnet for the men, if not so much for the women, who were convinced he was a chauvinist. What evidence they had for this was never fully inspected, but the group feeling was that a man with a car like that must be proving to the world that parts of his anatomy were impressive, and it became impossible to say anything else for fear of being told that one was on the wrong side of an established truth, and therefore talking nonsense. However people like Terri Thomas would have leapt into that car at the first invitation as, to be fair, would the very differently wired Chrissy. In fact all the singers present, male and female, amateur and professional, would have leapt if they'd been invited, despite disagreement over Jerry himself. The women generally found him distasteful, while the men were very happy to drink his drink, slap him on the back and declare him an excellent fellow, even if they did have to be at the office by 9am the next morning. But evenings out like this, especially after a good sing, and without responsibility for a few hours, were popular. The good cheer was genuine, and Ahmed was always delighted by it.

The members of The Gamut Range did not have to be at work by 9am, yet they were the ones being careful. Being younger on average than the amateurs, most of them had not yet started families. They were not rushing back home, but drinking moderately and saving their voices, happy in their own company. Neither side of this behavioural divide found the other particularly appealing – which in fact simply didn't matter. There was no hostility of any kind.

The conversation around Jerry also wouldn't have appealed much to the professionals either. It wasn't so much the content of it – they all loved music, after all – as the wildly enthusiastic way the music was discussed.

Young Fred II had started it: 'Don't you just find incredible the way Tallis piles up the voices at the beginning of *Spem*, slowly, slowly, until he suddenly hits you right between the eyes with all 40 of them, flat out, singing *fortissimo*. It's so awesome'; and he backed up his words with a clenched right fist thrust violently upwards, a fierce expression on his face and a selection of searing animal noises.

'Yes, but the best bit is when everyone comes in on that amazing chord – WHAM – and then everything seems to fall apart, and melt, and go all misty, and the choirs come in one after the other all subdued, and nothing seems to happen and the last 40-part passage just starts...'

'... and we all start making fistfuls of mistakes', Jerry chimed in.

Everybody laughed, and then started to talk all at once.

'The best moment in choral music I know,' said Alex Stout, a tenor, 'is the Amen at the end of Blair in B minor.' This was greeted with howls of delight, since everyone standing there, including Terri, had done their stints in college choirs. There was a universal urge to recreate this Amen, voices and organ thrown in together.

'Dah, DAH, da da DAH' went the general sing-along, accompanied by big hand gestures. This re-enactment had to be repeated several times before the rush of blood to the head which was behind it had been used up; and when it was, another glory of the Anglican cathedral repertoire was wheeled out and re-enacted with equal fervour, followed by another. They had just moved on to Stainer's *I saw the Lord* (DAH, da da) when Ahmed very gently informed them that midnight was at hand and that he would have to close.

Everyone accepted this without demur, since no one was very drunk and everyone had a sense of life outside singing and visiting The Blue French. Remarkably not all the local diners had left, and indeed some of them were tipsier than any of the singers. Old Mrs Pritchard, despite her reservations about singers without orchestra, had had the time of her life listening to everything that had been said and sung, and asked when the next in-house performance would be. 'Friday', said Ahmed. 'I'll be there', she said.

Jerry, catching sight of Christy still sitting with Tom and Chrissy, went up to their table.

'Hi Tom,' he said, pulling faces to suggest he was fully abreast of what Tom had supposedly been up to. 'Long time no see. Would you mind if I were to abstract Christy from under your very nose and take her home? I think she needs some TLC.' To most people this would have sounded creepy, but the three of them, steadied by Tom's insistence that Jerry hadn't been drinking at all despite appearances, accepted that there was no danger, either of accident or advances.

Christy smiled dreamily. She hadn't been this content for a very long time, fully realising that Chrissy had made it possible. She floated out of the restaurant on Jerry's arm, past Ahmed who nodded to them both, murmuring 'Just popping home now. See you Friday', and tucked herself into the Maserati. Her husband hardly recognised her when she arrived home. Chrissy meanwhile was left to contemplate an unexpected turn of events. Tom gently put his arm on hers.

'So you have a new friend; and I've had some, you know, thoughts about Regis. Life is going your way'; and they left as the restaurant emptied with them.

As Chrissy was putting on her helmet, ready to cycle home, she recalled that she would be back there in 12 hours' time. She wondered if either Tom or Christy would be back, but suspected not. They had other things to do in life but sing all day, not that she could remember what style of singing would be expected of her on the morrow – medieval, renaissance or baroque. Whatever it was, she would take it in her stride, whenever it started.

Ahmed bade good-night to his customers, his kitchen staff, and Eugene. He turned out the lights, leaving the cleaning to a private firm who sent people at 8.30 every morning. In many ways midnight was his favourite time, standing in his doorway, smoking the one cigarette he allowed himself each day. It was still warm. He went upstairs to bed.

Chapter 2

WEDNESDAY, 5 JUNE 2019

BY THE TIME Ahmed next stood in his doorway the lines of perspective tracking away from him down Tippett Avenue were beginning to bounce and liquefy in the midday haze. A long, humid day was already under way. His first customers arrived hot and thirsty.

The very first was a stranger, tall and ample.

'Hello,' said a thick Russian accent, flashing a dazzling smile. 'I am tell there will be singers. This is truth?'

'Welcome,' said Ahmed, folding his arms lightly over his chest. 'There will be many singers during today. Have a juice or beer and wait for them.'

'I am here for audition,' said the accent, holding the smile. 'My name is Leonid Moudrich, from St Petersburg. I would like for audition please.'

'I know nothing about that,' said Ahmed, gently. 'But there will be people who do.' At this moment, and with some relief, he spotted Joe approaching. He introduced Leonid to him, and explained his situation.

'That's odd,' said Joe, nodding encouragingly nonetheless. 'Only The Gamut Range are due in today, and they never audition?'

'I am real Russian bass,' pursued Leonid, and without further encouragement let out a bottom B♭. 'Maybe I can sing round you?'

'Let's sit down and get out of this heat?' said Joe, leading the way inside. He asked Ahmed for 'the usual' and an Arabic coffee, which was duly called out in the direction of the partitioned kitchen. It was Joe's task today to sit in on The Gamut Range session, as they prepared for their concert in Cremona. They were due to rehearse from 2pm to 5pm, after which the plan was to have a meeting in the restaurant, followed by dinner for those who wanted to stay. This was the kind of full-on schedule which made him glad to be a student with a strong sense of mission.

'Who is that beautiful woman?' said Leonid, eyeing a new arrival.

'Ah, that is Caduta Massi, one of our best sopranos,' said Joe enthusiastically. 'I wonder why she is here now.'

'I have been summoned,' said Caduta, sitting down at their table, having ordered her 'usual' which at lunchtime was humous with some pitta bread. 'There is illness, and there is a tour tomorrow, which I shall now be on.' Caduta, coming from Caltanissetta, spoke with an Italian accent, but her use of English was pitch perfect, along with her singing, never causing misunderstanding. 'Who is this unfamiliar gentleman?' she asked, 'please introduce me.'

'Well, I've only just...'

'I am Leonid Moudrich, from St Petersburg. I must audition. I am bass', and he let out another B♭.

'That is quite something', said Caduta, instinctively wiping her cheek.

'I can sing on you?' said Leonid.

'Well, not on me,' said Caduta, smiling. 'But our conductor will be here soon', not mentioning that Anton never auditioned.

Joe began to view Caduta through the eyes of their Russian visitor. He himself knew that he was too young to attract the attention of such a legend in the profession, but he appreciated that the Russian didn't know who he was dealing with.

For Caduta was famous in the singing world, not only for her uncanny ability to sound more like the English than the English, but for her exceptional beauty. Many a conversation among the men at Ahmed's had tried to pin down her allure. The one that was most easy to agree upon was her natural grace, something she had come to wish she could turn off at will. Ever since she was a teenager she had had to get used to dealing with those moments when she was singled out by meaningful whispers – from across the street, from behind her in a shop, from the audience when she was on stage – and learn to react in a way she could live with. She couldn't find it in herself to be dismissive or unpleasant. She wasn't coquettish or haughty or manipulative; she was just a straightforward country girl abroad, with a voice which could find no meaningful employment in Caltanissetta. And the women she sang with liked her too, genuinely impressed. Her exotic foreignness seemed to preclude any jealous comparisons: in a crucial sense she wasn't seen as being one of 'us', and so escaped judgement as such. Her good fortune in finding such a scene so far from home still amazed her. How had she done it? She had asked her friends this many times, with heartfelt gratefulness.

But it was Ahmed who had come up with the only complete answer: 'You can sing'. And indeed it was her singing which defined her unique status in London, for foreigners were not common in the profession. She quickly came to realise that people like her were immediately assumed to be too slow in rehearsal, no matter how good their actual voices. She knew only too well she had not gone through the training which the English cathedral tradition offers its choristers – with its emphasis on fluent sight-reading and ensemble discipline of an almost military precision, from an early age. Despite her preparations before leaving Sicily, she was surprised at just how little rehearsal English groups devoted to learning new repertoire. She had to learn very quickly that where ensembles in Italy might take a week to rehearse a concert programme, their

English counterparts expected to get it right more or less first time in rehearsal, with the luxury of leaving the interpretation to the heat of the concert itself. The threat of sinking in this environment tested her more than anything she had ever experienced.

In response to the warming-up noises, low in his throat, which Leonid had decided should accompany his unblinking appraisal of Caduta, she turned away to look about the room. 'Where is Anton anyway?' she asked, adding with a touch of irony, 'he needs to have a word with our Russian visitor.'

'It looks as though he may not be coming along after all,' said Joe, as Steve Taylor walked through the door, closely followed, as inconspicuously as possible, by Eugene. 'What are you doing here on a Wednesday afternoon?' he asked Steve.

'I am having...' – and here he addressed the welcoming Ahmed – '...one of those salads you do full of red and green bits, and a normal coffee, none of that over-sweet Arabic sludge.' Once again he decided this time not to try to quote the menu but go for a more direct approach.

'Coming up', said Ahmed, wincing afresh at Steve's turn of phrase and noticing how he never could bring himself to give the name of the dish, in this case *tabbouleh*, as stated in the menu. Ahmed had long ago divided his guests into those who had a go at the printed titles, and those who refused to. There were other ways of categorising his guests, of course, but this way amused him the most. Caduta didn't bat an eyelid at pronouncing the Arabic titles, for example, even though her native Italian was the only linguistic advantage she had over Steve. Of course Steve, the singers, and all the locals assumed she was fluent in every language under the sun.

'Have we both been summoned, then?' asked Caduta of Steve. 'Illness?'

'Well, fellow travellers. I don't know whether his Lordship is ill, exactly,' said Steve, 'but he sure isn't bothering to turn up', his descent into the demotic designed to make him seem easy-going. 'I have his most recent edicts inscribed on this little screen here,' and he indicated his phone. He was introduced to Leonid, who looked at him expectantly. But Steve's mind was on other concerns, like taking a professional rehearsal on no warning. 'Are we looking at the Allegri this time?'

'In fact no,' said Caduta, 'that's for Saturday. I'm in for Angela, who has lost her voice. I imagine the other three sopranos will be here in a moment', she added, knowing that Angela must indeed be ill, since no freelance singer in London would willingly give up a concert fee unless he or she really could not sing a note. Since arriving in London Caduta had come to understand that it was the professional rigour which these English singers displayed that made the ensembles they sang in cheaper, leaner, and more matter of fact than their competitors. Foreign critics complain that with such haste in the preparation English singers don't have time to think themselves fully into the music. Caduta knew from early on that this was special pleading. So quick were her new colleagues onto the actual notes that they could become bored with them with embarrassing rapidity, having mastered and assimilated them in a few minutes. She came to understand that rehearsals in London were little more than a chance to make sure that everything was rock-solidly in place, so that everything meaningful could be left to the performance itself. Few words were to be heard at those rehearsals, either from the conductor or the singers: musicianship and group understanding would take over.

She was able to make her way in this environment because she had the necessary quickness of mind not only to learn to sight-read, but be able intellectually to process the information without getting stuck or panicking. The notes flew by, and she learnt to fly with them. She found she could stand and deliver a solo which she had only sung once through, possibly several days earlier, without forever worrying about whether it was good enough. She had noticed how the English singers simply assumed that they were good enough; and who was going to dare tell them otherwise? They were going to do it in the way they wanted to do it, they were going to enjoy it, and then they were going to sing the next phrase, and the next, without looking back. She found this attitude, and the confidence which lay behind it, enthralling, since her training in Italy had represented the polar opposite in almost every respect.

'Well, it'll be good to have your experience available to us, Caduta, and let's hope there are no hiccups that will cause argument. You'll be by my side, won't you?' Steve asked Joe, in a whisper, trying to master the panic which always welled up in him when he was about to work with professional singers, realising that the eventual concert was going to be more testing than usual. He could easily imagine the scene as it would unfold. The two amateur ensembles that he was due to conduct would be on display, set alongside the 15-voice Gamut Range. This crack outfit would eventually be conducted by Anton Wellbrooke, which meant that it would go as it always did. Onto the stage these professionals would come, capping everything that had gone before with effortless precision, while his work with the amateurs would be 'appreciated'. There were to be other pieces of music in the concert, of course, but in the final item – Tallis's *Spem in alium* – when all the groups would come together, he would be relegated to singing one of the eight bass parts, while HRH Wellbrooke conducted and took all the plaudits. For what? Spending rather less than an hour at the afternoon run-through hoping this very difficult music would fall into place without any bother on his part, while he, Steve, had spent weeks dinning the testing lie of the score into recalcitrant throats, so that that afternoon rehearsal could indeed go smoothly.

But he had to get on with these people, partly because he was generous enough to recognise how good they were, and enjoyed the beauty which resulted from their collective discipline; and partly because when he did work with them, as this week, he was given a prominence he would not have in his normal appearances before a public. And, to be fair, he was glad that his amateur singers would have the chance to hear one of the world's top a cappella groups in the flesh, and maybe even get to stand next to one of their members during Saturday's concert. These were experiences, he knew, which were simply priceless to some of his charges, especially the younger ones who wanted to go further with their singing.

JOE AND STEVE nodded to each other, like old partners in crime, feeling that hiccups were likely to be kept to a minimum, given the collective know-how of the people due to be at the rehearsal. 'Who else will be singing?'

'It must be the full complement of 15 singers,' said Joe, 'the members of The Regis Quartet, plus the other eleven regulars. I'm rather looking forward to hearing them sing Tallis's *Gaude gloriosa*, as a matter of fact. They're singing it in Cremona, and again on Saturday?' he added. But they were interrupted before anyone could react.

'I like to sing this glory piece,' said Leonid. 'Does it have super-crazy low ones? Can I audition for you Mr Steve? Then I can sing round everyone. I can sing a low B♭ any time' and was about to launch himself again when Caduta spoke.

'In fact it does not have super-crazy low notes, I'm sorry to say, Leonid. We are doing it at high pitch; but even if we weren't there are no really low notes in the English repertoire at all. Not what you would call low anyway. The lowest is probably a fifth higher than your B♭.'

'I can also sing super high,' countered Leonid. 'It is very beautiful my high. It is much adored in Russia. You should hear it. Right now.'

Joe was about to sacrifice himself for the greater good, and take Leonid off to a piano in The Bunker, when a gaggle of singers darkened the doorstep. At the same time Bob and Sally Gallagher arrived for their customary weekday lunch. Ahmed stood among them, hands resting lightly on hips in a pose of easy-going authority, nodding. 'Be careful of Mr and Mrs Gallagher,' he said pleasantly. 'Are you all coming in?' he asked the gaggle.

'We haven't got time now, Ahmed' said Jonathan. 'We have to be over the way in a few minutes. Where is Angela? And come to think of it,' he said looking round, 'where are the usual basses?' At this point he caught sight of Caduta and Steve, sitting inside. 'Is there illness?' he asked, repeating an expression that was part of their collective argot. 'Has the much demonised summer flu laid us low?'

'There is illness,' said Caduta, for the second time that day. 'And I fear it is going to make the rather difficult programme we are due to sing tomorrow that much more difficult.' Steve began to revise his opinion of what would be required of him at the upcoming rehearsal. Everything would depend on how good the deputies turned out to be, which in reality meant who was free at short notice. Singers of the calibre of The Gamut Range regulars and their preferred replacements were hard enough to book months in advance, let alone a few hours. However it was a matter of long established pride not to change a programme once it had been agreed with the promoter, and it was just unfortunate that Anton had chosen not only *Gaude gloriosa* but also substantial pieces by Josquin and Pärt for this trip, all sporting split parts, some requiring solo voices. As it turned out no half-reasonable deputy was found to be free for this rehearsal – the notice had been too short – but some could manage the journey to Italy the following morning 'if they moved one or two things around.' The problem at hand, then, was Steve's. He was going to have to take the rehearsal with voice-parts missing. This furthered his edginess. 'Come on then, fellows,' he said, keen to take charge. 'Let's get going.'

'Maybe I can sing you exactly now, and then I can join', said Leonid, standing up.

'No,' said Steve, brusquely. 'You wait here. We'll be back soon', he lied, hoping Leonid would vanish in the meantime.

Bob and Sally Gallagher looked at each other meaningfully, having picked up on the burgeoning atmosphere of crisis. 'They are missing some of their people,' said Bob. 'I wonder what they'll do.' And a little frisson of pleasure passed between them.

WHAT THEY DID was what they always tried to do in difficult circumstances: get on with it as well as they could, not ask too many questions, and go home. If Anton had been there this approach would have suited everyone perfectly. There would have been a general shrugging of the shoulders, on the grounds that there was nothing to be done, and leave the worrying to tomorrow when circumstances might have changed. But for Steve it wasn't good enough. He felt he had to leave a mark of some kind, if only to show that he had a point of view of his own, something he didn't often have a chance to exercise at this level. As they entered the rehearsal room he started counting heads.

'What a shambles. Even with Caduta, we're missing three people,' he said. 'We are going to have to rescore things.'

Joe saw the imminent danger. 'My phone tells me that you'll have three good deps with you tomorrow?' he offered.

'In which case I can't see much point in like rearranging everything just for this rehearsal', said Stewart. There was a murmur of agreement around the group.

'I would literally just like to sing one or two solo passages – perhaps you could fill in what is missing somehow on the piano, Joe – and leave the full sections to tomorrow', said Chrissy.

'Yes, I would like to sing my solo...' came a chorus of sympathisers, which goaded Steve into action.

'Well you can't. We'll sing everything through properly', he said.

'There's like no point,' insisted Stewart. 'I'm not wasting my voice on lines I shan't have to sing in the concert', he added, to a further murmur of agreement.

'Look here. I'm running this rehearsal. We'll start with the first piece' said Steve firmly, and opened his score of the Josquin.

An hour later everyone in the room was hot, tired and dissatisfied. The more the singers went onto auto-pilot, the more Steve tried to impose his authority. Everyone realised that there was no getting round Steve in this situation; they all recognised that to openly defy him was not acceptable. The problem for Steve was that, unlike the amateurs he had rehearsed the day before, these singers had little respect for his ideas. They knew as much about how this music worked as he did – and much more about how to sing it – with the result that they just sat there, functioning, while counting the minutes until the session would have to end. They were very familiar with rehearsals like this: a good result was neither possible nor expected. The serious work would be done tomorrow, in situ.

Unfortunately these were niceties which Steve, coming from a different tradition, had long failed to grasp. During the course of Ingegneri's *Cantate domino* it became apparent to all the singers present that there was a wrong note in the scores they were using. The second sopranos – Chrissy and Fran Moody – were being asked to sing a D in a chord of C minor. This D could not be explained by any of the normal grammatical justifications – it clearly needed to be changed. Someone somewhere along the line, either a modern editor or the original scribe, had miswritten it, an error which, if original, had been blindly reproduced every time the piece had been written out again, for hundreds of years. This was so common in modern editions of renaissance music that it was often said groups like this only rehearsed in order to weed out the mistakes in the copies, since they expected to sing every written note accurately first time. They liked to boast that the only danger was that the copy would force them into error. This being a regular occurrence the singers were quick onto it, and started to make suggestions among themselves.

'What's going on? Is there a problem? Tell me', said Steve, testily, feeling he ought to be consulted.

'Yes, there certainly is,' said Chrissy. 'We think the second soprano D on the first beat of bar 45 should be an E♭ – the D is obviously wrong.'

'What makes you think that?' asked Steve, on red alert.

'Well, for Christ's sake, it sounds terrible,' said Chrissy, 'didn't you hear it?'

Steve hadn't heard it, but he wasn't going to say so. However he could now see that it was wrong on the page. 'Surely it should be a C. It needs to fit into a chord of C.' His tone of voice became more flustered. As it did so all the singers who were not immediately involved in the question of what to do about this rogue note, switched off, waiting for the moment when they were required to do something which did concern them. It was of no interest to them that a second soprano note was wrong, and it was of equally little interest that Steve was floundering. It was simply none of their business. Surreptitiously, behind a convenient copy or hidden by a music-stand, out came the phones, and gazes were lowered.

Steve monitored this with mounting discomfort. He recalled the superficially similar moment in the rehearsal with Voces Civitatis he had taken yesterday, when his academic credentials had been called upon by singers who cared passionately about the issues involved, even though they were unqualified to give an answer. It had been up to him to find a workable solution, aware that everyone would back him if he sounded authoritative. Here he had a room full of people most of whom were perfectly capable of solving this little riddle, bound to be supportive of Chrissy and Fran whatever they decided, and glad of the pause in the singing. He would have done better to ask the sopranos what they thought the right answer was. But he was too proud.

'Well, anyone can see it has to be changed,' he continued, adding redundantly 'it was probably the fault of the original scribe. I'd like you to try a C here.'

'We don't think it can be a C,' said Fran. 'C creates consecutive octaves with the tenor; and anyway the imitation in the other parts suggests an E♭.'

'Leave it for now,' said Steve, 'I'll check it with Tom Morris when I next see him – he'll know immediately what's right.' Chrissy and Fran pulled a face at each other and said nothing more. Suddenly the whole group was ready to continue. 'Let's continue', said Steve.

The rehearsal duly ran the full three hours. Everything was more or less covered, ending, after the final chord of the final piece, in total silence. Irritation and exhaustion vied for the upper hand in the singers' minds until finally someone said 'How about a beer at Ahmed's?' and everyone trooped off, looking at the floor. Joe, who had spent the time filling in where necessary at the piano, patted Steve on the back. Neither was experienced enough to understand what had gone wrong.

The plan had been to hold a singers' meeting at Ahmed's after the rehearsal at 5pm, but with so many people missing, and no sign of Anton, no one felt the need to mention it. Nonetheless everyone who had been at the rehearsal was now at Ahmed's, sensing an opportunity to relax in time which originally had been set aside for group business. Suddenly Steve and Joe were part of the team again, the rehearsal and the responsibilities of giving a scarcely-rehearsed concert on the morrow forgotten. Bottles of beer and glasses of wine were ordered. Not long after those were delivered, *mezze* plates were ordered too. Ahmed called out a succession of requests, the kitchen began to hum, and a convivial mood spread irresistibly about the tables.

As it did so the conversation reverted to the standard jogging-along topics that inform every gathering of these professionals, wherever they may be in the world: illness, bargains online, children, scandalous goings-on reported in the press, obviously stupid decisions made by right-wing politicians, films, dresswear, hangovers, parties, cooking, types of beer, shared bars, travel horror stories, incredible true stories, unbelievable lies told by agents/ conductors/ festival promoters and so on and on for hours on end, all managed with a generosity of spirit which came quite naturally, everyone meeting on the same level with the same hopes and fears. A more perfectly equitable society would be hard to imagine, and it was made possible by the fact that all the participants were self-employed. It was essential to the congenial nature of these gatherings that when they came together to drink and talk there was no boss breathing down their necks, implying dissatisfaction.

It was here that Steve was at an advantage. He might misjudge a rehearsal, but in the end he was part of the singers' world, and was accepted as such. His humble background, state education, assumed cockney accent and obvious inability to command large fees, coupled to a well-liked talent for encouraging ordinary people through singing, made him immediately sympathetic. The singers might disagree with his decisions, but they would always want to imply fellow-feeling.

Something like the opposite was true for their director, Anton. He obviously did not come from a humble background, did not have a state education, did not have a cockney accent, and seemed quite good at being paid satisfactorily (or so it was widely assumed – no one actually had any figures). He hardly ever misjudged a rehearsal, knew the business inside out, was friendly and supportive to the people who worked for him and was an enthusiast for the music they did together. And yet his employees were not instinctively sympathetic towards him, for the simple reason that they were his employees. They wanted the employment he offered them, they needed the money, but they did not want to be obliged to show gratitude for it. They would also not question Anton disrespectfully, but this was more from fear of the consequences than because they agreed with him. Instinctively they would disagree with him, whatever he said.

It was perfectly possible for conductors with the kind of international reputation Anton had built up, to ride roughshod over this divide between employer and employee. There were plenty of them, sometimes admired, but never loved, living a separate and, it was assumed, more privileged existence somewhere out of sight, most tangibly in the business-class end of aeroplanes. After all, there was no absolute need for the two sides to talk to each other: everyone would do their best in the concert, the employed were just as proud and independent-minded as the employer. The divide was caused by the unequal pay, the unequal fame which was dealt out at the end of a successful concert, and, worst of all, any impression that the conductor might give of having contributed more than anyone else to the performance. This was the minefield which Anton was about to have to negotiate yet again, as he entered the restaurant with his wife, Lotte.

'Uh-oh, here comes royalty', said Steve, as he caught sight of them approaching. Ahmed's guests braced themselves to make an effort.

Anton felt the collective effort, but knew he would not be left to feel out of place. He and Lotte had been in the profession since before some of his younger singers were born. Anton had made legendary recordings more than 30 years ago, and Lotte had sung on them. These achievements were not forgotten, but somehow they never seemed relevant either: they were part of the mists of time to the younger members, along with Arthur Scargill and Harold Wilson. Lotte had separately carved out a career as a soloist in recitals of music from the renaissance and early baroque periods, long before such things could be relied on to interest a general concert-going public. She had been at the top of this tree for a long time, retiring just a year ago to sustained applause. Both now in their 60s, well-preserved and of a youthful disposition, they offered an unusual bridge between the kind of aristocrat of a profession who feels awkward talking to people in the same line of business half their age, and elderly celebrities who are a little too desperate to show how well they still do fit in.

'Well, your Highness,' Steve started up, after Ahmed had taken his and Lotte's initial order for the evening. 'Where were you when we needed you most?'

Of all the people in the room, Steve was the one who most immediately put Anton on the back foot. Underneath the surface there was too much obvious discontent in him, too much niggle.

'Oh hello, Joe,' said Anton, dodging the bullet and smiling sideways. 'Has there been a difficulty? I gather one or two singers were absent sick. Will they be there tomorrow?'

'We thought you might be ill?' said Joe.

'Oh no,' he replied without evident concern. 'I was setting up a television session for tomorrow morning. In here as a matter of fact. I need to talk to Ahmed about it. I couldn't turn it down, and it had to be discussed this afternoon, or the opportunity would have evaporated. Television always wants everything right now, however inconvenient but with the utmost urgency. Or someone else can do it. In our line of business they don't really mind who it is, and they assume they are doing you the most colossal favour. Anyway, I thought you might enjoy a Gamut Range rehearsal for once, Steve.'

Anton sensed the condescension in this remark just too late to think of a way of phrasing it differently. It was enough to get Steve going. 'Come off it, mate. I was landed a totally unenviable task,' he fumed. 'How was I supposed to rehearse this kind of music with half the voices missing? I'd thank you to take your own half-cock rehearsals,' and he moved to another table, avoiding everyone's gaze.

Anton was not good at confrontation, he hadn't been brought up to it. He liked to smooth things over if possible, and if not possible he would pretend the awkwardness had never happened and walk away. Some conductors thrive on arguing with their performers, even starting disagreements in order to impose themselves, nurse their egos and so feel better able to lead. Anton was the opposite, preferring to lead through consensus. Nothing pleased him more than a group opinion coming to the surface, which he could defer to. Then he could retreat into himself again.

He went to find Ahmed, who was talking to Bob and Sally Gallagher, in the process of settling at their favourite table. Without in the least intending it, something of a regal manner came over him. 'Ahmed, would you mind very much if I were to be interviewed for television here tomorrow morning? I would love to do it here. It would be good for you I think, and I would feel relaxed in such familiar and pleasant surroundings.' Even his accent had acquired some old-fashioned inflections as he spoke, so that it sounded more as though he were demanding something that was a foregone conclusion, than that he was asking a favour. It had never occurred to him to ask the BBC to pay for the privilege.

'Wow,' said Sally Gallagher, 'that's an honour, Ahmed. We shall all watch this one. What do they want to interview you about?'

'It's to be part of a series on recent trends in classical music-making', replied Anton, the regal manner departing as the reality of having to do the interview at all began to hit home. He didn't mind the invitation, nor talking about it, but underneath he was already dreading what he would have to go through. One problem was going to be the interviewer, Barbara Prentice, a woman who had a reputation for making people squirm in public. She felt she owed her viewers entertainment.

'That will be pleasure,' said Ahmed, rising to the moment. 'I'll open early so everything is finished before customers come. What time would be OK?'

'They were asking to set up from 7.30.'

'No problem. Anyway how was your interview last night?' Ahmed asked, the only person in the room to remember that Anton had been on the radio, too.

'A doddle, compared with what this is going to be', sighed Anton, his confident persona slipping further.

'You'll be fantastic, as you always are,' pursued Sally, looking at Anton with mindless adoration. 'We are so lucky to have this wonderful restaurant just round the corner, aren't we Bob?' and for a moment they gave the impression that there was nothing more important in their lives.

'But do you not go to Cremona tomorrow?' pursued Ahmed.

'Yes, I'll have to go straight to the airport from here. It should all just about fit', though he shuddered some more at the thought of how much rushing about was involved on such a day. And uncertainty.

He avoided Sally's intensified gaze and looked for a quiet corner to have an early dinner, wondering how much he ought to drink the night before so much responsibility. He decided on quite a lot. He knew his limits, and he deserved relaxation wherever he could find it. The Blue French always hit the spot.

But he was not to be left in peace. Lotte came to sit by him, accompanied by Araminta Flatt, who found in Lotte's career a comforting reference point, made more comfortable by the fact that Lotte had retired. She felt they were now on a par, and could talk like equals. Lotte was happy to reminisce with her and they were about to continue a conversation started at another table, when Leonid, forgotten by everyone except Eugene, who had watched him drink his way slowly through the afternoon, sat heavily down.

'I must sing by you, and by you perfectly', he began, re-engaging his smile.

Joe came up. 'Leonid would like to audition?'

'Well he can't,' said Anton wearily. 'I never audition anyone for anything. I acquire singers by word of mouth. Everyone knows this.'

'Leonid doesn't', said Joe affably.

'How does he come to be here?' asked Anton.

Leonid had followed this patchily, but at the mention of the word 'audition' he sprang to life. Standing to his full considerable height he unleashed a top F which shook the walls and silenced the room.

Noticing he had made an impression on these famous English singers, he started to hum some Russian music, not recognised by any of the distinguished panel of experts sitting and looking up at him.

'Who is that by, Leonid?' Chrissy called, feeling an obligation to break the ice which was rapidly forming.

'Yes, it is. I promise', he replied. His audience then watched as he consulted with himself, deciding which of speech or song would best represent him and his culture. Finally he smiled again, prepared himself to act as an ambassador, and launched forth:

'Покаянные стихи» написаны Альфредом Шнитке к 1000-летию крещения Руси, завершены в 1987 году, и впервые исполнены Государственным камерным хором Министерства под управлением Валерия Полянского в 1988 году. Тексты «Покаянных стихов» взяты композитором из восьмого тома «Памятников Древней Руси» под редакцией Д. С. Лихачева, вышедшего в 1986 году. Это издание и содержит одиннадцать «покаянных стихов», положенных на музыку Шнитке. В 1986 году Шнитке перенес инфаркт. Почувствовав близость смерти, он обращается к покаянной поэзии в качестве источника текста для своего последнего хорового сочинения. Ему предшествовали следующие произведения для хора a cappella, также написанные в творческом сотрудничестве с В. Полянским: Три духовных хора 1984, Концерт для хора на текст Григора Нарекаци 1985. Композиция «Покаянных стихов» выстраивается таким образом, что за одиннадцатью «стихами» следует заключительный двенадцатый номер, написанный без слов. Сочинение устремляется, через это послесловие, в молчание.'

No one moved. No one was sure whether he had finished, and no one wanted to be rude. But Leonid himself had run out of steam. He heard the suppressed giggles of the likes of Fran and Caduta, and deflated like a soufflé in a draughty oven. He sat down heavily once again, radiance gone, allowing Joe to speak softly in his ear and then to lead him out into the fresh evening air. Joe propped him up at a table outside, made sure he had beer and cigarettes, and rejoined his friends.

'Blimey,' expostulated Araminta, as soon as Leonid was out of earshot. 'But you never know, do you? Apparently Chaliapin had a very uncertain technique when he started, and it was Toscanini who gave him the confidence to carry on. Maybe you would like to be to Leonid what Toscanini was to Chaliapin,' she twinkled at Anton. 'Have you ever been to Kazan?' she continued. 'I have. It might seem from London to be an unlikely place for a singer of Chaliapin's stature to be born and raised – he was brought up in appalling poverty – but like so much in rural Russia, despite the poverty, culture is the one thing that keeps them going. It is so heartening to think of. I went there to give a masterclass at the Conservatory of Music. I had learnt some rudimentary phrases in Tatar, only to discover...'

'Excuse me a moment', said Anton, and got up to find another table. Lotte looked at him with an expression he knew well, a carefully graded mixture of resignation and passive aggressive complaint, which he hoped would not lead to anything more detailed when they got home. Tomorrow was shaping up to be a day to remember, without domestic silences to herald it.

He found another table, hosting only Robin and Fran, who were deep in conversation. He felt not much would be required of him if he joined them; they were anyway two of the team that he particularly liked. They continued their conversation, allowing Anton to lean towards Eugene, who had stationed himself near enough to Robin to feel her presence, and order a bottle of Reserve du Couvent and *mulukhiyah* chicken stew. Eugene pirouetted away, disinclined to call out to the kitchen staff over a full room. Anton was ready to share his bottle if need was, but he was equally ready to see how far down it he could get by himself, determined nonetheless not to finish it.

He fell to thinking. What was it about Araminta, Leonid, Steve and, in diminishing perspective, just about everyone he met that annoyed him? He was under the impression that he liked people, often being told that he was encouraging to those he worked with, and reliably pleasant to the countless organisers of concerts whom the group met on their travels. Yet when he sat down by himself, all he registered was how little sympathy he had for them. He didn't wish them dead, he just wished they would vanish without trace, a middle-ground, generalised rejection. He acknowledged that they had every right to exist, as he did; but he wanted them to exist only when what they were doing intersected with what he was doing, when they could have a business-like relationship, benefit from it, and go home.

He had long ago worked out that forming casual rejections was different from forming lifelong hatreds. Hatred was something much deeper than instantly dismissing someone for how they dressed or arranged their hair. Dress, hair, accent were merely incidental accessories, hardly noticed except as supporting evidence when the chips were really down. Hatred had to do with points of view, and the kind of people who were capable of holding opposing views to one's own and sticking to them, often backed up with offensive language. Hatred was personal. Anton didn't fundamentally disagree with the legions of people he took against. He anyway hadn't the slightest interest in finding out what their defining points of view were. He simply automatically and instantly disliked everything about them. It was as random and as impersonal as road rage. And that image, once it had come to him, gave him a clue which made him shudder: if he had come across himself driving a car, he would instantly have taken against himself. Perhaps he disliked in other people not what made them different from him, but what made them the same. Perhaps in fact he disliked himself.

He wasn't much given to deep thought, or to making his life unnecessarily uncomfortable through it, but – and he noticed he was already halfway down the bottle Eugene had noiselessly placed in front of him only a few minutes ago – he felt, as he had done so often, that he was a hypocrite. If he was pleasant to Robin and Fran now, would he really mean it? If they stopped singing well, would he continue to be pleasant to them? He knew he wouldn't. In fact he would hope that they too might vanish without trace or complaint. Yet he longed to get to know them better, to behave well towards them. 'Would you like a glass of this excellent red?'

'That's very sweet of you,' said Robin, 'yes, as long as you aren't cross with us tomorrow when we make mistakes.' She giggled nervously. She never knew what to say to Anton, never quite sure whether he was making an older person's observation, the point of which she had missed. As it became apparent that Anton was being friendly a second table was brought nearer to the first, and a group began to cohere. Anton duly ordered more wine from an ever-hovering Eugene.

'What time are you planning on getting to Heathrow tomorrow?' Fran Moody asked Anton, trying not to sound either too familiar or too polite.

'Well, I have to be here at the crack of dawn to do a television interview', said Anton.

'Oh, that's exciting,' said Fran, the interest fading in her voice as she spoke. 'Any idea what it's about?' and, in her disinterest, she put on a jokey accent, full of curves and bubbles.

'I imagine it will be about the history of the group.' (Before he had even started to speak Fran was making soothing, encouraging noises low in her throat while nodding her head in appreciative agreement.) 'About where we think we fit in the history of the early music revival, which originally was concerned with authenticity, pure and simple.' (Fran instinctively changed noises: 'mmm', then 'mmm' more urgently as he continued, and finally 'MMM' as he finished.) 'And how singing fits into a revival which was essentially an instrumental phenomenon.' She had been quietly rummaging in a pocket for her phone while he was explaining, which prepared her badly for when he fell silent and began to observe her more closely.

'That's quite a privilege, isn't it?' she essayed, floating every syllable in a childlike tone, her face alight with picture-book excitement, itching to see what her screen said.

Anton looked around the table. He had noticed that the moment he started to speak about himself, even though he had been encouraged to do it, everyone had started to concentrate on something else. *Sotto voce* conversations had immediately started up all round, mobiles were brought out, the small talk of people who knew each other, worked with each other and liked each other had started to flow, at first as a trickle but, once he had gone quiet, as a torrent. He had felt particularly exposed when he had reached the part about the history of the group – a topic which he hoped might be of interest to everyone – and had heard Fran say to Robin, in a low whisper, 'why is it that whenever I like pluck my eyebrows I always like sneeze?', followed by uncontrollable giggles, which had spread like wild-fire to the tables nearby. Fran did her best to smother a tickle in her throat.

He wasn't offended really. Perhaps he had sounded pompous, or at least self-satisfied. But what was he to talk about? He didn't live the lives of these people half his age. To him they had an astonishing number of reference points, from being technologically savvy in a way he could never be, to being fluent in such a wide spectrum of musical styles that his specialist knowledge in Renaissance polyphony seemed tediously academic, or 'beardy' as they might call it. When he sat with them in a social gathering, when everyone genuinely wanted to treat each other as equals, the irony was not that he was in some way exalted, but that he knew less than everyone else. The only advantage he had was in years. Soon even this would not be an advantage, but for now it was accepted that he had used his time gainfully in setting up something which employed them all, and he knew what he was talking about. They understood and appreciated this, but his employment of them wasn't a topic that could be referred to casually. The singers were after all employed by a host of other conductors; they were not obliged to be nice to him. The imbalance in how they all met around a table in a social gathering fascinated him. But he still didn't really know how to talk to them.

'Mind if I join you?, said Joe, the youngest person around those tables, who had been watching his patron flounder.

'Please do', said Anton who, like Steve, felt relieved at being able to relax with someone so easy to approach.

It helped that Joe was coming at his career from a different angle. He wanted to be accepted by these top professionals, in the hope that he would work with them in due course. He also wanted to learn the choral repertoire; it didn't matter which part of it. Unlike Anton, who had started out decades ago in a different world, he wanted to be the best at every school of composition, not just in one specialised area. He knew that what Anton had shown in his career was important, that renaissance polyphony could be the most rewarding choral music in the whole spectrum of ensemble singing; but that had been done now. Anton had mopped up the last untapped repertoire, relentlessly touring and recording it, until there wasn't much room left around the edges. He, Joe, had to make his own way, find his own repertoire, which was now bound to be a mixture of things. The challenge was to make it individual, different from what all the other young conductors, not least the ones on his course at the Academy, were hoping to launch for themselves.

He alone around the table was interested to hear about what it took to land a television interview, and how one would handle it. 'Would you mind if I came along tomorrow morning?' he asked Anton.

Noting that Joe's voice was free of child-like bubbles designed to please, Anton brightened. 'Of course not. You would be most welcome. Perhaps you can help me out in ways not yet apparent', and they had a laugh together. To say that Anton felt a fatherly concern for Joe's career would be to state the obvious, but Anton knew that Joe was a capable conductor. He had watched him in action, noting that he was able to hear everything in the sound in front of him, was able to listen into a polyphonic texture and hear the middle parts as few people can, and correct them. He had a clear beat and a non-confrontational way of correcting errors. In addition he wanted to do what Anton did, taking his career from there. They buoyed each other up.

'I know young hopefuls like me are always coming up to you, asking how they can repeat what you did decades ago, but what actually do you think is possible now?' he asked, reaching over to repossess an unfinished bottle of wine he had left behind. Fran and Robin turned away, keen not to be thought eavesdropping, though they couldn't help overhearing.

Joe already knew the likely answer, but wanted to hear it again, from Anton. 'To make any kind of mark you will need a first-rate instrument and a defining repertoire,' replied Anton. 'Nowadays that repertoire will have to be mixed, and it will have to include contemporary writing, preferably including a female composer; or some outside-the-box performing practice which will seem refreshingly new – electronic, Indian, African rhythmic, monkish, infusion, stellar, spherical – you know more about what's out there than me. It would help to find a composer with an individual voice who can tap into one or more of these modern alternatives and produce a genuinely involving hybrid. Then back him or her to the hilt and perform their music alongside Palestrina. Nothing to it.' And he grinned.

'Did you mean "instrument?"'

'I meant your ensemble of unaccompanied singers will form the instrument. Focus on what it takes to make a group of singers sound like an instrument of the finest blend and tuning known to man. They should become an instrument which you then play on, as an organist plays his instrument, only you will have the added excitement of knowing that the pipes which are collectively making your sound are human beings.

Remember that an out-of-tune orchestra, with bad blend, is simply not acceptable these days. Nor are mistakes in the playing. Why are these elementary requirements watered down when it comes to vocal ensembles? Is it the long reach of the amateur tradition, where having fun is the prime concern when singing? Playing the violin used to be fun until the professional orchestras began to require something more committed. And the concert-going public began to care about the difference. There's a long way to go with this. You could be part of a revolution which has only just broken out', and he stopped to down the contents of his glass.

He looked to see whether any of the human voice-pipes sitting nearby had taken an interest in what he had been saying, and caught Robin's eye, which she had been unable to focus somewhere non-committal quickly enough.

'Do you think of us as organ pipes?' she found herself saying, not knowing whether to make a joke of it, or show that she didn't like the idea much. She glanced at Fran.

Anton was grateful. For once he didn't feel like a hypocrite. 'I meant that the wonderful thing about what we do is that we form a melodious instrument, of human pipes. It is a beautiful concept – and none of you looks like an organ pipe, I promise' and they all tried to laugh it off, without finding it funny.

'And I suppose,' said Joe carefully, keen to keep the subject alive, 'that if I get the instrument right, it won't matter very much what repertoire I play on it', and he filled his glass, raising an eyebrow to the table, to ask if anyone would like some, Anton's bottle having been passed around and finished. The women took some, realising too late that it would now be rude to try to escape.

'That's true,' Anton replied 'but be aware of the other young conductors who have come to the same essential conclusion. You'll not be alone in wanting to form this choir of the future. The standard of ensemble singing is rising quickly, as I notice in a host of young groups starting out now. You'll need a repertoire to define you.'

'And money,' chimed in Fran, who was employed by a number of these new groups, and was aware of how different the pay could be. 'How did you get over this problem when you started, Anton? Did you inherit a load and blow it on unwanted concerts of renaissance music, to the delight of your parents?' It was now possible to laugh without restraint.

Anton was grateful again. 'I inherited nothing apart from an expensive education; but the difference was that the kind of singers I wanted to use in those days had the kind of voices that didn't think they would ever get much payment: amateurs, students, and the occasional professional who relied on earning proper money from singing big-voice stuff. It was just that some of them actually preferred singing in small ensembles, preferred to go on tour with friends who thought like them, instead of sweating it out alone for weeks in a German opera house. To do this they had to run quite serious professional risks – hoodwink their agents who always found ensemble work anathema, keep their names off ensemble-work publicity, run the risk of being expelled by their union. Essentially singers like you didn't exist then, Fran.'

'I didn't exist then', said Fran happily.

'This scene has moved on, and levelled up,' resumed Anton. 'There are plenty of singers now who make a good living from ensemble work, like you two, and expect to be properly paid for it. Add this to the fact that very few amateurs these days can match the standard of what the professionals do, and it's a no-brainer that you'll need to start paying from the beginning. Anyway let's order another bottle,' he added, eyeing the two now empty ones in front of him. 'So, Joe, how do you make ends meet?'

'I have a few choirs that employ me, one night a week kind of thing, to prepare a concert at some point in the future, usually several months away. One's based in a hospital, one's a community project in Reading not dissimilar from the Whyte Chorale, and one is a Cambridge college choir. So quite a range.'

'They do sound very different from each other. Do you need special skills to manage them all?' said Anton, reflecting that he didn't have any of these likely skills, and that the prospect of acquiring them was unappealing. He felt relieved that he had started when he did, on the few skills that he had possessed, and had somehow made it work. He wouldn't trade places with Joe now for twice what he earned. And yet. The future of his profession lay somewhere out there, and if not with a musician as capable as Joe, then with whom? He did realise that if that question had been asked in the early 70s, no one – but no one – would have been able to predict that it lay with someone like himself.

'I suppose I just apply the same method across the board,' replied Joe. 'I don't have any magic spells that can make people sing well together. The Cambridge one is the most fun. It's just a pick-up chapel choir, consisting of undergraduates from the college and around, unpaid, though they get a free dinner in hall afterwards. No one claims to be a good singer or even a good musician, but they're so intelligent that although I have to tell them everything once, I never have to tell them twice. So I choose my words carefully and get a very good approximation of what I had in mind first time through. I go up every Sunday for a 4pm rehearsal, Evensong at 6pm and dinner. A lovely day.' Ahmed approached with the new bottle, and filled their glasses.

'Mmm,' mused Anton, half to himself. 'I also get a very good approximation of what I have in mind first time from my singers, with the difference that I say nothing at all.' The four of them looked at each other, raising their glasses in salute. 'Did you sing in a college choir like that?' he asked the two women.

'Oh yes,' said Robin, not too young to wax nostalgic. 'I was at Merton, supposed to be reading modern languages, but all we really wanted to do was sing.'

'And party,' said Fran, coughing. 'Choirs make excellent party units' and she turned away to cough some more.

'Poised between the amateur and professional worlds,' said Anton. 'You were lucky to have the chance at that age to come anywhere near the latter.' He decided to take a risk, and talk about the past. 'If you had been around when I started there would have been few opportunities for women to get a feel for the singing profession at all, and almost none of them at undergraduate level – men or women – went on to make a career out of it.'

There was a pause while they separately considered how they could best handle what might come next. Fran took the plunge. 'But they must have been good singers. I mean, here we are.'

'They were good singers,' said Anton, liking these people enough to try their interest further. 'The strange thing is that although we paid them very little, they continued to sing in the face of odds they ceaselessly represented as unacceptable.'

'What odds?' said Robin.

'Not enough money. Everyone trying to take advantage of them, from promoters to recording executives. Constant recourse to what their union laid down as the basic rules of engagement. Fundamental dislike of the world they found themselves in. And me, the privileged one, not caring how they were treated.'

Fran and Robin began to feel out of their depth. So far as they knew they didn't have a union, and didn't see the need for one. Anton seemed to treat them alright, at least they supposed he was ultimately responsible for their treatment. The terms and conditions of The Gamut Range, endlessly updated by themselves, were as good as any. And they didn't want to hear how an older person, who they relied on and admired, might have been trashed when he was their age. Joe, however, wasn't prepared to give up so quickly.

'Yes, I've been in situations with singers where my youth and inexperience has not been an advantage. But I always assumed someone like you would never have had those problems.'

'Why would my position 40-plus years ago have been so different from yours now, at least in this respect?' asked Anton, briefly wondering what he would have said to a prominent conductor in such a conversation, if he had had the opportunity when in his early 20s.

Joe realised that this was a fair question, to which he had no answer. He carried on, sounding exasperated. 'Well, haven't there been any arguments at all in the present group?'

'There are tensions now,' said Anton, deciding to sidestep the details in present company, 'but nothing like there used to be. One way of finding out what people fear in themselves is to see what they instinctively dislike in others. I found out a lot about my colleagues by observing what they disliked in me.

There was a lot of mutual dislike in those years, which just seemed like being par for the professional course; but actually, looking at it with hindsight, I realise we were all scared. Scared of being judged harshly, scared of our limitations as musicians and as people. And one way we could run away from examining ourselves unflinchingly was to bury our doubts in immutable political beliefs. We formed cliques, which made it easy to blame others who thought differently from us – people we could blame as being responsible for all the disasters that we felt afflicted us. In the 70s and 80s political positions, inherited from the past, were very much still alive: in The Gamut Range we had hard-line communists alongside Thatcherites; and these positions were maintained through thick and thin, exactly like a religious belief. In fact the results of this intransigence would remind you of many a religious war. Such instinctive divisions created a terrible working atmosphere. Interestingly I think everyone sitting around this room tonight would all have the same opinion about Brexit, a kind of togetherness that was quite impossible in the 70s.'

'How did the atmosphere change so quickly?'

'It changed in The Gamut Range by getting rid of people born around 1950, and replacing them with people born nearer 1990. Replacing them with young people who expected to enjoy their work, and could find other groups to sing with if they were dissatisfied. Upset sticks in the gullet, you know, where the notes come from. Do away with tension and you get better singing. Increasingly we enjoyed coming to work, and the standard rose, just at the point when most groups lose direction.'

'When is that?' asked Joe, who was determined to follow this to the end, wherever that might be.

'After 20 years, 25 at the most. They run out of repertoire and/or the public gets bored with the repertoire they made famous when they started. Or new ways are found of doing it. They start sleeping with each other. Tensions between personalities, never resolved, come to the surface when things start to go wrong professionally. Then someone has a better idea and splinter groups are formed.'

Fran and Robin, who made their living largely from groups which had been going five years at the most, felt relieved. Twenty years from now, even 15, was unimaginable. They were sure they would be quite different people by then, with quite different needs and priorities. None of this concerned them.

'I never heard of a group falling apart over political differences, though', pursued Joe.

Anton stared through the window at the deserted pavement outside. 'Interesting, isn't it? There was endless trouble with the singers' union in those days, all of it politically driven; but you're right, that alone was not enough to destroy any of them, as far as I know. I reckon they all survived by believing in the music. They simply couldn't bear to do it badly, and were talented enough to do it well. Once the concerts were under way, nothing else really mattered. I never worked with anyone who wasn't carried away by singing something as unbelievable as *Spem in alium*. Something in the original call to become a professional singer made it impossible for them to foul their nests in that way. We are all lucky that in the end everyone took that attitude. If they had been doing something less fulfilling it might have ended very differently.'

'Well, it might have ended. So how did you manage to defy the 20-year rule?'

'By being...'

At this point four unmistakeably tipsy young men arrived for a meal, raising the decibel level to the point where Anton decided not to fight it. He made a throat-cutting motion to his companions with a wink, and fell silent. A slight draught to their right announced the swift approach of Ahmed, who welcomed the newcomers, half-smile across his weathered features. He recommended some starters and the visitors went to sit at a table away from the door, near the kitchen wall. Eugene floated up to them. 'Yes?' he said, and further dishes were ordered: *kebbeh* and *falafel*, with *tabbouleh* and *fattoush* to back them up. The hubbub level rose further as everyone re-engaged with half-finished conversations, and the kitchen progressed from hum to vibrate. Ahmed looked with pleasure across his domain.

Anton, however, had had enough for one visit. It was still early. He also loved this scene of conviviality and hated to leave it and the half consumed bottle, but tomorrow was a killer, and he still had to pack for Cremona. Joe said that if he was coming back for the session in the morning he ought to be going, otherwise he might as well spend the night here, at which Anton offered him a bed in his house nearby. Fran and Robin realised they could stay at their table for as long as the mood took them, though Fran began to think she might do well not to talk over the hubbub, and aggravate an incipient cough. Joe and Anton left together. Anton waved a hand across the room at his wife, who was still talking to Araminta. For all he could tell she was enjoying herself. As he and Joe passed Ahmed they promised to see him sooner than anyone had thought or expected, and said good night.

Several tables were still going strong, small groups dotted about the room. Anton's disappearance coincided with a general reordering of alcohol, which took into consideration a *digestivo* which Ahmed had developed some years ago, called *arancello*. It was a home-made variant of *limoncello*, based in orange rather than lemon. In the hope of catching Robin's attention, Eugene now wafted about the restaurant brandishing the unmarked bottle. But he was unlucky. The journey to Italy had made people cautious, and all he could interest them in was 'one more' beer. Memory of the *arancello* was shelved for a later date.

During this short lull in serving Ahmed caught Eugene in mid flight. 'You like that girl, don't you Gene?' he said, looking him straight in the eyes. 'What is good about her?'

Eugene wasn't used to having his private thoughts examined, and especially not by Ahmed, from long experience. Since he hadn't examined them himself in any depth he had difficulty answering. He avoided Ahmed's gaze, choosing to look at the floor, trying to maintain some dignity.

'I don't know why her,' he said sulkily. There was a long pause. 'Why are you asking?'

'I care for you. You are my brother in life. Your welfare is one main activity.' Eugene looked wretched.

'Why shouldn't I like her?' he blurted out. 'She's lovely.'

'She is lovely. She has lovely atmosphere. Does she remind you of anyone?'

'No,' said Eugene emphatically. 'Who could she possibly remind me of?'

Ahmed hesitated. He knew his next comment would be badly received, but he couldn't go on pussy-footing around Eugene and his multiple hang-ups forever. At some point they would have to have a proper conversation about something – anything. Certainly the place not to start was here; but the strange thing about accumulated silences is that the easy, carefree entry-point retreats as the silences build up, leaving a kind of desperation. The unwanted result is a sudden lunge into familiarity which appals and embarrasses. 'Eliana?'

At this Eugene let out a howl of pain and vanished, not to be seen again that evening. The howl had not gone unobserved by Robin, who had understood for some time now that she meant something special to Eugene and been very intrigued by it. She looked up at Ahmed, concerned. 'Is he all right, Ahmed?'

'Not properly,' he replied. 'Eugene is not happy person – because he has no idea what would make him happy. He's had many difficult experiences, but hasn't learnt from them. Or rather, he has learnt not to learn from them. He closes his mind, and runs.'

'Is there anything I can do to help?'

'Probably, but you see what happens if you get close. He needs people to be gentle with him, but too much gentleness will not sort him. It can only be beginning. Some difficult questions need to be asked and faced.' He sighed unhappily.

'Did I hear you mention a woman?' said Robin.

'Yes. I think...'

But here he was obliged to break off, realising he was the only person left to serve a busy restaurant. Coming Miss Caduta...'

THE ONE PERSON who had not joined in with the group drinking was Caduta. She had found a table in a corner of the room and ordered her food and drink on her own. She hadn't meant to be solitary – she didn't mind whether she was alone or in company – but at least she liked to start an evening alone, and await developments. As the group tables slowly broke up, some of the boys saw that there was space around her, and went over to ask whether she would like to chat. She gave nothing away, neither encouraging nor dissuading, though she knew she would have to be very firm if she was going to stop them joining her. Three of them sat on the three available chairs. A familiar difficult silence followed.

The singer most taken with her was Jonathan Williams, the burly falsettist. This wasn't to say that the others were impervious, but Jonathan went further. Caduta maddened him; and although there was nothing new to her in this, she knew she had to be careful. She had no desire to encourage someone who, whatever they might say, really only wanted casual sex; and she had to sing with him tomorrow. Unfortunately for her admirers she had no desire to settle down. She was naturally gregarious in the Italian way, and was generous-spirited enough to want to take an interest in anyone who took an interest in her, yet the playing fields were so unlevel that she was in danger of spending her life misleading people. Nor did she want to spend all her time talking to women. The bind she now found herself in had started in Sicily, of course, introducing her to the boundaries she would have to respect. But nothing at home had prepared her for the way English boys dealt with their desires. They were so self-important about them.

'Have you got a young man waiting for you somewhere?' asked Jonathan eventually, as if there was nothing else to talk about.

'No', said Caduta, without smiling.

'That seems incredible', pursued Jonathan.

'Why so?' said Caduta. 'Haven't any of you got young women waiting for you?' She looked round the table.

They hadn't, not really. 'Is being in London like being in Italy? I mean when it comes to seeing someone', said Alastair, the tenor, who had been brought up by elderly parents.

Caduta braced herself to make an effort. 'Where I grew up there weren't very many boys of my age. We all went to the same school, we all knew each other from being toddlers to being young adults. Some then moved away, like me, but the sense of belonging to an extended family was and is very powerful, and doesn't seem to fade. People of my parents' generation almost never moved away, so they have lived in the extended family through their lives. But there will be a strong and welcoming community there if I ever go back.'

'Didn't you want to like settle down with one of these fellows, then?' said Stewart.

'No, I wanted to sing.' She paused to collect her thoughts. 'I wanted to sing more than I wanted children.' She paused again. 'And making love to boys who were like brothers to me didn't appeal.'

'We are not your brothers', said Jonathan, without a glimmer of hope in his voice. The pathos of this remark got through to her. She wanted to convey sympathy, she even relaxed and made a movement of her hand towards him, but an alarm bell ringing in her head stopped her going further.

'We'll be in Italy tomorrow,' she said, hoping to sound positive. 'None of the pretty girls we'll meet there is your sister. You can go for it.'

Jonathan looked utterly downcast. He wished the other two would vanish. He felt stupid, cumbersome, clunky. 'Maybe you can show us round a bit', he said, in desperation.

'I don't know northern Italy very well – and I hardly speak the language,' she joked. 'But they have some unusual specialities there – you should try the *mostarda*.' But Jonathan's mind wasn't on food and, to make a point, called for his bill and soon left without saying another word.

Bob Gallagher had been watching this exchange from a distance. He turned to his wife, who had been watching him. 'That young man has clearly never heard of the Gallagher Principle', he said.

'I'm not sure I have,' Sally replied.

'It states that beauty only enthrals as long as it remains beyond rational explanation. The moment it is identified and explained it ceases to fascinate and becomes normal. And one forgets the hold that that object of beauty had over one. Not that I think her beauty is going to be rationalised in a hurry, at least not by him. He is in for a rough ride.'

'What makes her so attractive in your opinion, as a man?'

'Her small features. Small nose, small mouth, eyes of real power, all packaged into a neatly shaped head framed by irrepressible hair – that's what attracts attention, at least from a distance. And,' he added, knowingly, 'the small features thing doesn't work on men. If anything the reverse is true.'

She regarded him analytically, and they nodded the nod of people who have worked out a way to live together.

ARAMINTA, having waxed lyrical, now waxed confidential. She and Lotte were the only two people left at their table. 'Tell me, my dear, how did you meet Anton?' she asked, pushing a half-finished bottle in Lotte's direction.

'We met under a table in the Examination Schools in Oxford, during the 1973 student revolt and occupation.' Lotte smiled both at the memory and the phrasing. She had tried this line out a number of times over the years, to a number of different people, but she had realised from the second Araminta started to speak, that she was the perfect target. She poured herself a glass from the proffered bottle, offering some to Araminta, who declined it.

'I beg your pardon,' said Araminta, struggling to make sense of any of these words. 'Goodness me! What kind of table, and what did you do when you got under it?'

'It must have been a wooden table, intended for students to take their exams at. First of all we kissed, and then we made love.' She loosened the chiffon scarf around her neck, as if these memories had raised the temperature of the room.

Araminta struggled to find expression. 'Heaven's alive! Why there? You mean in public?'

'There were several contributing factors,' Lotte went on dreamily. 'One was that we were both reading English, and had just been studying Graham Greene. We had read, separately, that when he wasn't trying to blow his brains out in Russian roulette, he was confronting his boring life by fucking women under the altar in churches all over the known world. We admired this very much, of course, and, seeing as how we were also stuck in a place we rejected, we decided to rival his daring. Another was that we had found a common interest in Marxism, and had joined Militant.'

'Not Militant Tendency?' said Araminta, shuddering under waves of half-remembered rejections. She had of course been gently nurtured, which meant a complete mental block when it came to Marx, Trotsky, social upheaval and related armies of unwashed proletarians. When she had recovered enough to think clearly, she realised she was surprised that Lotte had not been similarly brought up. 'Do you mean you took up with those ghastly bolshies, who wanted a communist revolution on England's green and pleasant land?' She looked with loathing at the emptying bottle.

'More or less,' said Lotte happily. She stared hard at Araminta, clocked her self-satisfied demeanour, and decided to go for it. 'I found I reacted almost orgasmically to slogans like "Stuff it up the scumbags", and "We'll squeeze the rich until the pips squeak". And I found I had a social conscience. It seemed to me – and to Anton as it turned out – that the left-wing arguments were very powerful ones.' The scarf found itself being tugged back and forth, as Lotte warmed to her subject. She took another drink.

'Well, I'm sure we all wish that the poor were not so poor; but honestly, Marx wanted an upheaval which would have destroyed everything we English hold sacred.'

'Actually the founding spirit behind Militant was more Trotsky than Marx. Trotsky, you will remember, advocated permanent revolution.' She was beginning to enjoy herself, as the old verities, encouraged back to the surface under Araminta's influence, began to reassert themselves after many years in the wilderness. 'He believed that capitalist property would inevitably be forfeit as the workers moved to address inequalities in the government of their countries; and that this should be based on an understanding that different nationalities of workers were not in competition with each other.'

She stopped, flushed and breathless, the scarf had migrated and was now wound round her left wrist. She was keen not to sound too fanatical and so give Araminta an excuse to laugh the whole thing off as obviously ridiculous.

'But that kind of talk is obviously ridiculous,' said Araminta, not laughing. 'I mean look what's happened since. The whole ghastly commie vision has collapsed on its face. All those dreadful dictators have ended up being excoriated by the very people they said they were helping. And they were all male.'

This last remark took Lotte by surprise. Was it possible that one could be an unreconstructed right-wing traditionalist, and care about sexual inequality? But she was too lost in her memories of how good it had been as a student to campaign for things one believed in passionately, with no prospect of being responsible for the results, to pursue this thought further.

'Their argument was fundamentally sound, though,' said Lotte, determined not to lose sight of what had motivated her intellectually years ago. 'We loved the way Sartre and de Beauvoir wandered the corridors of the Sorbonne, during the 68 occupation we modelled ourselves on. Sure, what we all stood for was speedily hi-jacked by unscrupulous politicians, whose failure was surely the greatest failure in the history of the human race to date. But the truth in Trotsky's arguments remains irrefutable: the uneven distribution of wealth in the world is a scandal beyond describing.'

Araminta decided she had had enough of this undergraduate, girly tittle-tattle. She was fortified by the thought that what she had believed in as a young person had delivered over the intervening decades a stable democracy with a lifestyle that everyone, so far as she could see, had benefited from. Her own situation showed exactly what political stability, coupled to strongly rooted national institutions, could achieve. If she had been a middle-class Muscovite, born at any time in the first half of the 20th century, with her comfortable inheritance, she would either be dead by now, or so poor life wouldn't be worth living. She could hold her head up high.

'Anyway what have the Examination Schools at Oxford to do with Trotsky?' she asked, diverting the flow.

'Well, in the early 70s student agitation towards the extreme left had led to the demand for a proper Student Union – incredibly this had been repeatedly refused. By November 1973, students like me and Anton, and hundreds more, decided to take matters into our own hands by barricading ourselves into the Examination Schools building. This really was the real deal. We were confronting authority, just as our communist heroes had done, with our friends rallying round with deliveries of food, medicines, reports on hostile authority – the real deal I tell you. And the university was such a ripely suitable target: a breeding-ground of privilege and reaction, stuffy and out of touch. I doubt that any of us has done anything as thrilling as that again in our lives, not even, in my case, performing the solos in *Messiah* in the Albert Hall. And with the heady atmosphere came other heady things – free sex and under the counter drugs. I had always fancied Anton, across the lecture room in the English faculty, and suddenly here we were, euphoric. And we weren't the only ones.'

Araminta couldn't restrain herself. 'Was he the only one?' she asked.

'Arguably not completely the only one', said Lotte, resorting in her confusion to doublespeak, annoyed that she had given Araminta the chance to look yet smugger.

'Sounds heavenly,' stiffened Araminta, thinking of the pasty-faced, spotty physical types normally associated with left-wing student marches. 'What was the upshot?'

'We stayed in there for a week, but the threat of more occupations loomed large over the authorities for months to come. In February 1974 we issued a flyer saying "You have had three months and your time is up. Negotiations have failed, talking has failed" and we occupied the Indian Institute. Heady times and heady stuff.'

Araminta not only began to lose face – she couldn't remember anything she was doing in 1974 except, vaguely, singing – but interest in the whole dreadful, defunct topic. She would never again be able to view Lotte's career with the same detached equanimity. 'So what happened then?' she said, looking around for Ahmed and her bill.

'We were turfed out by a posse of 'relatively elderly gentlemen who were working in the Clarendon Building', said Lotte, noticing Araminta's failing interest and striving for a bathetic conclusion.

'Oh?' said Araminta, briefly arrested.

'...and some rather controversial violence, involving the University Police, the Proctors and the City Police, some out of uniform.' Even this impressive catalogue now failed to prevent Araminta from paying her bill.

'Are you still a red?' she asked, as she collected her things and stood up to leave.

'Yes and no. It was an intellectual interest, soon overtaken by the business of establishing myself as a singer. I still go on marches in support of ideals I believe in – like the anti-Brexit march just the other day – but I wouldn't campaign for world revolution any more. Anyway it wasn't really like that in England, even in the heady 70s. Infiltrating the Labour Party was as far as we went', and she waited with pleasure to see if her words would hit home.

'I think the European Union is an abomination,' said Araminta, 'run by unelected old men with criminal pasts', and with a toss of her head she walked out.

AHMED WATCHED HER GO, and turned his attention to the now solitary Lotte, aware that all his other customers had paid up and left. He had always been fond of Lotte. She was the kind of woman he instinctively admired – modest but effective. Someone who could achieve much by saying nothing while standing their ground. He knew she had been a great singer in her time, and that she had done it by sheer talent and determination. He had no time for the noisy kind, who occasionally came into his restaurant with the others – the kind who self-advertised at every opportunity. None of them had done as well as Lotte in the long run, so far as he knew. She was attractive too, an example of how youthful you can look if you spend your life doing something you enjoy.

'Can I get you something to cap?' he asked.

'No thanks,' she said; and then, recalling that Anton would be away tomorrow and she wouldn't have occasion to revisit the restaurant for at least two days, changed her mind. 'Some of that *arancello* would hit the spot I think. Can you spare some?' As she calmed she smoothed her scarf on the table before her, before slowly putting it again around her neck.

In an Italian restaurant the owner, knowing a client so well, would have sat down to continue the conversation. But Ahmed never thought of it. He stood politely to the side of the table, hands resting easily on hips, gazing out of the open door at the empty streets beyond. 'This is favourite time of my day,' he said almost to himself, thinking of his upcoming cigarette. 'The houses round here are so beautiful – I believe you live in one?' he turned discreetly to Lotte.

'Yes,' said Lotte, keen to talk. 'We were lucky to buy one before the housing market went through the roof. Most of the houses round here were built just after the Napoleonic Wars ended, in the 1820s and 30s. It was as if a dead weight had been lifted from everyone's thinking, resulting in a wild expansion of London's ambitions. This whole area had been fields for many centuries, originally belonging to religious foundations and then, after the Reformation, to private land-owners. In no time – about 20 years – hundreds of acres of arable land were covered in squares, ringed by very similar housing and a green space in the middle. There must have been tens of thousands of these houses built, some of them destroyed in the blitz. Since I retired I've had more time to explore the area. I have quite a collection of old maps,' she added, looking apologetic. 'Walking around with them makes me feel old-maidish.' She laughed. 'Someone asked me yesterday whether I was lost, to which I replied that the street names had changed since 1871. I felt rather foolish.'

'Foolish is not a word I would use to describe you, Mrs Lotte,' said Ahmed, marshalling his best English, knowing that a compliment would please, but too much of one would offend. 'How is the retirement for you?'

'You know, Ahmed, I was born to sing. There is nothing else I really want to do. I was advised to retire while I was still ahead of the game, but in many ways I wish I hadn't. I would have carried on doing a good job – I'm not the sort of person who assumes I'm doing as well as ever and has to be sacked. I think I would have known when to stop. But I had a big concert last year, a kind of showcase performance partly designed to encourage younger singers not to give up hope as they approach older age, by which everyone always means 60. I was 65 by then, and decided that I really had had enough of the travelling. The wear and tear was not on my voice, but on my body. The ideal was to find work in London – gigs I could walk to.

'Does Mr Anton want more travelling? He is same age as you I think.'

'Oh yes. He'll be able to wave his arms around well into his 90s, assuming he hasn't permanently fallen over by then. His thrills are different from mine – he actually likes the travelling, or at least the arriving; exploring languages and cuisines and wines. He is an inveterate traveller. He loves the concerts, but he would travel anyway. You must have travelled a lot in your time?'

Ahmed hesitated. There was a limit to how far he wanted to confide, and his travels had not always been pleasant. "Not as much as that. I was born abroad, but came to England at young age, and have hardly ever left.'

Lotte understood that that was as far as he was going to go on this occasion, and asked for her bill. She smiled as she said good-night to him, happy to walk slowly home in the warm air.

Ahmed cleared the tables, and went outside to smoke, with time now to worry about Eugene. It couldn't go on for ever like this. He was responsible for him. He sighed as he remembered the early start in the morning.

Chapter 3

THURSDAY, 6 JUNE 2019

AHMED WAS BACK AT HIS DOOR by 7am. The light was clearer than he had ever seen it in London, reminding him of early mornings in the desert. There the portents were more dramatic. Such light only lasted a brief moment and one did well to catch it. Too early and it was still freezing cold; too late and the magic had dissolved into a dusty haze which would last until dusk. Too late and one was already sweating, finding the shade, finding the light itself oppressive. In London, as in England, physical things were relatively tame. No drama. He was glad of it.

He thought of the breakfasts of his youth, always framed by apprehension of the day to come. If he was lucky he would have *labneh* or *shanklish* cheese, olives, unleavened bread and Arabic coffee. Those were simple products, costing nothing, but, ordinary as they were, they had given him a sense of taste. If one of these items were taken out of the mix, the experience fundamentally changed. He learnt never to see a meal as a package of flavours which was delivered as a completed whole. Every ingredient counted and so had to be chosen with due respect for its individual character. For this reason he loved Arabic cuisine, and regretted the English habit of lumping together all manner of faint flavours in a hopeful melting-pot, reinforced by salt. But then, he reflected further, should he ever regret ending up in a rub-along and make-do place like England, he knew that beggars cannot be choosers. And he had been a beggar.

He watched as an elderly van drew up outside, parked by the sign which announced that they had arrived at The Blue French, and waited. The driver's window was rolled down and a middle-aged man with a heavily lined face raised his chin in a brusque manner: 'Is this The Blue French restaurant?' Ahmed pointed to the sign. The driver and two fellow workmen got out. 'We've come to set up for an edition of "Places Where Musicians Relax".'

Not many minutes later Ahmed's tables had been largely displaced and his floor covered in lights, cables, cameras, microphones, stands, special chairs and different tables. 'What is all this for?' he asked, more out of bewilderment than irritation.

'We need to make the place look normal', said the foreman.

'Normal for a local restaurant called The Blue French?' asked Ahmed, beginning to feel aggrieved.

'No, more normal than that. The sort of place that people talking about proper music might sit in', was the rejoinder, delivered with the air of someone who has offered an irrefutable argument to someone assumed to be too stupid to understand it.

Slowly a completely fake environment was constructed around the bare bones of Ahmed's business. When it was finished the foreman stood back and admired his work, saying he wouldn't mind visiting a place like this. Ahmed registered that noone like him ever had, but shrugged his shoulders and waited some more.

At 7.30 Anton and Joe walked in, Anton carrying a suitcase. 'Dear God, has a bomb dropped on this place? It looks gutted,' said Anton, turning to Ahmed, seeming for a moment to imply that he was responsible for the carnage. 'It was meant to be an environment I'm used to relaxing in.'

Ahmed was in the process of explaining he had cancelled the cleaners for today when the foreman butted in, ignoring him and addressing Anton. 'Are you the geezer who's doing the talking? This should look just right, don't you think? Mind what you say', he added with a wink; and the three of them got back in their van, broke open three packs of home-made honey sandwiches, and applied themselves to flasks filled with instant coffee.

As they left a small posse of miscellaneous people arrived, all of whom had made the effort to get out of bed early in order to be present at that miraculous fascinator of contemporary life – a television session. These were Barbara Prentice, the interviewer; the producer, Rustin Samson; three technicians; Eugene; Chrissy, also carrying a suitcase; and Bob and Sally Gallagher. Barbara strode ahead with a proprietorial air and looked about. 'This looks very homely. Just the sort of place I would drop by for a snack. I think it will do us very well. Ah, hello Anton, I haven't seen you in a month of Sundays. How the devil are you?'

They shook hands as Anton privately recalled the last time they had met – about a fortnight ago, at the BBC, when Barbara had been hosting a panel of choral conductors and priests for a discussion under the title 'Where shall I sing the Lord's song?' The conclusion, framed for the contemporary all-inclusive BBC, had been everywhere, at any time, and to any Lord you cared to identify. However, despite the broad-sounding starting-point, it had quickly become apparent that only religious buildings in the UK were considered relevant or interesting. As a result Anton had said nothing until, with three minutes to go, Barbara had finally turned to him and asked him point blank where he personally preferred to sing the Lord's song. 'In symphony halls, preferably on the other side of the world, in Latin', he had replied, exasperated. He had not been included in the general air of self-congratulation when the programme was finished.

This crowd of arriving facilitators and well-wishers were variously attired. At the shabby end of the scale came the technicians, shapeless trousers covered in small but bulky pockets, full of bits and pieces; three-layered undershirt, shirt and floppy jacket, worn in all locales and in all temperatures; topped by mats of unwashed hair. Rustin Samson was distinguished by his cream silk shirt, which he wore as a kind of talisman against hot weather. The non-combatants were united in their loose-fitting cotton-wear, Chrissy ready for yet hotter weather in Italy later in the day, Joe looking crumpled. Anton also had prepared himself for Italy, but knew he must look good for the cameras, and so had chosen a blue linen suit, carefully pressed. But if looks could kill, or at least sweep the board, Barbara was the winner. Combining business-day efficiency with touches of almost-hidden vulnerability, her grey suit was the picture of contemporary feminine tailoring. As neat and polished as a pin, her face gleaming, her breath super-fresh, she was ready to encircle and demolish anyone's wagon.

Ahmed greeted them all with his customary half-smile and solicitous manner, asking if anyone would care for coffee. Having raised an eyebrow of enquiry to Eugene, he went to the kitchen himself to prepare the refreshments. Joe, Chrissy and the Gallaghers made themselves comfortable at one of the imported tables. Barbara waited for the lead of a portable microphone to be fed through her clothing before she sat down in a carefully positioned chair, a sheaf of papers, ostensibly with her questions printed on them, held in her right hand. Anton went through the same procedure, and sat down opposite her. In order to do a balance, Rustin invited them to tell him what they had had for breakfast while he adjusted his headphones for comfort. The cameraman applied himself to his framing.

The minutiae of breakfast having been dispatched, everyone in the room, watching an imported clock with exaggerated markings for the second hand, waited for the countdown. The live version of this was conveyed by muffled noises from inside Rustin's headphones – for some reason, possibly related to the sensibility which encourages doctors and nurses to hold the needle behind their backs before injecting a patient – the details of such a countdown are never played openly and, true to form, were not on this occasion. Instead a red light had been placed just out of sight and its winking capabilities carefully explained. When it winked, Rustin shared, they were about to go live. He did not need to explain that from this point onwards everyone had to be on excruciatingly good behaviour for a very long time.

The light began to wink; Rustin pointed at Barbara, mouth working. Tensions, already high, rose further.

'Today it's my pleasure to spend time with one of the founding fathers of the early music movement, whose pioneering work with The Gamut Range has introduced millions to a new aural experience. He not only established new audiences for 16th-century polyphony, he also showed how a certain kind of choral sound could raise the bar of excellence for choirs and vocal ensembles world-wide. I am talking of course to Anton Wellbrooke...' The camera turned to focus on Anton for the first time, who was caught between the desire to look approachable and intriguingly distant. The result was a grimace. '...who we are thrilled has chosen his favourite local trattoria as the place where he feels most relaxed.' She smiled a gleaming smile.

'So, Anton,' said Barbara, happiness informing her every syllable, 'you seem to have made a big success of your life's work', and she waved the sheaf of papers up and down in jovial support of these words.

'It's kind of you to say that, Barbara', said Anton, moving uneasily in his chair.

'You must be thinking of retiring soon', she twinkled.

'Oh, you know, the desire to explore further hasn't dimmed. Don't rush me away just yet.'

'I wouldn't dream of doing that...'

They continued briefly in this vein, deploying the kind of alternatim the psalmists would have recognised, and not in a good way. But suddenly, as so often happens in these things, with no time set aside for sliding gracefully from one register to another, the essence of the matter arrived unheralded.

'Obviously you've become a role-model for many young conductors of a cappella ensembles, what advice would you give them?'

Anton, seasoned pro that he was, was ready. 'They need to know that if they intend to be pioneers in any category of music-making but especially in unaccompanied choral music, they immediately and probably permanently put themselves outside the accepted channels of appreciation and, indeed, financing.'

Barbara smiled some more, tilting her head to make her gaze more penetrating. 'What does it mean to be a pioneer, then, and why bother to be one?'

'It simply means not doing what everybody else is doing, just because it is the accepted norm. It means finding music which is supremely worthwhile and proving to a sceptical world that it is so.' He stopped to decide how best to express himself, his eyes darting around the room. 'You take a risk. Why give yet another performance of *Messiah*, or the Matthew Passion? You will please the audience for a few hours, after which you and it will be totally forgotten until the next outfit comes along to do it again.'

'In your determination to be a pioneer, then, was it obvious to you from the start that you had a career ahead of you?'

'No, not at all obvious. In fact I never set out on a career in music. I just put on a concert many years ago with some friends and find myself still doing it. None of the calculation which the logic of hindsight seems to demand came into it', he added, by mistake looking straight into the camera.

'But surely at some point it turned into a career. You must have given up other forms of employment in order to concentrate on giving concerts and travelling' and she pursed her lips to reinforce her increasingly no-nonsense, questing tone.

'As a young man I planned nothing except one move ahead. It was like living one of those mind-games where the end is stipulated and the challenge is to work out how you get there.'

He allowed himself a glance at his audience, hoping for some gesture of support. A rigid silence greeted him, as if even breathing might be thought against the rules.

'Would you say you were helped by your timing? The late 70s and early 80s saw the advance of early music in every field', pursued Barbara, the sheaf now receiving an admonitory tap.

'Yes, in those days the battle-cry was all for "early music" and a return to a sound which modern people thought the composers must have had in mind. For a while this was known as "authentic performance" until everyone got sick of the "A" word; and then it was referred to as Historically Informed Performance or HIP, an even more tiresome label...'

'But you haven't really answered my question,' Barbara interrupted, tapping more vigorously. 'What you are describing refers to instruments from the past, which can be played and their sound incorporated into modern music-making. But voice-boxes from the 16th-century don't survive, so in that sense you could never be authentic. Yet the dialectic was there. To some extent you did hitch yourself onto the authenticity bandwagon, when there was basically no justification for it.'

Anton noted the clear thinking behind this question, and acknowledged to himself that he would rather be interviewed by someone who knew what they were talking about, however uncomfortable the questioning, than by someone who wasn't worthy of his full attention. Barbara was good.

This time he eyed the camera deliberately, smiling confidently. 'I never said there was any justification for it. I have always been completely straight about the fact that we have no evidence, and will never have any evidence, of how 16th-century singers sounded. All I've claimed is that we are at the forefront of a new standard of choral singing.'

'Well, that's nice,' said Barbara, deciding the time had come to take the metaphorical gloves off. 'But is it possible that your Anglican, rather hands-off approach as some critics have said, might not be the whole answer for a full-bloodied 16th-century Italian, like Palestrina for example?'

Anton caught Joe's eye. There was a glint of something in it. Something like the unveiling of the jugular? Anton was not going to let the younger generation down now. 'Possibly not; but then just as possibly he might be absolutely delighted with the way we sing his music. Perhaps standards have risen since his day. I often dream of Palestrina hearing us sing, and turning his eyes to heaven in ecstasy.'

Barbara had also caught Joe's eye, and was not in the mood to be set up. 'That doesn't disprove the competence of the Sistine Chapel Choir in Palestrina's day to sing his music. After all, it was written for them, for a sound he knew well. You are entitled to say that you are doing his music in a modern way, and that that way may be effective, but not that it automatically must replace every other way, especially not his.'

'I simply find it hard to believe that if you respect the nature of the music, as we have tried to do, and then ask for the highest standards from its performers, you can better the results. My point is that this not only has nothing to do with authenticity, it is a kind of opposite.' Anton, feeling himself to be projecting exasperation, now looked anywhere but the camera.

Noting his discomfort it was Barbara's turn to look straight into the camera and smile. 'So am I right to assume that you are happy to take this music out of its original context and put it in completely new clothes for modern consumption: symphony halls, paying public, digital recording, evening dress for the performers, a piece written for Lent followed by one for Christmas followed by one for Advent?'

To her surprise Anton picked up the theme gratefully. 'Comfortable seating for the audience, heating in the winter, enough lavatories in the building so that the audience doesn't have to trail through our dressing area backstage, proper lighting on stage, enough money to have all the texts printed, a good income for the promoter and hence to us, in short a thoroughly professional environment for a thoroughly professional ensemble. So, yes. As to liturgical propriety it is completely irrelevant to what we are trying to do.'

Barbara, sensing the indignation in many of her listeners, quickly regrouped. 'Doesn't it make any difference to be able to look up during the performance of a deeply religious setting of some beautiful words and see an altar or a devotional object, or even just the walls of a building that has been used for worship for centuries? How can the interior of a modern hall substitute for that?'

'My eye glances off the routine surfaces of the standard symphony hall and moves on to the packed seating. What excites me, and spurs me on to do as well as I can, is the sight of large numbers of people having come to hear us.'

'That's telling them', Anton said to himself, looking away from Barbara in triumph, ready to acknowledge the applause he felt was his due. But his audience remained resolutely silent. He looked back at Barbara, whose combative instincts threatened to get the better of her discretion.

'So to sum up: not only are you asking us to take on board your wish to be afforded the comforts and securities of big-time artists in the mainstream, you also want somehow to recreate the music in your own secular image. Do the words mean anything to you at all – or is the music just to be a series of abstracted sounds, made as pretty as possible?' The papers in front of her rose and fell ever more vigorously, as she whipped herself into indignation.

Anton sighed. 'What matters to me is what the texts meant to the composer. I am a musician who interprets sound. When I am choosing music to perform, I look for sound which moves me. At this point everything will depend on how much the words moved the composer – not how much they move me – and whether that composer had the ability to convey meaning in his music. And I do not apologise for making The Gamut Range's sound attractive. What on earth is reprehensible about that? It may sound easy to do, but it takes years of practice to bring off.'

Again he looked round for ecstatic applause; again he was grounded in a moment.

'The objection is that this smooth, polished sound is in danger of trivialising, even anaesthetising very powerful concepts. How do you react to the criticism that you make all this music – 200 years of it, as you are keen to point out – sound very similar?'

'That's obvious. A keyboard player, take a harpsichordist for example, will inevitably make everything that he or she plays sound similar because of the limitations of their instrument. The instrument is locked into its soundworld, and no amount of clever nuancing will change the sound it makes. My instrument is like this. The sound I want from it is fixed. Knowing this, I can say something very simple – to the singers, and through them to the audience: "Here is music I believe in, we are going to sing just as it is, as well as we can".'

Anton heard the crowd go wild.

Barbara was unmoved. 'In other contexts that kind of unvarying consistency over many years would be held to be dull and uncreative. No one would want more than 20 years of the same way of performing Shakespeare, for example. Or the same fashion in clothes. When you are conducting a piece you sing often don't you long for something different, something surprising, if only to keep you on your toes?'

'No, when I get restive with a piece I cease to programme it for a while. There is so much else for us to sing that we are not obliged to find new angles on old favourites, as the directors of Shakespeare's most popular plays are – and I'm not prepared to make one up just because journalists have got fidgety and can't think what new to say about us' and he gulped down some water.

Barbara turned again to eye the camera meaningfully, projecting the very picture of wounded probity. 'So you mean to go around the world producing identikit performances wherever you go. Aren't you worried that the world might get bored with this? And aren't you worried the singers might get bored with your approach? How do you keep them interested year after year?'

'Well, interested is what I've kept them, as you can see. Over nearly 50 years now I've been lucky in having an unusually slow turnover of regular singers. On those few people the sound was built and has been maintained. As in an artisan's workshop, knowledge and skills from the past have been passed along. I like the idea that we are craftsmen...'

Rustin, earphones clapped to his head, began to make windmill gestures as the monitor neared the end of the available time. Barbara braced herself for a final sortie. 'Despite this you have managed to hold the thing together all these years. What do you think are the qualities which have kept you on the road for so long? You have pointed out that the natural lifespan of a group is about 25 years and even that length of time presupposes a constant cycle of reinvention. You don't seem to reinvent, and you don't seem to be on the verge of extinction.'

'My original conception has turned out to be surprisingly robust, centred on nothing more complicated than a sound which can be applied indefinitely to great music. And that great music is in endless supply. Renaissance polyphony is a chronically underexplored repertoire, unlike that of those poor bastards who are forever hailing another minor baroque "masterpiece" because all the major ones have been performed to death.'

'Well I sense there will be plenty of people who will disagree with you there,' said Barbara, huffily. Nonetheless she was professional enough to find the gleam in time. 'I'm going to have to bring this insightful discussion to a conclusion, but is there a last word you would like to share with us?' She laid the sheaf to rest on the table in front of her.

'Well, how about this. Abbot Suger, a French divine of the 12th century, once wrote: "We can only come to understand absolute beauty, which is God, through the effect of precious and beautiful things on our senses".'

Anton was flying, spurred on by the support of thousands of wildly cheering fans. He looked across at Rustin who had become unaccountably motionless, distracted by something in his headphones. Anton took this as a sign to continue. 'Suger also said: "Marvel not at the gold and the expense but at the craftmanship of the work'. I am not a Christian in the accepted sense of...'

A sudden and intense panic had descended on the room, as can only happen when live broadcasts are in question. Somehow the orderliness of millions of living-rooms throughout the land becomes so important that a few seconds can decide the fate of a presenter. Rustin returned frantically to windmill mode while Barbara, finally flustered, interrupted:

'Well, there we must leave Anton Wellbrooke, and The Blue French restaurant, his charming first choice for a place to relax. My heartfelt thanks go to Bakhmet, the charming owner, and everyone here for making this fascinating encounter possible' (eyes turned to see how Ahmed had taken this moment of forgetfulness, but his face remained impassive, as professional as anyone else in the room). Next week I shall be interviewing Nigel Kennedy. Until then...' and she was cut short by the second-hand of the clock, and both hands of Rustin. The red light was flashed on and off again.

The world in Anton's head evaporated. For a few seconds there was such a silence that all he could do was to look incredulously about him. Then, as if at a signal, everyone fell noisily apart, the air thick with congratulation. Joe was ecstatic. 'OMG, I learnt so much. Everyone should see this. That bit about the meaning of beauty will haunt me for ever.' Anton wondered whether anyone else would be so diligent, but said nothing.

'Bloody brilliant, Anton,' said Chrissy, putting her arm round him, an unheard-of familiarity. "That must have taken some doing, eh?' and she looked into his face. He looked silently back.

'Maybe I can get you a quick something before you go?' asked Ahmed, indicating to Eugene that a table should be prepared.

'There isn't time, much as I would welcome it', Anton slowly replied. He saw the Gallaghers standing hesitantly to the side, looking shell-shocked. 'It was just lovely,' gushed Sally. 'I'll never forget it. To think that I was there', and she clapped her hands together. She was aware that she had only understood a fraction of what had been said, but she took home a sense of fulfilment in having been talked up to.

'You are very kind,' he said, 'I'm delighted you were there. Now unfortunately Chrissy and I must mount the underground railway network, and ride away', at which he fumbled in his jacket to make sure he had his tickets and passport. No one laughed at his imagery, but a bitter-sweet pause was felt, as ordinary life too rapidly reasserted itself. This was surely the moment for everyone to act out the theme of the moment, and relax in The Blue French.

Barbara, meanwhile, was readjusting her clothing in the aftermath of the clip-on microphone. She saw Anton pick up his case and make for the street door. She quickly caught up with him, happy to promote a kind of truce, as if they had exhausted themselves in a hard-fought battle, now behind them. They both felt they needed some common ground where they could pause and take stock, tired as they were. Stopping just inside the door, Barbara, for the first time remembering the interview they had done together a fortnight earlier, asked 'What did you think of that college chaplain who did his best to control the Lord's song discussion the other day?'

'He seemed like so many others...' Anton replied, treading the welcome common ground with circumspection. When Barbara said nothing, he put his suitcase down and continued. 'A man who has got large and noisy on college hospitality. Where is that humility, solitude, penitence, eschewing wealth, giving to the poor that his training, if he had really believed in it, required of him? I see precious little of these things in such a man.'

'Yes, I was told he had been in the job for 30 years and, frankly, I wondered whether he might have forgotten what it is to be one of Christ's foot-soldiers, as someone once put it, I forget who. Why do these priests seem so distanced from getting their hands properly dirty? Isn't that what they're for? One feels a stint in a slum parish might have toned this one up.' She was no longer turning on the professional beam, but just speaking straight. Anton warmed to it.

'He certainly needed a bit of toning.' said Anton, and they had their first mutually sympathetic moment of the day. 'I've observed these people over years of being involved with their colleges, and without fail they are hypocrites. They cannot avoid temptation, of various different kinds – I suppose one expects that, they are only human after all – but the worst of it is that they derive all their considerable authority and income from espousing Christian values, yet when the chips are down, and keeping strictly to those values is inconvenient, they suspend them.' His tone became harsh. 'This makes them like the rest of us of course, but it is their job not to be like us. They have a duty to not give way to the inconvenient, but to be absolutely unbending in their adherence to Christ's teaching. Otherwise what is the point of them? They can't have it both ways', with which his voice seemed to retreat back into him, his mind already having moved on to the next thing, despite himself.

'You sound as though you have suffered at their hands.'

'I have certainly been scarred by one or two of them. I can't help remembering that it is the job of any priest, but especially college chaplains, to rise above careless behaviour – however bad it is – take a proper human interest in our misguided situations, and put Christ's teaching into evident practice. Instead of which they would descend into petty likes and dislikes, queeny huffs and fits, little stand-offs on points of minute protocol. And it was no one's place to correct them.' With an exaggerated gesture he opened the restaurant door, unsure whether she would continue the conversation in the street.

'Which was what gave our cuddly friend the balls to tell a panel of people live on the radio how they should be singing.' Barbara looked at Anton with fresh eyes. She saw that he had come off a script he had been perfecting over the years and was at last speaking impulsively. She wished they could have started their interview again from scratch, and with a different brief.

But this was impossible. The equipment had been taken down as they spoke, allowing Ahmed to prepare his restaurant in time for midday. Rustin, caught socially between the technicians and Barbara, waved a vacant hand and departed on foot. The technicians made for the BBC Outside Broadcast Unit which had brought them, spooling up trails of cable as they went. Joe bade the professionals farewell. Barbara, suddenly keen to re-establish a connection with ordinary life and the people inhabiting it, accepted Ahmed's offer of refreshment, and sat down again. Eugene decided to spoil her, dipping round her table like a bird-of-paradise. Barbara was quite sure she would visit again.

ANTON AND CHRISSY made their way to the tube stop, awkward with their cases as they went through the barrier. This hour-long journey from central London to Heathrow airport was one they knew so well they could predict when the carriage would empty along the route, and where it was likely to fill up again. They also knew that having a conversation was effectively impossible unless everyone in the vicinity was to hear it, and Chrissy was keen not to tire her vocal chords. They sat next to each other in silence as the train launched their journey to Cremona. In 24 hours' time they would be most of the way home again.

At the airport they parted, keen not to imply any sense of congregation, and disinclined to meet up with the others. Professional musicians go their own way in airports, just as they refuse to sit in a middle seat on the aeroplane itself. The last thing they relish is the possibility of three of them sitting in a row. None of these nods towards privacy was done with any desire to be antisocial, they were simply a mechanism by which some semblance of independence could be maintained in the relentless routine of their travelling. Some of them were close friends, but they still wouldn't plan to sit next to each other on transport to work.

The group didn't meet as a unit until they had gathered on the far side of immigration at Milan Linate, to take a private bus to Cremona. There were now 15 of them: four sopranos (including

Caduta, who had stood in at the last minute); three altos (there should have been four, but the agreed deputy had failed to clear her diary in time); three tenors (there should have been four, but no acceptable replacement had been found); four basses (one being a deputy); and Anton. It was highly irregular for missing members not to be replaced, but the virus which was doing the rounds had found easy pickings among the London singers, leaving few spares. To make matters worse Fran, who had arrived in Linate with the others, had stopped talking, in the hope of not aggravating the cough of the previous evening, now a sore throat.

Anton considered the devastation which had been visited on his 'instrument'. The programme, which had been chosen at least a year previously, was a difficult one:

Josquin: *Praeter rerum seriem*
Pärt: *Tribute to Caesar*
Lotti: *Crucifixus a 8*
Monteverdi: *Crucifixus*
Monteverdi: *Adoramus te*
Monteverdi: *Domine, ne in furore*
Ingegneri: *Cantate domino*
Monteverdi: *Cantate domino*

INTERVAL

Josquin: *Gaude virgo*
Josquin: *Tu solus qui facis*
Josquin: *Pater noster/Ave Maria*
Sheppard: *Verbum caro*
Tallis: *Gaude gloriosa*

He had never changed a programme once it had been agreed, and although this one came into the category of 'dog's dinner' for various reasons, he wasn't inclined to change it now. The illnesses and shortages of personnel would have to be managed.

He surveyed the order of pieces. It contained the necessary nod towards the two composers most associated with Cremona – Monteverdi and his teacher Ingegneri – alongside music by Josquin des Prez and two English composers – Sheppard and Tallis – which they were previewing for the concert on Saturday. These had unusually high top parts, which would be much better sung by people who were not ill. Unfortunately he didn't have the necessary number of singers to perform *Spem in alium*, or he would willingly have included that too. The sheer scope and virtuosity of Tallis's *Gaude gloriosa* was going to have to stand in for it.

BY THE TIME the bus had reached Cremona the singers had carefully gone through the scores, trying to work out who would be capable of singing which parts, where the usual performer was absent. It wasn't so difficult replacing the ones who were actually missing – there were enough members present to sing the lines as solos in the full sound – but trying to guess what Fran would be capable of by the evening was a different task. One option was to rule her out altogether from the start. But this would create a problem in the Tallis, where a major section calls for all four sopranos to sing solo lines, reckoned too high for altos to fill them in.

Anton knew that the best solution to the crisis lay in letting the singers decide for themselves, and so he kept silent. The negotiations went fluently, as they always did when the chips were down, each singer quickly accepting the role they would have to play to save the day. The requirement wasn't so terrifying. The odd note might be uncomfortably high or low but the ensemble sound would give everyone a solid context, and in a reverberant building much could be disguised. The person who now really came under pressure was Fran, who would surely spend the rest of the day drinking gallons of water and worrying. Like all her colleagues she was not one to worry unnecessarily. But sooner or later even the hardiest singer will be forced to admit that illness has cornered them, and Fran realised she was dangerously close to this ultimate state. Nonetheless she said nothing. Nothing would make her ask to be relieved of a prominent solo which no one present could easily perform. That would be to let people down by choice.

There was little time to rest in the hotel. The rehearsal had had to be lengthened to accommodate all the changes made to the scorings, and there was a rule that for 90 minutes before a concert there should be time to recover and find something to eat. Within half an hour of arriving, they were lined up in the baroque church of San Marcellino.

Anton had prepared himself for a tiring afternoon, but even he was surprised by the pressure he now found himself under. Added to the need to drive everyone through the programme, trying to guess which sections were secure enough to leave to the concert, there was the issue of very evident radio microphones set up in the church, a broadcast not having been agreed to in advance. These were as a red rag to a bull so far as the singers were concerned, and their knee-jerk reaction that Italian entrepreneurs were 'always' trying to get something for nothing when it came to photography and recordings, instantly soured the atmosphere while draining energy.

No one outside the narrow parameters of the London singing world would understand why the free publicity which came from a nationwide broadcast would be unwelcome to any group; but there was a sensibility among singers like these that if the radio employees were being paid to be there, so should they be, in addition to their concert fee. This was an area where the assumptions of the amateur singing world clashed most elementally with the professional, leaving incomprehension in its wake. The Italian radio personnel, knowing no different, assumed the whole concert was proceeding on the usual amateur basis. A violent argument broke out between the radio producer, Anton, and the local agent, which used up 20 minutes of crucial rehearsal time and ended in the radio team derigging noisily, amid highly audible imprecations.

Anton turned to his colleagues, hoping for some support. He found that everyone was now involved and expressing an opinion, while he himself was caught in the crossfire. The singers knew that he was not entirely in agreement with them, that he did think that any publicity was good publicity, even if he himself was not being paid for it. But, then, for all they knew he was being paid more than them anyway and in that respect, if in no other, he wasn't digging with the same foot. The employer versus employee stand-off of years ago was stalking the wings, ready to leap forward. Before it could, however, concern about the minutiae of how they were going to get through the concert finally took over.

They half-sang their way through the sections which gave them most cause for worry, before limping off. It didn't help that the church was dusty, the temperature outside nearing 40 degrees and the sanitary arrangements medieval. They now had just 90 minutes to go back to the hotel, change and find a snack. The one aspect of what remained of the day that gave them simple pleasure to contemplate was the Ristorante Duomo, whose outside tables were ideally situated in view of the west end of the Cathedral, which some of them knew from previous visits was beautifully illuminated until midnight, the restaurant staying open as late as necessary. There had been many happy gatherings at those tables over the years, and it was intended that there should be another on this occasion. As a result of relentless touring the regular members of The Gamut Range had built up a network of preferred hostelries all over the world, places looked forward to months in advance of going to them, with an obsession which had led to questions about whether the meal or the concert was the more important element in their travelling. The stock answer was that the concerts had to be booked first.

Very hot weather makes what is already uncomfortable in being on stage, worse. Clothes become scratchy and irritate, paper scores begin to disintegrate, the physical effort involved in singing generates sweat, everywhere. San Marcellino is a cavernous building, capable of holding a thousand people, with a sweeping vault and spacious aisles. In normal day-to-day usage the hot and bothered might sit in there for hours and escape the glare. But a thousand bodies, plus the extra lighting on stage – so demandingly stipulated in the contract rider sent round by The Gamut Range management – had begun to turn the interior into a cauldron. The organisers had half predicted the problem by installing some electric fans, borrowed from friends nearby who could lend one at short notice; but the end result was an audience that fanned itself with anything to hand, making the kind of relentless low-level susurration one might hear from an army of cicadas.

This constant motion was soon found to be distracting to sing to, aggravated by the way people like to talk when they are uncomfortable and cannot forget themselves. And the singers had other concerns. The heat generated by the stage lights on the back of their heads had caused so much sweat to run down their faces that those who wore glasses, which was most of them, found that the beads either obscured the notes on the page or, worse, created false notes, which had the alarming property of moving about. Some of them decided that it would be prudent to take their glasses off altogether, which in turn meant they had to hold the copies close to their faces and so eliminate any contact with Anton and any singer who was not right next to them.

By the time the concert had been running for 15 minutes, The Gamut Range presented an unorthodox spectacle to their public. Several were holding their spectacles as well as their copies, while juggling handkerchiefs as best they could. Jackets for the men had been abandoned of course, but this only drew attention to the unflattering effect of sweat on black shirts. Uniformly puce in the face the singers were trying desperately to keep abreast of music they had hardly rehearsed. The sense of stress was palpable. By the interval some members of the audience, suffering themselves, were beginning to ask anxious questions. But there was nothing to be done, since the sound itself was as good as ever, and no one showed signs of leaving.

Fran's failing voice had thus far not been exposed to close scrutiny, since The Gamut Range sings most of its repertoire with two voices on each vocal part. She was singing with Chrissy, who was a most reliable partner, today in her element. This state of affairs came to an abrupt end at the passage for four solo sopranos in Tallis's *Gaude gloriosa*. Fran had been saving herself for this moment, aware of the responsibility. The previous section ended with a resounding cadence and Caduta duly began the new passage. When Fran was due to come in and join her she missed her first note, vaguely identified the second, missed the third, croaked her way through a handful more, before finally dissolving into a coughing fit from which there was no return. Water being very much to hand, she swallowed half a bottle of it and looked at Anton, distraught. The audience, however, far from being shocked by this unprofessional behaviour, which was what Fran desperately feared, murmured their appreciation of what they took to be courage, and gave her a spontaneous round of applause.

This didn't solve the problem of the missing part. But when the singing, which hadn't stopped despite the applause, re-established itself in the building, it became apparent that no line was missing. Keen to make use of his unusually high range, Jonathan Williams took up where Fran had left off, and blossomed. He was encouraged by the way Tallis had written the music in two sets of pairs – two voices accompanying each other in each pair. His partner was Caduta. He couldn't believe his luck. Slowly they began to sing to each other. Then they began to sway in sympathy. Soon they were smiling and gesturing as they swopped phrases back and forth, sometimes in parallel motion, sometimes answering each other with brief melodies. The other pair in the mix – Robin and Chrissy – began to join in, so that by the end of the section it was as if the four of them were taking part in an elaborate medieval dance, to music which is usually staged with the utmost reverence.

The audience went wild. The sight of Caduta, an Italian girl with film-star good-looks, dancing alongside a handsome Englishman who now had tears in his eyes, was too much for the tender-hearted polyphony-lovers of Cremona – and soon the whole church was filled with tender-hearted people, whipping themselves into a frenzy of delight. The fact that *Gaude gloriosa* does not finish at the end of this solo section was of no interest to anyone. Anton essayed a preliminary downbeat for the start of the next passage, but quickly decided that the best thing he could do was acknowledge the applause, bringing the four soloists forward. This only encouraged some members of the audience to rush to the foot of the stage, the better to photograph Caduta, shouting out in terms well-known to her to embrace her young lover. Puccini could not have managed it better. And as may happen with verismo opera crowds, the move of some of the audience to the front, encouraged everyone to get to their feet and surge forward.

Needless to say none of the musicians on the stage had seen anything like this, not even Caduta. Nor had the promoters, whose day jobs did not involve staging Puccini. Delight in the singers turned to apprehension mixed with relief, as they realised they would not have to sing the rest of *Gaude gloriosa*, but also that it was unlikely they would be allowed to leave the building without singing several encores.

Encores are the bane of professional musicians' lives. Haven't they sung enough? Aren't the audience satisfied? Didn't they enjoy the programme as it was, whole and entire? But this time normal rules didn't apply. Further singing was going to be an exercise in crowd control, since without it they were not going to escape. The crowd flooded around the foot of the stage, blocking off the exits, baying. The only way to re-establish calm was to start singing.

What happened over the next half-hour joined the lengthening list of topics for argument and debate over many communal meals for months to come. They sang a short piece, after which the audience went wild again. They sang another one, during which some of the more elderly began to leave by the doors at the west end of the church, and the hubbub diminished. They sang a third one, now seriously dehydrated, after which a critical moment was reached. The sopranos on the left-hand end of the choral line began to leave the stage, determined to sing no more. Nonetheless the crowd broke into a chant – 'bis', 'bis', 'bis' - and some even tried to touch Caduta's dress as she passed. But at this, out of nowhere, an instinctive brake was applied. Reasonable people asserted their authority, and the madness of the moment had passed. The singers slipped as silently as they could through one of the doors into the street, and so into evening temperatures and a gentle breeze. Few could remember a more delicious sensation in their careers than leaving that church and standing outside in the night air.

The group that eventually arrived at the Ristorante Duomo caused the Sicilians who ran it to look twice. Accustomed as they were to judging people by appearances, these English had them floored. They remembered the group, and especially Anton, well from previous years, but had never seen them so neutral. They were giving nothing off – there was no atmosphere to catch hold of. Were they happy, should they be greeted with smiles and exclamations and embraces? If not, what did they expect? The Sicilians knew they weren't very good at judging glum expressions, at least not in their guests. They knew them well enough amongst themselves, off-duty, but that was private.

The singers pulled the chairs back from the tables in silence and sat heavily down. The cooling air and the sight of the cathedral, beautifully illuminated, raised their spirits, but nothing was going to put significant life into them unless it were liquid. Claudia, the youngest of the servers, decided to break the ice. She went up to Anton, who squeezed out a smile and a kiss on the cheek. She looked at him searchingly. 'Salutamu,' she said, deciding to keep it simple. 'Stanchizza? Vinu?' 'Si', said Anton, grateful for all the help he could get. He indicated Caduta and sat down.

Two-litre jars of the house special, red and white, started to circulate, alongside chilled Italian bottled beer. Menus were passed around. The cheaper items began to be discussed as relaxation and rehydration went hand in hand. Alastair, who had been on previous visits, reminded those near him that there was an excellent antipasti selection inside. Pizzas were identified and their ingredients rated. Anton observed that a *bollito misto*, and the *mostarda* which always accompanies it in this part of Italy, was available. Knowing how it would be received, but unable to stop himself, he recommended the *bollito* to those sitting near him. At this the trenchant mood the singers had brought with them to the table turned easily into disgust.

'It's revolting,' said Judith Brooks, who had also been here before and hadn't tried it. 'Full of naughty bits.'

'Oh yuk,' said Nancy, right beside her, 'what's *mostarda*?'

'A kind of opaque mustard with caramelised fruit in it', said Anton, encouragingly.

'Yuk', said Nancy.

Anton reflected that the people who were so vigorously demolishing some of his most treasured cultural references had just sung a concert which no one else on the planet could have sustained. The instinctive gap between the one and the other, in him so narrow, yet in all his colleagues, including Lotte from the old days, so wide, appeared effectively unbridgeable. It must seem to them as though he had been brought up in the kitchens of Europe, where offal was a commonplace, which by extension, and in some obscure way, played into their default view that he was brought up posh. Neither of these things was true. He hadn't left the shores of England before the age of 18, and posh people in England don't choose tripe for their daily sustenance, let alone testicles. Something must have happened to him between the ages of 18 and 25 but, looking back, he couldn't see what it was; and whatever it was it hadn't happened to his colleagues.

Not once had any of them joined him for a tripe bake, or some Florentine *lampredotto*. He had once asked Ahmed if he would cook him some horse, to which Ahmed had replied that he couldn't get it in England. He said the English butchers wouldn't deal in it, though he had grown up on it in Jerusalem, as an inexpensive and nutritious meat. But he had added that if Anton could get it, he would happily cook it for him. This in turn had led Anton to import horse steaks, horse ribs and even a horse tornedos on one occasion, when they were available to buy, which tended to be in the Catholic countries. He found cultural cross-references like this the very essence of life, while realising that the people sitting round the table had quite different reference-points. What they had in common was love of the music they performed together. With that conjunction Anton had to be content.

And he was content. No plate of food in the world could rival the feeling of fulfilment when a performance was going just as he wanted it, and these people were the ones who made it come alive. They were nowhere near being the kind of careerists – medics, lawyers, academics, politicians – who have spent long training periods building up from scratch specialist knowledge that ordinary people will never come near, but people who were given a talent from birth. They had always been able to sing. And the first moment they could earn from it, they went out and did it, undeterred by anxiety over a career path. They made themselves available on the London singing scene, and waited to see what would happen. Along the way they had had singing lessons to be sure, but something completely instinctive had come first.

Anton looked round the table. The wine and beer was beginning to speak. He mentally clocked the singers who could be relied upon to say very little until they had drunk a bit; and the ones who made a lot of noise at any time in social situations, not much changing with the drink. The level of the chatter almost never rose above the tried and tested, which was more or less where the choice of food and drink also remained. Anton was neither surprised nor disappointed. Sometimes he wondered whether he would prefer it if he had an old friend on these tours, someone he could share his tastes and conversation with, someone like Lotte who had always at least pretended to take an interest; but being constantly on tour in close quarters with people who were neither family nor, specifically, friends, forbade anything exotic. It was necessary for him to be available to them all, no-nonsense and reliable in the classic English way. A friend from outside would dilute the constant need to join in with the whole team.

He sat back in his chair, noticing with relief that Caduta – an exception in every way – was engaging the staff in Sicilian dialect. Some members of the audience walked by the tables and recognised them. Various beautiful-sounding Italian adjectives came to the singers as they looked up, followed by clumsy attempts to say something pleasant in English. The singers beamed back, acknowledging vigorously that it had, indeed, been hot. Everyone smiled as they recalled the concert, the music and the camaraderie. The restaurant staff began to relax with their customers at last.

Anton returned to his glass of country wine and noticed that Chrissy was within talking distance. If he could converse with anyone in the group on topics interesting to him it was with her. Slightly older than the others, and a solitary person who did not intend to be anyone's dupe, she had thought round issues that most of the others preferred to think didn't concern them. There were limits – even she was not exactly his friend, not if he wanted to retain the ability to sack her, should that need ever arise. Given that she sang to perfection it seemed impossible that that need should ever arise. So why not be real friends? They were, and they couldn't be. Still, she was the only one of the standard group he knew he could consult without fear of getting a merely diplomatic reply.

'That was quite a testing little run-about', she said to him, deciding to plunge in first.

'I don't know how you keep going in conditions like that,' he replied. 'All I have to do is wave my arms around. I thought you sang really well', he added, knowing she wasn't going to say that he had waved his arms around well, and deciding not to wait for it.

'Yeah, well, singing soprano duets at high pitch with a countertenor was something of a novel experience', she said, and paused for him to comment on the result, knowing he would.

'It wasn't ideal, though I realise he got us out of jail,' said Anton, spearing a slice of beef tongue he had been playing with. 'If we had replaced Fran right from the start the audience riot would probably have been avoided. And I actually wish we had finished the piece, rather than have had to sing numberless encores. And I personally could have done without Jonathan's infatuation with Caduta becoming a public spectacle.'

'How unItalian you are. What you would have liked was a perfect performance of a perfect piece of music, sung in total silence, ending in polite applause. Heavens alive – the locals dealt with it in their own way, adding lustre to our reputation. I agree it would become rather wearying on a regular basis, though', she added, suddenly wanting to sound reasonable.

'That must be how it is for successful rock artists, though, day after day after day. And they don't get to sing Tallis.' He chuckled, taking a sip. 'What a grisly existence they must have.'

'They don't want to sing sodding Tallis, Anton', said Chrissy.

'They don't know to sing sodding Tallis, Chrissy. Do you like being in Italy? In the end you don't seem to be much derailed by all this Latin emotion.'

'To be honest with you I literally don't think about it. It's just another job, isn't it? Tomorrow it will be samey old London again, where we shall not bring the house down. It'll be London food, London weather and London people. Next week, if I remember rightly, it'll be the US. It could be Japan.' She stopped to stare at her colleagues as they discussed their daily lives at home, wondering how they would reply to this question, and thinking the answers might be rather different. 'Wherever it is I shall enjoy the singing, the company of my colleagues, the swimming pool, and then I shall enjoy coming home. I waste very little energy on sight-seeing, or doing any of the recommended cultural things. I don't even like shopping much. I literally wouldn't mind eating sandwiches all the way round a tour frankly. We move on so fast that I'd become a wreck in no time if I tried to soak up all these places have to offer. And I wouldn't be able to do my job properly.'

'Don't you enjoy meeting new people?' he asked, hoping he might get some insight into her personal life, an area of mystery for all who knew her professionally.

'Yes, but if you mean do I want to get off with them, the answer is no. I don't enjoy one-night stands, and I understand so little of what I really want that I don't know whether to eye a man or a woman. All I want to do is sing, and I dread the moment when I'll not be employable any more. Lotte handled that so gracefully – bowing out when she was still at the top of the pile. I always loved singing with her. Her retirement was an irreplaceable loss to the group in my opinion. But when the time comes I won't be lonely. I enjoy my own company too much. And too often find everyone else annoying', she added, smiling, aware that the people near them round the table had stopped their conversations in order to hear what she was saying.

One of these was Nancy Silver. Sure enough she had not tried the *mostarda*, but opted for a pizza that had concentrated on unthreatening ingredients like mushrooms, red pepper and rocket.

'Oh Chrissy, how can you like say such terrible things,' said Nancy, giggling all over her neighbours. 'Well, to make you feel better I want you to know I like spent the whole concert wondering where you got your earrings. They really are special. I imagine they must be like made of silver?'

'They were given to me by an admirer...' replied Chrissy, allowing her voice to trail away.

'Oh, wow, do we like know him?'

'Maybe,' said Chrissy. 'But you may be imagining the wrong sort of person...' more trailing.

'What? I don't get you. Like what wrong sort?' she clattered.

'Well, for example, it might not have been a man.'

'Oh you mean like a woman. Well that's no big deal. Is she a singer?'

'Nancy,' said Anton, gently interrupting. 'What did you really think about during that concert? You sang really well. You must have been thinking about the music a bit.'

'Well, to tell the truth I was completely distracted by the like sweat which I could feel running down my back. All the way through the concert. It was incredible. It like never stopped. It started in my hair and ran like a stream down my neck and all the way down my spine to my like bum. It was so itchy, I didn't know how to scratch it and hold my music.'

'And sing?', said Anton.

'Oh that was the easy part. I didn't have to think about that', and her voice in turn trailed off as she enjoyed having been a little shocking. Such repartee proceeded from the double security of knowing she was respected in her work, and happy at home with her partner Dave, a horn player. For her, at 29, experimenting with new experiences had come to a natural end, leaving her to go places to make a living she enjoyed making, asking very few questions. Anton found her exasperating because he knew from the way she sang that there was a deep intelligence hidden away somewhere inside her, but more than anyone he knew she always spoke in company as though she was really dumb. It was only when she felt threatened that she allowed a flash of something more demanding to show through: conductors chose their words carefully when criticising her work. Otherwise it seemed to Anton as though she must have learnt at an early age that the easiest way to get what she wanted was to play the attractive doll, always saying silly, beguiling things to grown-ups who would then spoil her because she obviously didn't know any better and they did. This act drove Anton mad, as Chrissy knew very well.

The party began to break up. Fran Moody had gone straight to the hotel after the concert, knowing she had plenty of singing to do in the next few days and hoping desperately that her voice would recover overnight. One never knew: a good night's sleep and plenty of water might be all that was needed, or, despite these precautions, her voice might vanish for a week, and she would have to hand over all her work and her income to a deputy. All the singers had to live with this doubt, though if there was no sign of trouble it was put out of mind. In this mood several of the men, equally knowing they had plenty of singing to do in the next few days, nonetheless repaired to a bar in the square which stayed open even later than the restaurant.

Anton, Caduta and Chrissy were the last to leave, having consumed a *digestivo* which had been offered on the house. Caduta had discovered that their hosts came from Agrigento, which was less than an hour's drive from her own home. She had spent the meal retracing Sicilian steps with Claudia, her brother and their parents, much to Jonathan's disappointment, who had hoped to build on the new intimacy he thought he had achieved with her during the concert. He had yet to learn, as Caduta had learnt years ago, that in the professional singing world what happens on stage stays on the stage. The emotion generated by a piece of music in concert starts and ends there. The amateurs they knew might come off stage reliving 'the good bits' around a convivial table for hours afterwards, but not these full-time singers. It was quite common for them to go to bed after a good meal having forgotten what they had sung that evening, where and with whom.

Caduta, keen not to seem standoffish, joined the men at the bar. Anton and Chrissy, walking slowly back together, hesitated. Neither of them particularly wanted another drink, though they savoured the air of freedom this kind of touring so often, and so briefly, offered them. They were mindful of what they had to do in the coming days, and yet knew from experience that 'one more' would make no difference. They would feel tired in the morning but not incapacitated, and although Anton, at 65, was at least 25 years older than Chrissy, they were both old enough to have learnt how to sleep on public transport. Younger people always seemed to find this much harder.

They leant against a wall, being non-committal. In silence they surveyed the scene around the square, as several bars kept up a barrage of good cheer. Caduta and the men of The Gamut Range settled into seats around a group table at one of the bars and ordered drinks. The lights illuminating the west end of the Cathedral had been turned off at midnight, allowing depth to the stars above their heads.

Chrissy, reacting instinctively to the silence, started talking. 'What do you say to a brilliantly perceptive thought I just had, that the mood and ultimate success of all the mixed ensembles that London has spawned recently has depended on how well the conductor treats the women.'

This took Anton by surprise. 'Which conductor?' he parried, shifting his position, while collecting what thoughts there were to collect.

'All of them. Haven't you noticed? All the groups we sing for are conducted by men. Those groups are astonishingly similar, at least on paper. English men and women – very often the same ones – directed by a man. It's literally a miracle all those groups don't all sound the same. But the main reason why they don't, is that each of those guys out front has his own agenda, his own hang-ups, his own skills. Yet the treatment of the women in said groups will be identical. Whenever a conductor's authority is questioned – by anyone - he feels rejected, he feels panic; and his first hiding-place is to think of the women as inferior, and try to dominate them. At the same time he still wants them to admire and support him. What on the surface seems like just another instance of a man being autocratic and dismissive is really a complicated sexual game. If this game is allowed to be drained of its humanity, the group in question will slowly die.'

'Does this only apply to the women?' asked Anton, struggling to see where this was going.

'Well, it usually is the women, isn't it, since the men tend to be better at not taking arsiness personally.'

'Is this a feature of the younger practitioners only?' He shifted his stance again, implying discomfort at the line of questioning, though the hardness of the wall didn't help.

'Disappointingly, no,' she answered, giving him a steady look. 'There are plenty of older men who literally cannot grow out of using their ensembles as an extension of their need to appear macho. To control their surroundings which, as they are so quick to point out, they have created to everyone's great benefit. Their version of everything has to be the best, and everyone around them has to worship this truth. But I tell you that if there is a whiff of insurrection it will be the women who are the first targets of the inevitable sarcasm. And something in them enjoys it, for a while, until it goes too far and becomes an unbearable and humiliating routine.' She stood up straight now, drawing circles in the dust with her feet.

'Why?'

'Because very few people are impervious to the sexual positioning implied in all this, a merry-go-round which is triggered by our hero standing out front, wanting to seem attractive to the women. With the men he just tells them what to do, and they either do it or they moan, but the transaction is on an even keel. As I say, with the women the transaction is much more complex. Whether they fancy him or not, most of them will not be impervious to the fact that the person who is telling them what to do, and not liking the results, is male. The proof of this is when a gay man takes a session – the vibes are very different. Much healthier.'

Anton wondered whether to play innocent, but he had been around too long. He decided to meet the issue head on. 'How are we doing?'

'Not badly. At least you try to run properly democratic rehearsals, where everyone feels their opinions will be treated respectfully. You seem to have grasped that your singers know as much about the business of giving a concert as you do, the women as much as the men. The groups that are in trouble are those where the women keep resigning, because they simply can't take any more of the condescension.' She scuffed over the circles at her feet, and started afresh.

'Which explains how our group has lasted so long?'

'Yes, though what I've never understood is that by all accounts you were as bad as the rest of them when you were younger. Yet we seem to be here.' She lent back against the wall.

'The benign influence of Lotte, years ago, at the moment when it could all have gone wrong?' he suggested.

'Actually, legend has it that you disliked the men more than the women.' They both laughed.

'I disliked all of them equally, apart from Lotte – and on that our democratic ways were established', said Anton, now standing up straight in front of her.

Chrissy felt a rush of emotion. What was it? A longing for something, for sure. To protect this daring person, who of course didn't want it? To be close to someone she admired? To get really close?

Anton watched her as he realised he was on the verge of what for him was danger. He decided once again to meet the issue head on. 'Are you hoping for something?' he asked. 'Forgive me, I'm a bit out of practice at this sort of thing.'

Chrissy registered the luke-warm tone of voice, the 'don't touch me' shape sinking back onto the wall. She hadn't meant much, just an affection which would remain, under the emotional rubble of the touring life. The occasional tourist looks forward to a bit of activity between the hotel sheets. The persistent tourist takes their whole life with them abroad, and is disinclined to treat a journey as anything other than another ordinary day.

'No,' said Chrissy. 'But put the thought in your back pocket.' And she turned into the hotel.

NOT MANY MINUTES BEFORE THIS, it being midnight in London, Ahmed had been saying good-night to the last of his customers. It had been an enjoyable evening, the clientele made up entirely of locals. In particular the Gallaghers had come to relive the experiences of the television session, looking round them in disbelief at how the scene of only that morning had been washed away, and the restaurant they knew rediscovered. They had spoken loudly as they ate, addressing anyone else who would listen, delivering a breathless account of what had transpired. At times the tables near them had fallen silent as they exaggerated what they remembered of the discussion, not least the part played in it by themselves. They recounted how they had voiced support for Anton's revelatory statements, many of which 'of course' they hadn't understood, while allowing themselves sufficient knowledge to know when to applaud. Anton was represented as a knight in shining armour, Barbara as a cunning person 'very dolled up', intent on trying to catch him out, which she had conspicuously failed to do. By the end of the evening there were many wide eyes around the room, and a comfortable communal sense of belonging.

Ahmed listened to all this with tact and his characteristic half-smile. He was not in the mood to prick anyone's bubble. It had been an eventful day for his establishment, and he knew it would be remembered. Eventually the diners had begun to tire of so much excitement, and paid their bills. By midnight Ahmed was alone again, Eugene and the kitchen staff having long since departed.

He cleared up the remaining tables and went into the kitchen to prepare himself an Arabic coffee. He was too alive to go to bed yet, preferring to position a table in the entrance to the restaurant where he could sit and enjoy the warm air pass over him. There were no clouds, just a display of stars which he had come to observe with care. In his childhood, in a place where there was little public lighting, he had marvelled at the infinite depth of space. Here, in a big city, the display was inevitably greatly reduced, but this made him all the more careful of the stars he could see and identify. He put his packet of cigarettes on the table in front of him, and decided that he was going to break his rule of one a day. He lit up, and sat back, his mind slowly replaying the interview he had witnessed that morning.

There had been plenty of music in his childhood home, guaranteed by his grandmother's interest in the three sopranos who had dominated the musical life of the Arabic-speaking world at that time – Umm Khultum, Mounira El Mahdeya and Fathiyya Ahmad. Of course Umm Khultum was her favourite, as she eventually became everybody's, but the rivalry between the three of them, and the renaissance of song writing which it encouraged, had led to a lot of amateur singing in kitchens up and down the

Middle East. In particular Umm Khultum's proficiency on the *oud* had led to a craze of manufacture which his grandmother had allowed herself to get caught up in. For as long as he could remember there was an *oud* standing ready among the pots and pans, picked up and strummed in the few unoccupied moments of a woman's day. In time the strumming became articulate, and the quavery voices of his mother and grandmother more confident, so that he too could join in. Music in this world was informal, improvised almost – at least the vocal embellishments were – something for everyone. What had surprised him about the interview was the way music was referred to as a kind of commodity, something to promote egos and careers, make money from, get annoyed with different-minded people about – to all of which the public was a willing accomplice. How had it got so formal, so professional, so aggressive and cut-throat?

And one could hear it in the music itself, or at least in the performances. How different this was from the music of his homeland! He knew how his customers performed from the discs they brought him to play, with their artificial perfection, not a glitch or a blemish. And the music itself, so complex, formal and stiff; so arid in its lack of any spontaneity. The songs he remembered from the past only had a single melody, artfully nuanced and embellished, perfumed. The instrumental accompaniment would follow that melody, providing its own brittle tones to the singer's swirling, faltering, supple narrative. At times nothing would seem to move forward, as the singer lost herself in ever-decreasing vocal arabesques, reducing to a central point of calm before rushing forward again. There had never been such a golden age of performance in the Arab world, and he had been just old enough to marvel at it.

One of the many things he found alien when he had come to England was the style of music-making, and especially of singing:

it was an irony to him that he now had so much connection to the classical singing community. The musicians he now hosted seemed to specialise in everything that was opposite to what he loved in Umm Khultum and her world. The English seemed to tie everything down, put their melodies into straightjackets, sing without any detectable heart. The sheer complexity of their music made sure that no single person could express their emotions through this song. They had to blend into each other, to produce a shining exterior with no chinks. The sound gleamed as it spoke of religious truths apparently no one cared about, in a language, Latin, no one spoke. The music he grew up with throbbed with emotion, projected through its words by a single, passionate 'interpreter'.

He sighed. He wasn't by nature a politically minded man, and he was deeply grateful to the English for their unquestioning acceptance of him. He had had no sense of rejection of any kind, in all these years. Yet there were moments when he couldn't understand how his instinctive reactions could be so different from theirs. They could agree on food, certainly on drink, which he had learnt to enjoy without a sense of guilt in recent years, and he was in awe of the sense of well-being which his easy-going clients always emanated. But when it came to the arts he couldn't sympathise with them. It wasn't just music. He knew this from the posters which festooned his walls and ceiling. He had come to notice that if he wanted to feel alien in his own house, all he had to do was scan the posters. There he would find publicity for theatre, film, concerts, stand-up, poetry readings, all appealing to what was clearly thought to be a shared intellectual starting-point. None of it spoke to him. There was a fundamental dislocation.

Once again, under the influence of Umm Khultum, he forced himself to let his eye wander over the shiny surfaces of the posters. He encountered Stewart Lee, striding across a stage, microphone in hand, joking for everyman. There was Eddie Izzard having just run a marathon, asking for sponsorship. Ballerinas in skimpy clothing were adopting unnatural poses for the delight of an audience who could but gawp. The King's Singers – all six of them – were there too, grinning from ear to ear in identikit fashion, as if the cream just never stops flowing. Finally he arrived at the poster which disconcerted him more than any. It was an announcement of an anniversary rerun of *The Sound of Music*, to be shown up the road at the Screen on the Green.

What was it about this image which so shook him? Clearly it didn't come from his having retained an Arab view of propriety: he had got used to that difference in his life in England long ago, and had come to terms with it. There was the heroine pictured in a pretty cotton dress, more than half of her represented by unmistakeably shapely legs. The rest of her attractive physique was made plain through the dress. Behind her were several children in bright yellow costumes, whose expressions indicated a delight in dancing around a mountain scene which made them appear to him either moronic or spoilt. To the right of the ensemble was a single adult male who had obviously lost control of all these unlikely people, to some of whom he was possibly related. And the cause of this brimming happiness? The banner over the top said it all: 'The Happiest Sound in All the World'. *The Sound of Music.*

It was the reference to the power of music which threw him. He could take or leave the vapidity of the scene, but he could not dissociate it from what music meant to him. He could recognise the songs from the film, certainly: over the years it had been hard to escape them. But however trite he found them, he was free to reject them without tearing himself apart. What he couldn't swallow was the idea that something so fundamentally important could be so dragged through the mud. It was offensive beyond rational explanation, and it taught him once and for all that for him music indeed transcended normal reactions. Here, at least, he was at one with so many of his customers.

He wondered when he had allowed music into his soul like this. Was it the *oud* in the kitchen, the strumming and the singing? Was it simply the power of Umm Khultum's performances, which had gradually stolen up on him? He liked that option; and sat back in his chair to observe the stars again, light a second cigarette and let his mind come to rest on whichever of her masterpieces his subconscious offered him. Eventually he focused on *Al Nil*, a song he hadn't heard since his childhood, humming the melody under his breath.

He had made his way through most of it, gently accompanying himself on an imaginary *oud*, when he suddenly felt anxious to the point of nausea. Suddenly his mind was crashing through layers of memory, trying to fix the moment when this particular melody had taken on such intense meaning. Had his grandmother sung it on a difficult family occasion? Had his mother sung it to him when his father had punished him, which happened often? His mother... like a blow to the stomach he remembered. It was in the refugee camp. Someone nearby had been singing it as the shooting started. He felt tears coursing down his cheeks.

Chapter 4

FRIDAY, 7 JUNE 2019

BY THE TIME Ahmed stood in his doorway the following morning, preparing to open, the members of The Gamut Range were most of the way back to London. He could reflect on a relatively quiet time in the restaurant the previous evening, while all his singers were about other business, but he knew very well that today was going to be different, and tomorrow different again. For Saturday evening, for the after-concert party, he had agreed to stay open for as long as anyone wanted him to, which would surely mean all night. But for today he intended that everyone should go to bed early. It amused him to think that he was uniquely well-placed to ensure that that would happen, accepting the responsibility for facilitating a good concert with pleasure.

As midday struck he saw an unfamiliar figure walking towards him, a man of a certain age, wearing ill-fitting clothes and a cloth cap, evidently not quite sure where he was, or what he was looking for. Ahmed's apron reassured him. 'Hello', he said, distractedly rubbing a cheek.

'Welcome,' said Ahmed, examining him. 'Can I get you something?'

'Well, maybe you could, if it doesn't cost too much,' the man replied, hesitating some more, while anxiously pulling the cap forwards and back on his head. 'You see I'm in this choir, The Whyte Chorale. Rehearsing at 2. I noticed this restaurant when I was up here the other day, and...'

At this juncture Ahmed would normally propose 'the normal', or wait for his customer to ask for something known to be on the menu. This man, however, confused him. He obviously had no idea what was on the menu, nor any very firm idea of what he might like even if he were to read it. 'No hurry,' Ahmed started, papering over a gap that had turned into a silence, 'and to see those clouds, maybe better indoors. I think this humid time is to be interrupted.'

The man decided he needed to feel more at home, if he was going to get through this afternoon. He knew the singing was going to stretch him, which made him nervous. However unlike his fellow trainees in the Whyte Chorale, he had decided to meet the challenge head-on and alone, rather than by hiding in a crowd of equally nervous colleagues, none of whom wanted to come forward and be identified. Steve Taylor's friendly manner in rehearsal had spoken to him just enough to suggest that here was an activity he might do something crazy for. He might dare to find out more about it. Why not? 'You see,' he began again, rubbing his cheek some more, 'I don't know much about music, and things like that. I wasn't educated in it, if you see what I mean. My parents didn't have money for extra stuff...' he stopped again, the cap doing the work. He realised he might have misjudged Ahmed. Did he know about this remote world that so moved him?

But he was impressed by Ahmed's air of authority. 'I'm Brian. Brian Wiggins...' and he stared hard at everything but Ahmed himself. Ahmed was aware that he had never been in quite this situation before, aware that he had become accustomed to dealing either with regular singers, or with well-heeled local residents, and not much else. He clocked Brian's shabby appearance, sensed his uncertainty, and warmed to him.

'Sit down and I'll get you a cup of coffee,' he said.

'Oh, OK,' said Brian, wandering after him into the restaurant and from there behind the partition into the kitchen. 'I'm actually training to be a supermarket manager, you know. With Highbury's' and he swallowed noisily, no idea how this information would be received. 'I've had loads of jobs before, and thought I might try this. So far, so good, you know.'

Ahmed digested this rush of confidence. 'That sounds a serious job. Well, sit down and I'll bring you good coffee.' Although Ahmed spent his days making small talk, and never seemed to be at a loss for something genial to say, Brian almost floored him. He resorted to the routine. 'Have you worked in supermarkets before?'

'Probably.' Brian tried a casual shrug. 'I've done so many different jobs I forget which ones were for shops, councils, night-clubs, you name it. They weren't much cop, any of them, and some of them were dangerous, but I've always paid my way. I never looked for charity.' Ahmed waited for an expression of defiance after this remark, but it never came. Instead Brian looked defensive, almost pleading.

'So this time it's supermarket?' prompted Ahmed.

Brian hung his head. 'I hate them. I liked it in the days when there were little family-owned shops all down the high streets, every shop selling a different item. You could spend all morning chatting to the shop-keepers. It was a slower pace in those days. But I appreciate these Highbury's people being prepared to give an old stager like me a chance. I've come in on a government scheme.'

Ahmed knew enough about English life to know that what Brian was describing in the business of daily shopping had been taken out of a picture book of golden memories, but he wanted to be sympathetic. 'Are there many older people on your course?'

'Quite a few. All sorts. Some are just starting out.'

'And you wanted to sing?'

Brian coughed nervously. 'Not really, but I'm game for anything, me. I liked Mr Taylor.' He paused. 'I wasn't really interested in singing myself, but I thought it might be fun.' He paused again. 'I hadn't the slightest idea of...' He swallowed hard. 'I had no idea...' he tried to resume. Ahmed said nothing. Eventually Brian pulled himself together. 'Do you know the singers, then? And Mr Taylor?'

By the time the next customer appeared Ahmed was exhausted. He had told Brian all he knew about what went on in The Bunker, which, since he'd never been there, wasn't very much; and Brian had lapped it up, as his imagination described ever wider circles. Ahmed had also outlined the characteristics of some of the principal players, focussing on Steve, Joe and Anton, always representing them as the most delightful people anyone could hope to meet. Armed with this minimum of information, Brian, more and more intrigued, waited wide-eyed for the singing world itself to unfold around him. He installed himself at a corner table out of the way. By the time he followed the others over the road for rehearsal he had consumed half a cup of cold coffee.

Steve, Joe and Tom Morris arrived together. Joe thought Ahmed greeted them with more than usual enthusiasm. They all stood in the entrance for a moment.

'Any news from all those talented people rushing back from Cremona?' asked Steve. He was preparing himself for a convoluted day in The Bunker, with rehearsals taking place all afternoon and evening, culminating in a dress rehearsal for *Spem in alium*. One of his responsibilities was going to be The Whyte Chorale.

A thought had occurred to Ahmed. 'How it is possible the Whyte Chorale, made up of many people trying to get jobs in supermarkets, are rehearsing at 2pm on a Friday afternoon?'

'Well, friend, there is a reason. How do you know this?' Steve answered. Ahmed pointed to Brian, sitting in the corner.

'Oh hi!' said Steve to Brian, forgetting Brian's name. 'OK?' He turned back to Ahmed. 'You may be interested to know, mate, that thanks to my exceptional negotiating skills, backed by my prominent media presence, I have just arranged for Highbury's to part-sponsor the concert tomorrow. What was happening on a shoe-string, is going to happen with extra cash. We can all relax a bit. But now, of course, the management at Highbury's has become interested in this concert. Now they want Highbury's to look good.'

'Oh?' said Joe, feeling uneasy. 'What does that amount to?'

'It amounts?' said Steve, mocking him, 'to some of the big bosses turning up. Get it? This news in turn has caused quite a stir among those worthy songsters who might yet join us.'

Joe cut to the chase. 'How many of them?'

Steve looked at the floor. 'Well, at least a hundred at the last count.'

'You mean a hundred people will be singing in The Whyte Chorale tomorrow?'

'At least a hundred' said Steve, beginning to see past the initial achievement of his negotiations.

'That is to say,' pursued Joe, remorselessly, 'in the performance of *Spem in alium* tomorrow, there will be five people in each of Choirs 1, 2 and 3, making 15 members of The Gamut Range; something like 40 members of a boosted-up Voces Civitatis distributed through Choirs 4, 5, 6 and 7; and a hundred or more singers in Choir 8.'

He examined Steve with the look of a novice who has spotted a tiny chink in the armour of the well-established. He grinned from ear to ear, thrilled to bits. 'This is something I have to see. Dear oh dear. I wonder how they're all going to fit on the stage. I wonder how they'll see the beat. I wonder whether they will even be able to hear the piano, which will have to be planted in their midst', and he doubled up with delight.

Steve stopped inspecting the floor and started looking longingly at the vacant tables. 'Well, brood on this one matey. A lot of people have been let off work this afternoon to take part in our rehearsal, which means there will be a big crowd in rehearsal room 3 very shortly. We're somehow going to have to turn the music of Choir 8 into something manageable by a choral society', and he stared glumly at Joe and Tom, who had been listening attentively.

'Maybe I can help,'said Tom thoughtfully, briefly rooted to the spot. 'After all, I'm supposed to be, you know, laying down the law about what notes people should be singing, and I'm here partly to do just that in the Regis piece Chrissy has identified', and his voice trailed away as he stood aside to let one of Ahmed's regulars enter the restaurant.

Steve, also moving aside, kept his eye on Tom. 'How can you help, pilgrim?' he said urgently.

'Did I hear you say there will be a piano?'

'Yes', said Steve.

'Is there a photocopier in the building?'

'Yes.'

'Can you rehearse something else for a while?'

'Well I imagine we could spend hours on *Greensleeves* and *Strawberry Fair* if we put our minds to it. How long do you need?'

'Long enough to write out all the leads in unison, with the correct number of bars between them, so the Chorale can, you know, sing the points of imitation as melodies together, and the piano can fill in what joins them up. What I shall have to decide is which melodies to extract, and how long to keep them going before everyone loses the plot. I brought a full score, just in case.'

'Someone is going to have a big score-reading job to do on the piano', said Joe, not for the first time in the week. He had stopped laughing.

'Indeed', said Steve, beginning to recover his good humour.

'Anyone seen Johnny recently?' said Joe, asking after his fellow accompanist and now alert to what was in store for him. 'Where is he when you need him?'

'Not booked for this session, esteemed colleague. He deppeth where he list. Much in demand', said Steve, and the three of them finally sat down at a table and ordered some food.

BY 1.45PM A LARGE CROWD of miscellaneous people had gathered outside The Bunker, full of noisy anticipation. They were a little nervous, since singing of any kind hadn't played a large part in their lives, and singing of this kind was scary. But there was safety in numbers – clearly no one was going to have to do anything by themselves – and, what was more, they had the blessing of their employers. Those who had bothered to attend the previous rehearsals with Steve spoke well of his user-friendly style. There wasn't much to be anxious about, really.

Brian Wiggins remained in his corner for as long as he could, soaking up the atmosphere of the restaurant and replaying in his head all that he had just heard. Nothing from when he had been a youth 20 years ago had given him any kind of preparation for what he was feeling now. He could scarcely find words to express it, even to himself: he was struggling with a magical mystery world, fascinating and incomprehensible, peopled by gods. He longed to be part of it, though he had no idea why. His only experience of it had been one rehearsal down at the training centre, followed by the one on Tuesday evening in The Bunker. Even the group work he had done with Steve had meant something important to him; but when he heard The Gamut Range sing the opening bars of *Spem in alium* at the end of the tutti rehearsal that evening, he felt a quite new sensation. What had been intriguing had become essential. The sound they had made mesmerised him. It was a kind of intangible beauty. He dreamed it at night. It haunted him.

And he wanted more of it, like a drug. At this moment joining his colleagues for a group sing-along didn't seem like the way forward, but he realised it was the only way forward for now. And so he reluctantly gave up his corner and followed Steve outside.

As he did so Francis Quirk, the critic, passed him at the door. Francis entered the restaurant, greeted Ahmed, and looked about him. The first person he noticed sitting at a table was Tom, who by this time had got out some manuscript paper, a pencil, a pencil sharpener and a copy of the part-score of *Spem in alium*, which Choir 8 would normally have sung from. He had laid them out before him, and started to adapt the music as best he could. Francis knew Tom a little, from gigs around town.

'Hi Tom,' he said. 'Mind if I join you?'

Tom glanced up. 'Hello Francis. I'm working to a rather tight deadline here. Steve Taylor wants this finished as fast as I can do it, and it's rather tricky. You wouldn't believe me if I told you what I'm actually doing, but I offered, and so, you know, it must be done', he said, his good nature on genial display.

'Got you. I'll sit at the next table and keep out of your way', said Francis, with which he spotted Eugene, who not many minutes previously had slipped into the room, and was now languidly donning an apron. 'Yes?' said Eugene, still fiddling with the apron's ties. He had not forgotten the little incident of a week or two ago, but his was not a vindictive nature. There was no perceptible difference in his manner towards Francis as towards almost all of his customers, at any time. He maintained a scrupulous hauteur throughout.

'I'd like a plate of *siyadieh* fish with rice, and a glass of Blanc de Blanc, please Gene', said Francis, hoping a little informality would melt some ice. Eugene said nothing but went behind the partition to place the order. Francis opened a copy of *The Times*, the newspaper he wrote for, and had just started to read when a voice nearby called out: 'I really enjoyed your piece the other day about boredom. Very well managed. You did well to stay awake while writing it.'

It was Bob Gallagher who, with his wife Sally, was sitting at their favourite table near the window. They were slowly making their way through two helpings of *mulukhiyah* stew, with a bottle of Kefraya to hand. Francis put his newspaper down and laughed it off.

'Aha. It wasn't so much about boredom as about the good effects of nothing in particular happening.'

'Yes, I know, I read it carefully. But you clearly want it both ways: surely being stimulated by blankness isn't really possible for people today. All those Chinese mystics you quote weren't living in the modern world. I bet they would have thought rather differently if they had had a telly.'

Eugene, with natural delicacy, placed a plate of *siyadieh* in front of Francis, along with some unrequested *tabbouleh*. Francis thanked him, took a mouthful and turned back to Bob Gallagher. 'Actually it wasn't the Chinese mystics. I got my lead from something DH Lawrence wrote or translated – I forget which – in which he said "A great deal of the meaning of life and of art lies in the apparently dull spaces, the pauses, the unimportant passages." Goodness, what a beautiful thought! I've been obsessed with it ever since I bumped into it. It relieves us of the obligation to pay automatic tribute to all that restless art, which so insistently demands our attention every split second that we are exposed to it.' He took another mouthful.

'I always wondered why the mannerist styles made me feel so tired and empty. They have eliminated the unimportant passages. We are brought up to believe that urgent art is the only type of art which deserves our respect, as if we have somehow failed as human beings if we are not thrilled by something which continually jolts us.' He paused, aware that whenever he lost his reading audience he was thought marvellously impressive, but when he lost a listening audience the feed-back could be less appreciative. Bob had been making signals to Sally.

'Maybe a glass of that *arancello* would help my afternoon nap', Bob said, and waved at Eugene. Francis smiled. 'Just remember,' he said, intending to round the conversation off in an elegant way, 'that between our memorable moods and deeds, there is blank space. There is something to be said for books and paintings which include that blankness...'

'...and music,' said Tom Morris, who had been diligently working on his transcription but had overheard Francis's remarks and couldn't resist joining in. 'It is one of the principal delights of renaissance polyphony that it, you know, carries within itself unimportant passages, to the point not of dullness' – he paused, looking for the right word – 'but of repose.'

Bob decided to have one more sortie before abandoning the field: 'You mean there have to be boring bits for you to get the most out of the exciting bits?' and with that he congratulated himself, feeling he could honourably retire. He and Sally turned back to themselves, as they drank Ahmed's homemade *digestivo*. Slowly they unpeeled themselves from their seats, paid their bill and left.

There was a brief silence between Francis and Tom, as the former wondered how much further to go, and the latter looked at his unfinished transcription, also in two minds.

Eventually Francis decided he would go further. He had done his homework for the article, which Bob had noticed recently enough, to be able to quote his sources without hesitation, though he kept the newspaper and his article by him. 'Flavour provokes attachment, and insipidity provokes detachment. The former overwhelms us, clouds our minds, reduces us to a state of dependence; the latter liberates us from the pressure of the external world, from the excitement of sensations, from all false and short-lived intensities. It frees us from fleeting infatuations and silences the wearying din and clamour.'

Tom was deeply impressed. 'Who said that?' he asked.

'Possibly Ni Zan. At any rate it was a long established tenet of Daoism by the 14th century, when Ni Zan lived. Of course it is hard to translate the relevant Chinese characters into a modern language which is not misleading. Our word "bland" has to do a lot of work for which it is scarcely suited. The same for "flavourless" and "insipid". But the underlying principle seems to me to be incredibly attractive.'

Tom sat back in his chair, happy for a moment to surrender himself to abstract thought. 'What you say reminds me of those pen and ink drawings the Chinese and Japanese were so fond of. You know, the ones which depict a vast expanse of water with basically nothing on it – so the viewer only sees untouched paper – with just a few marks here and there to represent a fisherman in a boat, or a pavilion on a rocky outcrop, with maybe a figure sitting inside reading a book or drinking tea, around the edges.'

'That genre of drawing was exactly what Ni Zan was famous for,' said Francis, picking up his newspaper and starting to read. 'Things rich in colour run out, dry up, while things that are bland grow gradually richer.' He nodded at Tom meaningfully.

'And you will be pleased to know that the Daoists applied this way of thinking to music as well. I quote: "The most beautiful music – the music that affects us most profoundly – does not consist of the fullest possible exploitation of all the different tones. The most intensive sound is not the most intense. Sound delivered to its fullest extent leaves us with nothing to anticipate, nothing to look forward to".

I am struck by how very opposite to this was the underlying impetus of the baroque. If you were searching for reasons to think any mannerist music, beginning with the madrigals of Gesualdo, overstated yet disappointingly predictable, there they are. I wonder,' he added, suddenly going off at a tangent 'whether the mystics would have had it in them to reject Ahmed's food for its astonishingly agreeable, at times strong flavours; its lack of blandness. One has to assume that something as good as this *siyadieh* was anathema to them', and he chuckled at the thought.

'Yes, indeed,' said Tom, ignoring the last comment and staring unseeingly at a poster on Ahmed's wall, advertising a play at The Royal Court. 'That constant need to push emotional boundaries ever further out, to develop a style which, you know, is designed to grasp the listener and not let him go until he is a wreck, is something I've always mistrusted. Why did the history of Western art have to go so relentlessly in that direction?'

'What interests me,' he continued, trying not to be aware of the passing of time, 'is that the music which came just before the "revolution" of the baroque – the music which Monteverdi was rejecting for the very reason that it was to him too uneventful – always in some degree contains the elements you're espousing. All good Renaissance polyphony deals in an even-tempered, undemonstrative surface, which, you know, beckons the listener in. The past master of this was Palestrina. Never was there another composer that everyone has so rushed to call bland. The negative side of all those words you've used – bland, dull, flavourless – has been applied to Palestrina, but in my view they only apply in the positive meanings you've just given them.'

'I've only really thought about this doctrine in the context of painting and literature,' said Francis, waving an airy left hand while pulling his baseball cap harder down onto his head with the right, making a windmill gesture. 'How does it apply to what you're writing down there?'

'Ah, well, to *Spem in alium* not much, since the size of it makes for a fairly constant headiness, but even in *Spem* there are signs of what I mean: passages where nothing eventful happens, passages which seem to mark time, passages where the music flows along to the next cadence in perfect serenity without, you know, demonstrating anything, or demanding a specified reaction from the listener.' Tom finally became aware that he hadn't ordered any food, and although not hungry – he rarely bothered with such thoughts – he felt vaguely guilty for Ahmed's sake. He looked round for Ahmed, who quietly brought him a menu.

'Are those passages lying low in order to build up to a climax somewhere down the line?' said Francis, reflecting that Tom used the phrase 'you know' in the same way that young people use the word 'like': to sound colloquial, disarming, and to add just a fraction of extra time to find the next word or thought. One was old-fashioned, the other flip, and both were pseudo-involving.

'Sometimes, but that's not usually the purpose of them". Tom's tone of voice, already distant, now acquired traces of longing for something once understood and now in danger of being lost. He ignored the proffered menu. 'The polyphonic style, you know, is essentially restful, which is why I like the Daoist analysis.'

'What you're describing reminds me of plainchant,' said Francis. 'Hours and hours of uneventful music, treating its text in an undemonstrative way. I was raised a Catholic, and used to attend the services of the Divine Office whenever I could. My favourites were Vespers and Compline, but I used to make an effort sometimes to get up in the middle of the night to attend Matins and Lauds, when the monks were singing them.' He fiddled with his cap some more, always worried that if it wasn't tight on his skull all the teeming details logged inside his brain would escape.

'Looking back I realise it was important that the monks did this singing every day of their lives. They were professional in a sense that's at complete odds with the professionalism of the singers who come to this restaurant today – the monks' focus was the worship of God, to which end they sang endlessly, without detectable emphasis. Their desire was to worship as ardently as possible through song, in a single day, joining with their fellow monks as part of an ensemble. Solo singing was employed sparingly and, like the music they sang, when it happened it remained anonymous.' He folded up his newspaper, to allow Tom to escape if he wanted to. Tom remained silent. Cautiously Francis picked up his theme again.

'For the singers here, as they train to be soloists, every note is important, every underlying hint of meaning squeezed out as they strive to express their personalities through the music, their unique view. In the course of a professional engagement they might sing a few hundred notes, at the most. The monks sang tens of thousands every day. There seems to me to be a big gap between this cloistered world and even the latter-day Daoist world of Palestrina, let alone the early baroque.'

Tom nodded and sighed. Part of him wanted to undo everything that had happened in music since the renaissance period. His research had taken him back to the simpler, more communal world that chant had represented, and he longed to go there himself. He knew that the renaissance polyphony he studied had just enough chant in it to be able to perpetuate that sense of timeless worship, though pieces as calculated as *Spem in alium* were already leaving this chant-based world behind. The worst aspect of it was that everyone – singers, academics and the general public alike – wanted to make everything that went before the baroque into a simple-minded prototype. His next remark took Francis by surprise.

'Singers who come at renaissance polyphony from singing later music are as likely to misjudge its real nature as academics who, you know, want it to be a kind of dry-run for baroque composition. The same interpretative mistakes will be made. And the blandness in the writing either laughed at and avoided, or ignored in order to get, you know, to the "good bits".'

Tom was about to expatiate on the misguidedness of those conductors who start a performance of a big piece with only the glories of the final bars in mind, when a very flushed-looking Joe stuck his head into his line of vision and said breathlessly: 'Have you got anything for us? We've sung *Greensleeves* to death? We need something new?'

'Ah. Not much yet. I got distracted. I can give you the opening melody, arranged so everyone sings it together, but you'll have to do a lot of filling in.'

'Better than nothing, said Joe, and took the proffered sheet back to The Bunker and the photocopying machine.

'I'd better be a good boy, and finish this,' said Tom to Francis, 'but before I do, in case all this seems rather old-fashioned and, you know, irrelevant to the world we live in, I would remind you what André Gide wrote, not so long ago. Let me see,' and he rummaged around in his satchel, extracted his mobile phone and started to type. 'Where would we be without Wikipedia? And I'm an academic saying this. Here we are: "The great artist strives for banality. The greatest work of art is the one that will at first be overlooked, the one nobody will even notice. It is necessary to contemplate classic works over a long period for them to surrender their deepest significance, so secret is their inner vibration. Then, behind their apparent aloofness one may discover their most exquisite quality: their reserve." You know there is some modern-day, Westernised Daoism for you', and with that he went back to his work, the menu still unexamined.

REHEARSAL ROOM 3, hosting the Whyte Chorale, had become airless, and the people in it sweaty, despite all the windows having been thrown open. There was no wind, and so no through draught. Initially Steve had had to work hard to get everyone going, but once their inhibitions had been overcome, and he had shown them there was nothing but fun on the agenda – fun sanctioned by their employers – they all began to relax. The singing went from tentative to well-meaning to raucous in not many minutes, as those who could not read music began to join in with confidence. The question of whether any of them would manage to sing their way to the end of *Spem in alium* – ultimately the task before them – bothered no one apart from Steve; and even he was happy to let himself be briefly carried away by the infectious enthusiasm which surrounded him. No one else was worrying about *Spem in alium*.

But they all knew the tune to *Greensleeves*. Steve's problem was getting them to start on the same note. Joe would diligently play the starting note on the piano, at which Steve would give a down beat and a murmur would follow. Slowly the note in question – Steve had chosen a G on the grounds that, as he had observed countless times, whenever *Happy Birthday* is sung out of the blue it usually starts on or somewhere just below a G – became identifiable. After that it was plain sailing. The sound swelled as the words of the eight verses they had to learn became familiar, and their maudlin message struck home. The seventh and penultimate stanza – 'and that yet once before I die/thou wilt vouch safe to love me' – was sung with such sympathy that Steve became aware he was directing something almost unbearably passionate. To manage it he also just let himself go, swirling his arms in the air and leading the sound at the top of his voice. He later reflected that this kind of singing, which was unstoppable once started, came so nakedly from the heart that the kind of person who was likely to attend the concert the next day would surely put up barriers to contain the emotion, and rationalise it. There would certainly be nothing else like it on the programme, for all its variety of repertoire and types of ensemble. Those who wanted an evening of pretty, contained, 'Anglican' sounds were in for a shock.

By the time they had all gone over *Greensleeves* 20 times, the passion had begun to exhaust itself and the atmosphere to close in. Yawning spread like a contagion. Steve could see that action was needed. In the absence of Tom's transcription, which he sent Joe to procure, he decided to extend the folk-song element and reached out of his bag some copies of *Strawberry Fair*. He knew that most of these trainees would have to learn the music and the words off by heart, so he passed around the few copies he had, and started the process of going through from scratch all over again. Progress was slower. Keen though they were, the eight verses of *Strawberry Fair* were found by the assembled company to be hot-making. They had now tasted the joys of communal singing, and all they wanted to do was revisit them, preferably without further effort, and not necessarily just yet. The concert was going to be great.

After an hour, the mood was sultry and Steve decided to call a break. Everyone went outside for a breath of fresh air, a cigarette, a cup of something if it could be found. Unfortunately at that precise moment there was an almighty clap of thunder so exactly overhead that even the hardiest instinctively ducked, and the heavens opened. In a matter of seconds where there had been about a hundred dry and sticky people, there were now about a hundred slightly cooler but completely drenched people. At Brian's suggestion they all made for The Blue French, Brian promising that they needn't buy anything if they didn't want to, but equally promising that they would all get a friendly reception.

Ahmed, however, was taken unawares. In normal conditions his restaurant could only hold 60 people, with everyone sitting down, and just now there were 20 or so late lunchers finishing their meals. The arrival of a crowd of dripping trainees, pressing against each other to get into the dry, tested even his equanimity. He retreated as they advanced. Catching sight of Brian, he called out 'There'll be problem serving so many people. There's nowhere for so many to sit.'

Brian approached Steve, who was staring out of the doorway, mesmerised by the ferocity of the weather. Thunder claps had been joined by flashes of lightening as the rain threatened to overwhelm every fault in the fabric of Ahmed's building. Water streamed down the window panes, forming rivers in the gutters outside. Tom, also staring at the display, recalled how he had seen storms like this in Venice, the waters of the canals whipped into a fury, the whole picture turning a fungal shade of green. Those standing near Ahmed's doorway couldn't avoid being splashed, which forced them further inside. Within a few minutes of the start of the storm Ahmed's carefully organised interior world had been colonised by pools of water and scarcely audible apologies. No one could get in or out. The rain showed no signs of stopping. The members of The Whyte Chorale became increasingly uneasy, worried they might soon indeed be expected to buy something.

BY 6PM the rain and the clouds were finally gone, leaving watery sunshine and gleaming surfaces. The Whyte Chorale had reluctantly returned to The Bunker, with Tom's best attempt at including them in Tallis's masterpiece in hand. Soon they were put to the task of singing it, where their heart-stopping unison singing of some hours earlier was not on such obvious display. The Latin text hadn't helped: in translation the bit about the God of Israel absolving all the sins of suffering man hadn't aroused much interest, and the 'melodies' were so brief that there was little for the Chorale to get hold of. Joe did his best at the piano to build the sound to their entries, left hand striding, but few were fooled that the structure of the music militated against such treatment. Finally, Steve had got out a third folksong – *The Lincolnshire Poacher* – whose anti-establishment rantings had immediately found favour, and off they went once more. It began to seem as though hours of this increasingly unbridled release from normal life were in prospect; and the session only ended when Steve and Joe together decided they couldn't face any more.

The plan was now for the members of The Whyte Chorale to join in the *Spem in alium* rehearsal, with all the other groups, which had been fixed for 7pm. After that, separate rehearsals could take place, as necessary. This timing had given The Gamut Range the chance to go home after arriving in London; and the members of Vocem Civitatis to finish work. When the Whyte Chorale finally emerged from The Bunker, and thought about how best to kill off some time, they instinctively avoided The Blue French, having collectively agreed, by a sort of group murmur, that it was small, dark and 'pricey'. In a matter of seconds, as long as it takes for a grenade to spray its contents in all directions, there was no one to be seen. Ahmed had watched this procession and its dispersal with trepidation, since his restaurant was undergoing its afternoon metamorphosis from canteen to bona fide restaurant, a process which required his close attention. The interior puddles and exterior rivers having by now dried as if nothing had happened, he was kept busy nonchalantly explaining to some of his more highly-strung regular customers, who were now coming in to start their evening meals, that indeed nothing had happened, was happening, or would happen.

Tom Morris had gone over to The Bunker to supervise the singing of his new version of Choir 8, and was now back at his table, feeling guilty. How could he have committed such a crime against good practice? It hadn't even brought any pleasure to the participants, and, as he knew well, his yet-to-be-revealed version of the Regis was just as much of a crime. How would his reputation as a serious academic suffer when all this got out, as Francis Quirk would make sure that it did? He was too gullible, too keen to join in with the quotidian world of performers, and not keen enough to concern himself only with the rarefied heights of pure scholarship. He suddenly thought black thoughts towards performers and how the siren beauty of their performances could ensnare right-thinking intellectuals. He should have remembered that a performance of a piece of music is a one off. Fascinating, if you were lucky, but gone in a flash. The scholarship behind it was for ever. Without the years spent in the archives by people like him there would be no notes for these choirs to sing at all.

Not that the singers cared. Tom recalled with distaste the mess they habitually made of the most basic aspects of performance practice when left to their own impulsive whims. One year the texts were sung nasally, with ill-tutored guessing at how Latin was pronounced in different countries of origin, the next they were sung all blended and with Italianate Latin. One year *ficta* would be applied all over the place, the next year only at cadences, the next not at all. And each group claimed to have found The Only Answer, which they implied all the other groups were too stupid to have spotted, leading, they hoped, to everlasting fame from a grateful public. It was all nonsense, pure hubris. The performing world was a landscape of quicksand, into which armies of very self-satisfied musicians regularly vanished. Scholarship had to stand up to this, and find the eternal truths. How was he to defend himself?

As he toyed moodily with a *tabbouleh* salad, the members of The Regis Quartet entered the restaurant. At first the brightness of the light glancing off the stones and tarmac outside, shooting across the darkened restaurant, blinded them, giving Tom a few seconds to find some balance. He looked at his old pupils and reflected that, on the other hand, performing was a living activity, at the mercy of the doubts which afflict human beings. Scholarship claimed to be super-human, yet it too was fallible. At least performers were not hypocrites – they were trial and error people, prepared to take risks in public to discover new horizons. Scholars aimed for immortality with their findings, and because of the grandeur of their claims, were far more pathetic when they failed. He felt worse.

'Hello, Tom,' called out Chrissy, as she finally made him out in the chiaroscuro. 'How bloody marvellous to see you. We've all just come back from Cremona you know, where we caused something of a riot.' She grinned affectionately at him.

Hearing the pleasure in her voice at the simple joys of travelling and singing, Tom was quick to thaw, allowing a second round of thoughts to take over from the first, and immediately feeling the better for it. 'How on earth did you manage that?' he asked, intrigued.

'I sang soprano,' said Jonathan, 'it was enough.'

'Oh. What did anyone else sing?'

'I sang soprano with him, and Caduta and Robin sang the higher parts,' said Chrissy. 'Someone had to sing Fran's part, because she was voiceless by then. He and Caduta put on a regular display of fated lovers meeting in music. It was the funniest thing.'

'Were you singing madrigals?'

'Christ, no. This all took place in the middle of *Gaude gloriosa*' and she, Alastair and Stewart giggled in unison. Jonathan looked woebegone.

'Poor old Jonathan has got a bit of a crush on Caduta', she added, knowing the information was redundant, but, putting her arm round him, hoping to make everything better, to mother him a bit. She failed, though the effort was appreciated. Tom suddenly felt embarrassed talking about such private emotion, and decided to move the conversation along.

'Well, talking of Jonathan's soprano singing, you know, I've done some work on this Regis piece for you.' He winced as he said it, but there was no going back. He decided to make light of it. 'You know how us academics are always rewriting pieces of old music, to make them performable? Inventing missing parts, transposing, interpreting the *ficta* rules of the period, and so forth?'

'No', said Chrissy.

Tom sighed, bracing himself. 'Well anyway, I've done a bit of rearranging of this Regis. To suit your voices,' he added encouragingly. 'As you may remember I mentioned it is thought originally to have been a five-voice composition, with two bass parts. So I've kind of, you know, deconstructed the whole thing, transposing the tenor part up an octave, so that it twins with the existing soprano part; transposing the second part down an octave and amalgamating its notes with those of the existing bass part; and writing a second, lower bass part below this amalgam, especially for Stewart. The result should be interesting,' he finished, lamely. 'I've brought some copies', and he handed them round.

'This is very, very good of you, believe me,' said Chrissy, with relief. 'Looks great. And I brought along some renaissance stuff, to fill out our slot.'

The lads inspected her selection. 'Ah, Tallis's *If ye love me*. And some four-part Byrd. A home from home,' said Alastair, 'and not something we shall have to spend hours rehearsing.'

With this they all went over to The Bunker, where they passed a bumpy 45 minutes sailing through the Tallis and Byrd and coming repeatedly to grief in the Regis. Towards the end of this time large numbers of people began to enter the building, soon to be marshalled by Christy Benningham.

Christy had predicted the kind of scrum she was going to have to organise, and made some provision. The space needed for Choir 8, marked off by chairs, took up half what was available width-wise, and went deep into the room. This depth required everyone else to come forward and bunch up, which caused them to sing into each other's anatomies. The members of The Gamut Range, tired both vocally and physically, just wanted the whole thing to be over as quickly as possible. They scarcely smiled at each other as they were jostled. But for the members of Voces Civitatis – 40 of them now – the whole experience was endlessly amusing. Sandwiched between the two other groups, they quickly picked up on the cold staring from the professionals on their right, and the utter bewilderment of the crowd to their left, which only made the experience funnier. For a while it seemed as though they would be unable to recover from giving the impression that they were all, men and women, children on a school outing whose sole purpose was to annoy the teachers; but they had reasoned without Tallis. Or Anton. Neither was interested in making life easy for them.

Anton arrived at his stand with a few seconds to go before the official start of the rehearsal. He was not feeling 'so great' as he put it; but he refused to admit he had, or had had a hangover, nor that he couldn't handle the travel inherent in his lifestyle as well as his younger colleagues. Dyspeptic nonetheless, he took one look at the massed choirs in front of him and felt simply cross. Surely he was being taken for a ride. Surely this was not what had been arranged with these other groups? At the rehearsal on Tuesday only a fraction of the number of people had been there. Even his own Gamut Range seemed to have sprouted some extras, since the illness which had afflicted them when it came to going to Cremona no longer seemed so troublesome. Voces Civitatis had doubled in number; and The Whyte Chorale had expanded beyond all reasonable calculation. He looked despairingly at Chrissy, then at Christy, then at Steve. No one said a word. From here on in, this was his responsibility, a buck he could not pass.

Like his fellow Gamut Rangers all he really wanted to do was retreat to Ahmed's but, as his oversize copy of the music fell over the back of his too-small music-stand and landed on the floor in a heap, and still nobody moved, he saw something like red. If anyone knew how to take choirs through *Spem in alium*, it was him. This was indeed his responsibility, and, what was more, his calling. If they didn't nail it now, there would be little chance of them doing so tomorrow. He had an hour; and they were going to wish it was less.

He surveyed the scene, conveying no-nonsense. As often with performances of this piece, the choirs had been ordered to help the audience follow Tallis's sequence of events. This begins with Choir 1 singing from the extreme left of the stage, with the music slowly sweeping round to Choir 8 on the extreme right, introducing all the intervening choirs in between, the sound gently thickening like a sauce. Having presented all the voices in reduced groupings Tallis then wrote a passage, beginning at bar 40, where all 40 voices come together for the first time. The first big challenge of any performance, therefore, is to reach bar 40 in good enough shape for everyone to know when to come in.

In short order Anton turned to his left, motioning to the opening voices in Choirs 1 and 2 to begin. These parts were all being sung by his colleagues, who he decided not to overtax just now: they sounded as near to the ideal as anyone could reasonably expect in the circumstances. A few bars later Choir 3 joined them, also sung by his colleagues, every lead secure. Next came Choir 4, the first to be taken by Voces Civitatis, soon to be followed by the other three choirs that the members of Voces Civitatis were due to sing, with the Whyte Chorale bringing up the rear. 'Once they have all done their bit they can look forward to letting rip in the big tutti' he told himself. Unfortunately at this rehearsal, by the time bar 39 was reached only Johnny Tissot and Joe Farrant, bashing out the leads on their pianos, were making any kind of sound.

What Anton had heard between the concluding phrases of The Gamut Range choirs and bar 40, focused his mind on what he was being paid to conduct this shambles. Whatever it was, it couldn't possibly be enough to cover the energy he was about to have to expend on trying to find some way of getting everyone through to the end. Bar 40 is the first challenge, certainly, but the piece is 138 bars long. It contains further passages where Tallis sweeps through the eight choirs, giving each a brief moment in the solo spotlight. It contains a long section where two choirs are answered by two other choirs, who would of necessity be standing some distance away from each other, and would have difficulty hearing each other from one end of the staging to the other. Good co-ordination would be impossible if the singers were to play safe and modest by losing themselves in their copies, instead of looking up and following the conductor. Anton knew from long experience that singers who rely on what they hear, instead of following the beat to identify where they should be, were asking for trouble, because sound travels fractionally late across big spaces, and amateur singers anyway tend to sing behind the tactus. The sound that they had to fit in with, like tiny pieces of a jigsaw puzzle, would come to them delayed, to which they would then react late. The scope for the whole vast structure to come unstuck, and for him to be buried in the rubble, flashed across his mind as a man is said to review his life in the split second before he drowns.

He was just about to launch into a full-scale rant when the door at the back of the studio opened and two modishly dressed 30-

something-year-old officials entered, followed by a photographer. Seeing that they had caught the conductor in a moment of pensive silence, they made haste to take advantage.

'Sorry to intrude,' they brimmed, 'but we've come to see how well our money is being spent' and they gave out a little laugh. By this time Steve had leapt forward, and Choir 8 had come alive with many whispers and nudges. Since Anton could only look at them with weary disbelief, unabashed they carried on. 'My name is Darren', said the male sharp suit. 'And my name is Penny,' said the equally sharply dressed woman next to him. 'We're from the marketing department at Highbury's,' she went on. 'In fact' – and here they looked at each other with satisfaction – 'it's our job to spend the money set aside for publicity, wisely. Your Steve sold us a wonderful-sounding package, and we're thrilled to see so many of our brightest stepping up to the plate to take advantage. So we took the opportunity to bring Jeff, our lovely photographer along, to help prepare our publicity. We'd like to point out,' she continued teasingly, 'that we intend featuring just one or two of our most photogenic trainees on the poster. Jeff will be looking for the most glamorous,' and she elongated the first syllable of 'glamorous' in a jokey, fun-laden accent. 'So keep smiling, and don't forget to look at the camera', with which, and with all the time in the world, they found two chairs and made themselves comfortable in the small space between Choir 8 and Anton.

After this the singing of Choir 8 became significantly more present, the younger participants vying with each other to be noticed. To keep them somewhere near the track, Joe played his piano reduction ever louder, until together they had effectively eliminated the contributions of the other choirs – which wasn't so hard to achieve, since the professionals immediately gave up trying, and the members of Voces Civitatis, two to a part, were anyway struggling to be heard, not yet fluent with the notes assigned to them and still finding the scene distractingly silly.

Jeff the photographer began his work, initially concentrating on the members of The Whyte Chorale. Since they were all packed into a small space, it was necessary for him to push between them as they sang, clicking as best he could. After he had captured a promising number of popping eyes and flapping tongues, he became aware that there were other people in the room, whose existence hadn't been explained to him. In fact he might never have noticed them if Stewart Hammond, the strongly-built bass in The Gamut Range who was hard to overlook even in a crowd like this, hadn't pointed out in a stage whisper from the other end of the room, that there was nothing in his contract for this gig which mentioned photography, and if he was photographed he would expect to be paid extra. The other members of the Range murmured approval, out of solidarity, and agreed not to look up until the nuisance had departed.

Undaunted, Jeff observed them more closely. There was something alive about these people when they sang, he thought, especially when they did glance up to monitor Anton's leads. Jeff decided there was a gold-mine of expressions and reactions in the split seconds these singers were inadvertently granting him, and as unobtrusively as possible he captured as many of them as he could.

Finally he returned to photographing Choir 8 from a distance, as if he had been doing this all along, and left the room to make up the poster which that evening would be splashed all over the internet as far and wide as the reach of Highbury's made possible. It had already been decided that the banner would read: HIGHBURY'S SUPPORTS THE ARTS, over the picture of a woman with excellent teeth. Darren and Penny left soon afterwards, not to help him with the poster but to coo in a nearby hostelry. As they left they caused further disruption by clapping their home team to the rafters, their smiles fading as they passed Choirs 1 to 7, unable to comprehend what these other people were doing in the room, so few in number and so ineffectual.

By the time they had gone, Anton had resigned himself to the fact that he was relying on the two pianos to hold the performance together. The oxymoronic sound effects he was getting from the various groups would have made a more detached observer smile a wry smile and shrug his shoulders, but Anton wasn't like that. He cared too much about the final product, a care which resulted from his own need to be taken seriously. He realised that forces beyond his control had conspired to put him in an impossible position, and his first thought was to blame someone. His second thought, given that he had agreed to the parameters of this unlikely concert in the first place and so couldn't easily find a scapegoat, was to paper over the cracks and trust, as people in his profession did so often, that the audience wouldn't notice the mishaps, that the performers would 'get away with it' as the common phrase was. He ploughed on.

When he had finally forced everyone once through to the end he looked round the room, his expression as neutral as he could make it. Clearly they needed to rehearse some more, but it didn't make his job any easier to realise that it made little difference which section he needed to concentrate on. Remembering difficulties from previous performances, his eye instinctively alighted on the legendary bar 108.

'OK. Not bad. We need to go over this again, so let's take the final section first. Please find bar 108, and note that if you get lost you will be in grave danger of singing an embarrassing solo. You will see that there is a silence for everyone on the third beat of this bar. If you don't want to make a fool of yourself I suggest you stay silent for that beat.' He paused for some indication of comprehension, but, as in his interview the previous day, his words were greeted by a universally blank expression from those he hoped might support him, left to dangle.

He went gamely on. 'And you will also see that Tallis has done a strange thing, by putting the big chord which follows this silence on the fourth beat. As you know,' and despite himself he couldn't resist touching on the academic, a longed-for place of sanctuary for conductors of vocal music who don't know much about singing, 'there were no barlines in Tallis's time, so maybe this wasn't so odd after all; but it sure makes life difficult for the conductor,' at which he smiled tensely. 'I shall have to make a big up beat to bring you all in, when you might expect it on the following down beat. So don't be fooled. Let's give it a try.'

They gave it a try three times, Anton calling out the beats and emphasising the FOUR. After the third attempt the sea of bemused faces looking at him persuaded Anton to lighten the mood, desperate to see someone smile.

'It might amuse you to know that I remember a performance in Germany when I misjudged this bar 108. I conducted the fourth beat as if it were of no consequence, obviously moving through it to give extra weight to the following downbeat. Since I had made nothing of it, no one had come in; and indeed all my doughty foot-soldiers did come in with the heavy downbeat that followed. So far so good. The problem came in what should happen next, as it suddenly dawned on just about everybody, however lost, that an extra beat had been added to the total, and no one knew whether they should lose it again, or assume it had been added across the board. Bar 109 began to sound like one of those modern pieces where choirs sing the same music, deliberately scored some beats apart, to give a sort of soft-focus effect through gentle but persistent dissonance. But I felt that on balance Tallis hadn't had this in mind.'

With this punch-line he smiled guiltily and, he hoped, winningly. There was a further total silence. Even Jerry, who had just arrived and was poised to start his round of nodding and greeting, decided it would be best not to make a sound. The professionals, many of whom had been there in Germany and had had the fright of their lives, were not pleased to be reminded of the fallibility of the world which meant so much to them. The members of Voces Civitatis were in two minds as to how to react to a noted conductor, about to lead them into battle, who was admitting to a total cock-up caused entirely by himself. In their professional world the people higher than themselves in their line of business kept very quiet about total cock-ups, in the interests of respect about the office. Meanwhile the members of The Whyte Chorale gave the impression that this was the kind of rocket science which didn't concern them.

Anton realised for the umpteenth time that he might have guessed this would be the reaction. He had been in this position before. Why didn't he learn that it is best just to keep going, as Steve would have done, keeping a tone of voice no matter what the provocations, giving the impression of absolutely reliable competence? What the amateurs needed was a sense of fun and a sense of achievement, however slight the actual achievement. Then they needed to be told how wonderfully they had done. For them self-deprecation from their leader was a luxury as selfish as it was out of place.

After exactly an hour the *Spem* part of the rehearsal was pronounced finished, and the various groups broke up. The Whyte Chorale had finished for the day; Voces Civitatis went on to rehearse their solo items under Steve; and The Gamut Range moved to a smaller rehearsal room to revisit some of the items they had sung in Cremona, now with some of their regular singers restored. It was decided to retain all the singers from the previous evening, doubling some of the parts with the returning regulars, paying for them out of the unexpected Highbury's windfall. This meant that Angela could sing with Fran, who still refused to say that she wasn't well enough to do the job. A day had passed, but the equation hadn't changed for her. If she didn't sing, she didn't get paid, and although she would never agree to be so weak on stage that she knowingly let herself or her colleagues down, there was a fine line, which all the professionals knew how to tread, between 'getting away with it' and ruling oneself out. This decision was never left to the conductor, who would come to rehearsal expecting a completely fit team. No one ever told him they were ill, for fear of being judged unreliable. If they really couldn't sing they pulled out and found a deputy who was known to be acceptable, if preferably not too good; but as a general rule there was astonishingly little sickness among these self-employed singers.

Angela's return meant that the love quartet in *Gaude gloriosa* was not going to take place in its most recent iteration. Anton was relieved. He preferred sonic correctness to stampeding publics, and hoped to reach the end of the music this time in good order.

Sitting at the back of the room, hoping not to be noticed, was Brian Wiggins.

THE SINGERS of Voces Civitatis had stayed put in rehearsal room 3, as had Steve, Tom and Joe. Several of their number, who had not made it to any previous rehearsal, decided they had done enough singing for one day, and sloped off, making 'so sorry, can't be helped' gestures. But the core of 24 had remained, aware that they had a lot of work to do if they were to be ready for the concert. Joe busied himself making sure everyone had a complete set of copies on their chair, a set which included Byrd's *Laudibus in sanctis*. 'Ah, Rowdy bus,' said Jerry, happily reconfiguring the word 'Laudibus' while flicking through the copies. 'I know that one. Let's start with that.'

A suggestion from Jerry, in his characteristic half-joking, half-hectoring tone of voice, was finely calculated to make sure Steve would not take it up. Anyway he was mindful of its crucifyingly high bass part and was disinclined to start proceedings with Jerry and his mates yelling out high E♭s. He was anyway feeling uneasy about the Highbury's business. The final sum in sponsorship had never been mentioned, so keen had he been at the time to say 'yes' to the heady package of money, publicity and future possibilities which seemed to be on offer. On mature reflection, which had started around the time Joe had doubled up with laughter as the size of Choir 8 had become apparent, he wished he had known more about the actual sum, more about the detail of the publicity, and more about the continuing relationship between his endeavours and Highbury's ambitions.

He knew that it was a standard error on the part of supplicants to think that the rich person or organisation they have finally broken through to is endlessly wealthy, when in fact their philanthropy may only be designed to make them look good, while giving as little as possible to achieve that. Nonetheless he hadn't been able to believe his luck when Darren and Penny had taken up his suggestion, and at first all he wanted to do was daydream. A little later he recalled that people tend to give money with strings attached, and may give very little money indeed with quite lengthy strings attached, but for a while he was not to be woken up. Now, looking at Jerry and his chums, he was fully awake. 'Let's start with Byrd's *Ave verum*,' he said coaxingly. 'Something straightforward to recover our strength.'

Byrd's gentle prayer was sung through without much deviation from his roadmap, helped by Tom's suggestion that it be sung down a semitone. He also suggested that *Laudibus* should also be sung in downward transposition, so that the high bass E♭s might become at least Ds, but this had set off a round of complaint from some members of the group, several of whom claimed to have perfect pitch. Steve closed his eyes in silent despair. Although it is popularly believed that perfect pitch is the sure sign of musicians with God-given magical gifts, he knew that it was really only an act of memory, and almost always of slightly differing memories. He had had long experience of perfect pitch 'merchants' as they were disparagingly called, always a pain, inclined to lay down the law and tell everyone else they are wrong with all the ferocity of people whose very existence is being called into question. The fact that these self-appointed experts never agreed on the exact note in question was, to him, symptomatic.

'We'll sing it down a semitone, as Tom suggests', Steve said.

'I'll sing sharp all the time', said one young tenor.

'I'll have to write all the new notes above the printed ones – you'll have to wait for me', said a soprano.

'I think you'll find,' said Steve drily, 'that it's already been done, since we've had this problem before.'

Off they went, unbridled from the first chord, audible in the rehearsal room above where The Gamut Range was gently picking its way through Allegri's *Miserere*, with Caduta Massi agreeing to try out just one of the five embellished verses. Anton smiled, remembering what Caduta had told him about the unorthodox path that had led her to this moment.

She had had no choice as a student, she had confided, but to go to her local conservatoire, to study 'voice'. Since the choral tradition in the churches of Italy had been destroyed long ago by selling out wholesale to opera and its performance practices, she knew she stood no chance of being trained at home in anything other than what opera requires, by professors whose reputation and outlook revolved exclusively around this restricting art-form, as they had practiced it many years earlier. Her voice would be manipulated into learning how to sing loudly enough to be heard over an orchestra, into a dry, airless house, packed to the nines with rich people. She knew from the internet that there was another world out there for a talented singer; and when she failed her final recital she decided not to give up, but prove how misguided the system was. The words of the chairperson of the judges – a soprano of international standing who had never sung a note in tune in her entire career – spurred her on: 'A voice without power or colour. A voice incapable of expressing passion or interpreting passionate music. We strongly recommend *la Signorina* Massi finds another profession.'

Of course she had not yet found the kind of singing she might excel at. She often reflected on the number of her fellow students whose fine voices had been wrecked, or at least rendered unserviceable, by the narrowness of the teaching at her conservatoire; and felt a sense of mission towards those who would follow. She began to collect recordings of English ensembles singing baroque music and, to the complete bafflement of her family, began to listen to Choral Evensong online. She secretly began to experiment with what her voice could really do, at first embarrassed and frightened at how high it would go – surely this was freakish, something of no use. Then, on the Ash Wednesday of her final year at the conservatoire, she heard a boy from a choir based in Cambridge sing the solo embellishments in Allegri's *Miserere*. What she heard changed her life.

The question which worried her most, as she left for London, was how to identify what she supposed to be the desirable middle ground between sounding like a boy, and sounding like an operatic soprano. She knew that the English choral scene was still largely predicated on the sound of boys' unbroken voices, and she knew she didn't sound like any boy she had come across. On the other hand she also knew that it was no longer necessary to sing in the tradition of Wagnerian sopranos like Kirsten Flagstad to be accepted as a female on stage. How would she be expected to sing? She had spent many anxious hours trying to put together from online recordings exactly what awaited her, but could never quite identify which path would guarantee acceptance. There was so much middle ground; so many gifted singers switching effortlessly between arias by Bach, madrigals by Monteverdi and the sacred music of Tallis and Palestrina.

As it turned out, she needn't have been concerned. By the time she arrived in London no native commentator would have dreamt of making such a mistake as to refer to the widely employed and internationally famous sopranos she would soon mix with as 'boys'. The idea had become as taboo as discussing religion at a dinner-party. And as to singing Bach, let alone Tallis, with a six-inch wide vibrato, such practice had been greeted for some years by critics and public alike as something that was clearly an offence against nature.

So Caduta made her way to London, where she established herself with astonishing alacrity. Of course men kept fancying her, and everyone talked about her, but what really mattered, as Ahmed had noticed, was that her singing was exactly what the conductors of the time wanted. Her vocal range was unique; her ability to deliver music in a variety of styles rivalled only by a very few – Chrissy among them. But it was the sweetness of her tone, the inflections she could put into her lines without disturbing the pitch, that quickly sent her to the top of her branch of the profession. It also did her reputation no harm that the sight of her singing solo in the Allegri, coupled to the beauty of her voice on a top C, became an international sensation overnight. Anton knew very well that he was not the only director who wanted to employ her performing it.

As Anton recalled Caduta's words he became uncomfortably aware of the sounds emanating from beneath his feet. Byrd's *Laudibus in sanctis* had gone at least a semitone sharp in the first few bars, negating Steve's attempt to muffle the basses. He heard Steve stop the singing, get out his tuning fork, and bang it impressively on a hard surface. Everyone, even those in the room above, could hear that the pitch had risen. 'I told you I would sing sharp', said the young tenor, thinking to boost his importance by taking on the pains of the many, caused by the stupidity of a few, not least the soprano who was still ostentatiously doctoring her copy. 'Just a sec. I thought you had a copy with the new notes written in', said Steve, unable to resist doing battle and immediately regretting it. 'I didn't write them in' was the rejoinder. 'They are nothing to do with me. They make no sense.' And she continued to write the same notes in again.

The trouble they were experiencing with *Laudibus* boded ill for the next piece they were due to rehearse: Tallis's *Suscipe quaeso*, a seven-voice motet, where the Byrd only has five, and so technically more difficult. And they knew they had to sing it well, since it had been chosen by Anton as a show-case for them, in a succession of pieces by Tallis sung by the different participating groups, a parade which would eventually build to everyone coming together for *Spem in alium*. Anton's plan was to have a proper survey of Tallis's music: very small Tallis (*If ye love me* for four voices, lasting three minutes); medium-size Tallis (*Suscipe quaeso* for seven voices, lasting seven minutes); and two types of very big Tallis (*Gaude gloriosa* for a total of nine voices, lasting 20 minutes; and *Spem in alium* for 40 voices, lasting ten minutes).

This was a public examination in which Steve and his team could not afford to falter. Once again Anton had effortlessly contrived to put Steve in a situation which made him uneasy. It should be alright, Steve had argued in advance: four singers on each part, giving each other confidence, none of the parts ranging too high or too low, the notes not difficult and the atmosphere strong. He examined the choir unflinchingly as he prepared the first downbeat. The singing stopped a moment later as the second sopranos failed to negotiate a leap upwards of a minor sixth. Since this opening melody is imitated in all the parts, and it became apparent they would all have trouble identifying this unusual interval, he made them all sing it together in unison, before returning to the second sopranos and starting the piece afresh. As he did so he looked over at Tom Morris.

'This reminds me of what you made me do with the Whyte Chorale earlier,' he said, essaying a wink, 'having all the voices sing the main melody together, counterpoint-free.'

'Yes,' replied Tom. 'The difference being of course,' he added lightly, 'that if these excellent singers don't grasp all seven parts between them very quickly indeed, we are, you know, stuffed.'

Thus put on their mettle, the team pulled all the harder together, the contours of the melodies slowly becoming apparent as they learnt to put them together in parts. Since this piece, unlike Byrd's *Laudibus in sanctis*, is scored low and proceeds quietly, it immediately went flat where the Byrd had gone sharp. Although the 'merchants' had been outraged at the sharp singing, no one said anything about the flatwards delivery, if indeed they had noticed it. Steve had noticed it, having seen it coming, and shrugged his shoulders. This was one thing he could guarantee the audience was not going to notice or care about.

THE PARTY which slowly convened at Ahmed's was not much different from the one of three nights earlier. When The Gamut Range rehearsal concluded at 9.40pm, and the Voces Civitatis one at 10.10pm, half of the latter and almost all of the former headed over the road. Ahmed had not ordered any special supplies for this occasion, mindful of the curfew he was going to enforce, and of the boxes already in place in the store room for use tomorrow evening. As he saw the singers crossing the road he quickly took account of who was in the restaurant already, remembering that he was going to close the kitchen early on the following night. He wanted his regular patrons to enjoy their meals while they could. He had put the Gallaghers at a table as far from the door as possible, up against the kitchen partition, and elderly Mrs Pritchard near them. Lotte had asked to be halfway in between, so she could join in when she felt like it, otherwise she wanted a quiet meal.

There was already a hubbub in the street, led by Jerry, his acolytes gathered around him. As he entered the restaurant he nodded at Ahmed, but said nothing until he had caught sight of Eugene, eyes twinkling. 'Hygiene!' he called out at the top of his voice, and roared with laughter at his own wit. The acolytes roared too, though they had no idea why such an innocuous remark should be funny. Eugene assumed he was being mocked, and tossed his head. At the same moment he saw Robin enter the restaurant and immediately forgot himself.

In fact his sensibilities were to be called upon that evening in more than one direction. Just as he had begun a little dance which brought him closer and closer to the table which Robin and some of her colleagues had chosen, Caduta had come in with two young men. She summed up the prevailing scene in a quick glance and chose the largest gathering available. 'May I introduce two of my friends from Italy?' she asked. 'This is Divieto di Sosta, and this Passo Carrabile.' The three of them began to talk *sotto voce* in Italian.

Eugene was not so preoccupied that he hadn't picked up a number of small details in this development. For a reason that he couldn't explain the sound of Italian was familiar. He longed to understand it, and to join in. He had also taken on board what he supposed to be the aristocratic use of the word 'di' in the name Divieto di Sosta. He had long found, quite instinctively, that the whole idea of aristocrats was beautiful to him – gentlefolk who lived genteel lives in lovely castles were people whom he dreamed about, who kept his faith and hope in something resembling the future in focus.

Suddenly he found that, on a perfectly standard evening at work, his attention was being drawn three equally fascinating ways. He wasn't used to this, and found it almost impossible to keep up the pretence of doing his job. Ahmed repeatedly found him standing immobilised at random places in the restaurant, staring intently at nothing in particular. Even now he didn't reprimand him. Fortunately not many of the singers were stopping for food, or only for small plates.

And Eugene wasn't far wrong. Divieto did indeed carry himself like the proverbial aristocrat, at least when compared with Passo next to him. For those who like to divide the human race into convenient opposites, these two friends offered the most complete example. Divieto was tall, handsome, beautifully dressed and always ready with the right word, in several languages. Passo was hunched, shabbily dressed and hardly said anything at all. When social push came to shove, Divieto could be relied upon to launch into a well-informed statement of a point of view, delightfully filled out with little smiles and engaging gestures, where Passo, if he was in any way moved, would start to boil at first noiselessly, move on to grunts and groans accompanied by chaotic movements of his hands, until eventually, if he hadn't been interrupted by then, he would blurt out monosyllables, based in Italian.

The team smiled greetings as they tucked into the food and drink they had ordered from Ahmed on entering. Plates of *hummus*, *moutabal*, and *sambusac* with flatbread had already been delivered and were being passed around, as the wine and beer flowed. It had been a hot and sticky day, as well as a long one for many of them.

'We were in Italy this morning', said Alastair White, hoping this might be of interest, sensing that everyone was intent on their own needs and thinking total silence rude.

Space was made for the newcomers. Suddenly Nancy Silver, who had been busy on her mobile, impervious to the world as it had carried on around her, exclaimed: 'My God, have you seen what Highbury's have done with their publicity?'

This was said in such a tone of voice that it commanded immediate attention. The table fell silent. 'No,' said Chrissy. 'Show us.' Nancy gingerly passed her mobile round, exciting a succession of expletives, the most heartfelt of which was Steve's 'Jesus H!' until it finally reached the Italians. Everyone waited for Caduta to react. Into the silence she slowly said 'How could they do that? It was meant to be one of their singers. That's unkind and unfair', she murmured as tears welled up. The silence persisted until Jonathan went over to her and put his arm round her shoulders. 'That must be illegal', he said. For what they had all seen was a picture of Caduta alone, captured just as she had looked up to see Anton's beat, her mouth half open, her tongue just visible, her eyes intensely expectant, the upper half of her body leaning forward in a suggestive pose. Above this vision were, as promised, the words HIGHBURY'S SUPPORTS THE ARTS, followed by an encouragement to experience these artistic people in the flesh at Marlowe Wharf tomorrow at 7.30pm.

The singers gently expressed their outrage, one by one, without much variation in their message. Divieto, eyes darting as he hoped to gauge the prevailing mood among these people he didn't know, and so charm them instantly, said 'it is a scandal', a remark which was received by a gratifying chorus of approval. Passo, on the other hand, unable to treat the liberty he was witnessing as anything superficial, started to overheat. Soon half-formed syllables were escaping from him under great pressure. The English, who didn't know him and anyway had nothing else to add to the discussion in hand, did nothing to stop him from exploding. Finally, and in a great torrent of Italian-inflected noises, Passo let rip, ending with just one word, clearly pronounced and comprehensible to everyone: 'Penetrazione'.

The reaction around the room was electric. 'What are those young people so upset about?' asked Mrs Pritchard of the Gallaghers nearby, as all the diners paused. 'I've no idea,'said Sally Gallagher, eyes everywhere. 'It seems as though that young Spanish girl has been insulted – they are all looking at their telephones. Something must have offended them.'

Caduta understood that she was going to have to represent her friend more fully. Struggling to control her voice, she said 'Passo is someone who feels very passionately and deeply about a whole range of issues which afflict contemporary society,' her lapse into doublespeak showing how upset she was. 'One of these involves the power of advertising. I have heard him go into unstoppable rants about how, under the guise of buying toothpaste or a pat of butter, the advertisers are always implying that you can have the pretty girl too. "If you buy the product the girl will approve of you", is the covert message.' Swallowing hard, she laid both her palms on the table-top, as if seeking solace from its smooth surface.

'Once you start thinking like this, you can't walk down a single street in the western world without feeling encouraged to become intimate with girl after girl after girl,' she continued. 'Why does this so infuriate Passo? Because he sees the cynicism in it. He sees the departure from innocence. All our reactions these days are focused in imagining the ultimate sexual act, which, it is assumed, is the one thing everyone on the planet really wants to do. Immediately. Right now. It used to be possible in Italy to buy a bottle of *digestivo* which was recommended and illustrated by a *putto* with curly hair and a sweet smile. Nowadays you get the *digestivo* and a very suggestive adult body. Maybe you buy the liqueur, but the anticipated pleasure is only half complete. The result is that the whole of society is in a state of suspended animation, dissatisfied, always craving more.' She reached for her glass.

Passo had been following this with rapt attention. When Caduta had finished speaking, to a round of supportive murmurs, he stared hard at her, then at his glass, then at Divieto, who summarised for him in a quiet tone of voice what had been said. Immediately he half rose to his feet pushing at the table with his fists. 'It is a scandal,' he cried, remembering Divieto's words in English and daring to carry on from there. With further help from Caduta, he went on: 'No one minds if every second thought is of copulation. These days there is an instant connection between seeing a pretty face or body and imagining fucking it. It is always sex, everywhere, all the time. Not long ago no one would think of it, let alone suggest in public that this might be on their minds. The vulgarity of it makes me sick. Non posso sopportarlo...' and he started to sob.

It was Divieto's turn to put his arms round a friend's shoulders, and pull Passo gently back into his seat. There he sank into himself and said no more. Caduta was left to reflect on the injustice that had been imposed on her. Jonathan, who had remained crouching by her chair, made a succession of comforting remarks. But Caduta was neither to be wooed nor defeated. Her eyes were dry now. She would do her best at the concert tomorrow, look as beguiling as she was able, flirt with the officials from Highbury's if called upon to do so, and then she would go. Go away. Leave these tiresome men, none of whom seemed able to have a normal conversation with her, for whom she only felt pity. She couldn't help her looks or her voice. If they could be turned to a good purpose, it was her pleasure to make them available. But in the end they were trinkets. Nothing permanent came of them; they would both fade. She needed to achieve something permanent, however small.

Embarrassed as always by displays of emotion, especially when surrounded by their colleagues, the English singers round the table quickly returned to more mundane concerns of the day, which centred, as so often at that time, on the inadequacies of the service provided by the Northern Line.

ANTON HAD ENTERED the restaurant after the singers, having stayed behind with Joe to sort out the chairs and collect stray copies. They came in together, and so had both missed the saga of Highbury's publicity. Anton took one look at it, closed his eyes in horror, and dismissed it from memory. Joe was struck dumb by Caduta's beauty in the photograph, secretly determining to acquire a printed copy for himself. They both saw Lotte sitting by herself. And then Brian sitting by himself. They also bumped into Chrissy, who had left the group table to look for Christy in the crowd just inside the door.

'Has anyone seen that Christy?' she asked.

'Ah,' said Joe, overhearing. 'I think she said she was tired and going home to look after her children. But she expected to do better tomorrow after the concert.'

'Oh, bollocks', said Chrissy, disappointed, and returned to the group.

Anton and Joe found a table next to their colleagues and turned the chairs round so as to join them, while giving the impression that this was a temporary arrangement. Anton, as was his wont, ordered drinks for those who would accept them.

'So,' began Steve, who was already installed at the table, 'were the television people nice to His Noble Lordship? And how was my dear friend Barbara Prentice?' His voice was full of irony, not least because he had made a deliberate decision not to get up early and attend the session, or even watch the broadcast, and was feeling he just conceivably might have been more supportive. He was also keen to deflect attention from anything relating to his dealings with Highbury's.

Anton sighed inwardly, regretting the question, the style of the question, the tone of voice in which it was delivered, and the trap which it opened up in front of him. 'I quite enjoyed talking to Barbara actually,' he said, falling straight into it. 'She asked me what advice I would give young conductors today, and I told her they need to realise what it is to be a pioneer, and be ready for the consequences. I made it clear that...'

The table, after exhausting the topic of the Northern Line and now interested in observing Anton's reaction to the Highbury's publicity, had fallen silent. However, as Anton began to explain what he had said on the television, a whisper started up among the basses, who had gathered in a group at the opposite end.

'When did you last eat Indian?' Stewart Hammond murmured to Ben Causton, a promising young singer, popular with his colleagues. 'There's a truck-load of cumin in this here *sambusac*. Go and tell Ahmed you like it. That's one way to curry flavour', and they both giggled, looking intently downwards. There was a pause, as the distant sound of Anton's voice excited further disinterest. Ben spotted an unconsumed chick-pea on the table, which he manoeuvred into a convenient position.

'Glad it tikkaled you,' Stewart continued, which was followed by further giggling.

There was another pause while Ben, working out what he could get away with, flicked the chick-pea with his middle finger as far as it would go. Finally he half-swallowed 'Shut your Gobi', as he watched the projectile lodge itself under Steve's plate.

Startled, and worried he might be the butt of someone's humour, Steve cried out 'Bloody hell...' and looked down the table.

Stewart was not to be intimidated. 'Ghee, you really are proper dum', he intoned, sweetly.

This was too much for everyone within earshot. Giggling, like yawning when you're not meant to, is a contagious crowd activity, something which these people, so often in best-behaviour situations, knew a lot about. They owed it to themselves to do both as nature dictated, without fear of official reprisal. The table began to shake, open laughter followed. Hearing this, Anton, who had just got to the bit about how he refused to do the music which everyone else was doing, dried up. Exuding tolerance he wearily rose from his chair and went to join Lotte, signalling Joe to come with him if he liked.

'Oh dear,' said Stewart, 'We seem to have pissed him off', and they giggled some more, with diminishing force.

As Anton and Joe went to join Lotte, they passed Brian's table. On a whim Anton asked him if he could buy him a drink. Brian, caught between being in a daze and needing to talk, said 'yes, please' and, uninvited, wandered after them.

An awkward silence followed their arrival. Joe broke it by explaining how Brian came to be there in the first place, and followed this up with 'So, how did it go this evening?'

Brian looked nervously around the room. 'Awful. They haven't a clue. Bloody appalling.'

Joe sighed and nodded. 'But didn't I see you at our rehearsal?' said Anton, indulgently. 'You were alone.'

'Oh, yes, my fellow partners in crime probably made a dash for the pub. I just wanted...' and he struggled to find the right words.

'Did you play an instrument or sing in a school choir, or something, anything that led you to be interested in classical music?' said Anton.

'Oh no. There were no music lessons at my school – all that had been stopped years earlier. No, I have playlists on my phone, like everyone else. But I always knew this was just stuff. Better than not having it. Silence makes me anxious, you see.'

'So how did you come to be at our rehearsal?' Anton pursued.

'Well, you see, I heard your group sing the opening bars of the big piece in the rehearsal on Tuesday. Up to then I had assumed that piece was going to be one big jam, every choir piling in with their piano, like a giant rugby scrum. To be honest I had rather looked forward to that, it sounded fun. I could let off a bit of steam and then go for a pint with my mates.' The words came piling out, as he lost a sense of himself. 'But what I heard was so different from what I'd expected that I realised what I'd expected was rubbish. I realised I was missing something I could never have gone looking for, because I didn't know it was there, you see. And what I heard this evening has just made me madder. That sound. Those people...' and he stopped, suddenly in the present moment again, and embarrassed to find he was referring to Anton himself.

There was another silence, less awkward than the first. 'You seem to have fallen in love with a sound', said Lotte.

'Yes, that's it,' said Brian, gratefully. 'It is like falling in love. It haunts me, and I want more and more of it, like a drug. Every other sort of sound seems dirty and used. I don't know how to describe it better.'

Just as the four of them were thinking about how better to describe something they all cherished, a 19-year-old woman from Voces Civitatis walked by. 'Hello, Becky,' said Lotte, 'fancy seeing you here. I suppose you've been doing some singing. Let me introduce you. This is my pupil, Becky Cavanagh. She sings for Steve, as her mother does.'

'And my dad, and now my little brother, though he doesn't really want to. He says five years as a chorister at St Paul's has killed his love of singing', and she pulled a face. Brian stared at her incredulously. To be born into this world, and voluntarily to give it up. This was beyond him.

'How are you finding it?' said Lotte.

'Well, I like the friendly atmosphere, my family all being there, and the good music of course, and I know we have achieved some really good results,' she said, projecting her best enthusiasm. 'But to tell the truth it is a bit slow. We set off on a phrase and it immediately breaks down. And try as Steve might, few of us are actually aware of what has gone wrong, or how to put it right. I know I'm no better really, and shouldn't complain, but all it would take is for everyone to concentrate a bit harder. Some of the men seem to treat it as a big laugh. The opening of Tallis's *Suscipe quaeso* took nearly 20 minutes to get even remotely right... despite the fact that my part is in from the start' and she reddened as she congratulated herself.

'That either makes you a second soprano or a second alto,' said Anton, 'and from your speaking voice, and from what Lotte has told me' – here he looked enquiringly at his wife – 'you are a second alto.'

'Lotte has been very good to me,' said Becky, blushing some more. 'She has taught me so much, and is such an amazing singer herself', at which her eyes nearly popped out of her head.

'Becky is a very unusual kind of singer,' said Lotte. 'She is that rare thing, a proper contralto. Nobody these days calls themselves that – they all say they are mezzo-sopranos. I assume they get more work that way, and decide not to develop their low register because everyone wants an alto who can sing low soprano, as opposed to a properly low alto who can also sing in the tenor register when needed. The contralto voice is in danger of disappearing as a professional instrument."

'But you made your career from singing contralto,' objected Becky. 'You got lots of work and were very famous. I would like to try to do the same.'

'There is plenty of work in the solo market for contraltos, though 90% of it could be sung by one of these mezzo-sopranos. It's just that it would have a different timbre if sung by them. The problem is that very few people are born with the defining low notes – it's just the same for low basses. And that must have been true in the past, because there are few arias from any period which set out to explore those notes. It's the timbre of a real contralto which is unusual, like those astonishing Russian counter-basses – we hardly have them in this country – but I think Becky could develop the right timbre.'

'At the risk of missing out on a lot of work?' said Joe, who had noticed Becky in the rehearsal, pencil poised, and thought she might go far, preferably with his help. He felt a twitch of jealousy at her easy connection with Anton.

'She wouldn't miss out on work from me', said Anton, with a different motivation.

'Can I audition for you some time?' Becky asked Anton, looking at him with a mixture of youthful deference and determination.

'No,' said Anton. 'I'm afraid I never audition; and anyway you're a little young for what we get up to. What you'll need to do is establish yourself in the London singers' market and get a reputation for your singing, which will inevitably find me. You need to get some experience under your belt – for example of singing music you may not know very well to a packed symphony hall without amplification, on crucifying jetlag. For this privilege you won't be paid very much, at least not for a single concert. Long-distance tours, with a concert every night, are not so bad,' he continued, ever the salesman. 'So just get out there and get stuck in. Anyway you have my wife as your advocate, which is a very good start.'

As midnight approached the noise from the crowd near the entrance to the restaurant steadily increased, scaring up phlegm-related noises in Ahmed's throat. These in turn generated more noise from the lads, who once again had taken to singing their favourite hits from the cathedral repertoire, fists banging the rhythms in mid-air. Steve thought it would be morale-boosting if he joined them for the final moments of the evening, sporting his wine-glass in the manner promoted by Jerry – nearly full, but giving the impression that it had just been emptied and refilled. In fact neither of them had drunk anything, though this detail was lost on one middle-aged man, swaying around the edge of the circle, attempting to sing everyone's favourite Anglican bass solos in falsetto. With Malcolm Sargent to his right and Fred Fellony to his left, they were well away.

'Who on earth is that?' Steve asked of Jerry, loudly over the prevailing din.

'My name, young man,' said the man in question, more alert than Steve had given him credit for and fixing on him a steady stare, 'is Caius ffrench Beytagh. And don't call me "Keys". I won't stand for it. My name' – and here he accessed his maximum available height – 'is pronounced as in Latin. Kai-yus. Not as in that egregious Cambridge college, named after my brother Gonville, or just possibly the other way round. Not that I care. I would appreciate it if you remembered this detail the next time you wish to address me in rehearsal.' And with superb nonchalance he rejoined Malcolm and Fred mid-phrase.

Steve wracked his brains. He had no memory of this man, his singing, or the need to speak to him in rehearsal. It was true that during the course of the evening the members of Voces Civitatis had fluctuated in number, with quite a few leaving after the *Spem* rehearsal, but it seemed as though Caius hadn't left at that point, or at least hadn't left the area.

'I don't remember auditioning that person', he said to Jerry, more quietly.

'You didn't,' said Jerry, obviously sober. 'He came along with Malcolm to have some fun in the *Spem* rehearsal and then came here. He's been here ever since, hasn't he Ahmed?'

'Sure yes,' replied Ahmed. 'He was quiet at beginning, but when his friends arrived, he became loud. My job now,' he continued, looking at his watch, 'is send them all home. Or tomorrow is going to be nightmare.'

At this Jerry resumed the address of someone who was evidently the worse for wear. He climbed onto a chair, fell off it, climbed onto it again, gripped Steve's forearm, and with flaming eyes yelled: 'Tomorrow is another day. Why don't you all piss off?'

In the ensuing fracas Jerry could be seen gently guiding his colleagues into the street, leaving the more peaceable patrons from the further reaches of the room to make their own way out. The sight and sound of the Maserati caused a brief hold-up in the street, as several people stopped to ogle it: the Italians, Eugene, Brian, the Cavanaghs, and elderly Mrs Pritchard. 'That car reminds me of the finest stroke-play at Wimbledon', she pronounced, leaving the simile hanging in the air for anyone to pick up and run with if they so wished. No one coming forward, they all nodded 'good-night', and departed.

Ahmed, having joined the group around the car, now patted his top pocket to find the cigarette he had been saving up for when everyone was out of sight. He decided not to have a second one, weakly attributing the distressing memories of the previous evening to too much tobacco. The weather was still very warm. He rubbed his eyes, followed the lines of perspective, lost the detail in the far distance, and rubbed his eyes again. He refused to wear glasses, though he was not a vain man: where he came from it was such a rarity he'd never got used to it. He reflected that in 24 hours' time the evening would only just have started.

Chapter 5

SATURDAY, 8 JUNE 2019

TWELVE HOURS LATER Ahmed was standing again in the street door to The Blue French. Thunderstorms had been forecast for later in the day, which encouraged him to remove everything from the tables outside, except their blue-and-white chequered oilcloth coverings. He had heard his musicians mention many times how sticky weather made their job more difficult and uncomfortable on stage. Nonetheless he wasn't sure whether to hope for storms, which would cool the air down, but also make it more difficult for the public to get to the concert. He was just wondering how people coped during a performance which was interrupted by thunder, when Eugene slid past him, unusually early and uncharacteristically alert.

The general rehearsal at Marlowe Wharf had been called for 3pm, allowing for a proper run-through of all the items and leaving time for repose and some food before the show. Ahmed had made it known that he and his staff were not prepared to serve anything more complicated than *mezze* plates at the party afterwards. He intended to open as usual for his local clients until about 10.30 and then close the kitchen. Anyone wanting to stay on would be welcome, but the fare was essentially going to be liquid. Anticipating the pleasure that Ahmed had in store for them, some of the singers – those who tended to put the meal after a concert alongside the concert itself as the event to look forward to – had spent their precious free time trying to work out the quickest way back from Deptford, where the venue was situated. Ahmed wondered for a moment what kind of building this was they were to perform in, since so many of his clients were talking about it. But nothing in his experience offered any clues, and he soon had to turn inside and serve his first customers.

In fact Marlowe Wharf was a building of considerable antiquity, only recently turned into a public space. Like all its sisters along the banks of the Thames, it had spent centuries receiving goods from around the world, in this case grain. It had been standing on 30 May 1592, when the playwright Christopher Marlowe was murdered in a property nearby, from which event it derived its name. And from some time in the 19th century it had had a pub attached to it, called the Kit Tavern, after the same connection. It had fared better than many other wharves in the vicinity in not being burnt down during the heyday of trading; and it had also miraculously escaped being bombed during the Blitz. It was in fact a very rare survival of a wooden building from the 15th century, specifically listed in Elizabeth I's 'legal quays' act of 1558 under the name 'Black Eagle Wharf'.

But beautiful and old and historic as it was, its practical use had faded in the 1970s. Trade had come to be handled in different ways, and there was no faking it, just to keep history going. As Francis Quirk was heard to say: 'there are so many lovely old things in our country which once had a purpose, and now don't, so what happens next? Slap a preservation order on them and expect someone else to pay?' That was what had happened with Marlowe Wharf, except no one was prepared to pay. The building had stood there unused for nearly 50 years, officially preserved but abandoned and rotting. The Kit Tavern had also been forced to close as its customers drifted away, and it too was an unmodernised relic from the past, though a more recent past: décor, pumps, bar-stools, mats left just as the last customer had left them some time in the seventies.

Eventually a syndicate of City businessmen had taken pity on the two buildings and decided to turn them into an arts centre, with hospitality attached. One of the members of Voces Civitatis with a love of music and a philanthropic streak, Martin Clark, had joined this syndicate, and immediately proposed it to Steve as a possible venue for a concert. 'Obviously there's a lot needs doing to bring it up to regulation standard, but come and have a look and see what you think.'

Steve and Joe had gone to have a look, and were duly impressed by the sheer physical danger involved in entering. The floor-boards were unsound, the ceilings dripped cobwebs and there were thick layers of dust everywhere. Nonetheless it had an unmistakable allure. They started to imagine a stage, proper lighting, a box-office, rows of chairs and glasses of wine. Martin Clark suggested they return in six months' time, when he promised that there would have been improvements.

By then the structure had been cleaned up and made as safe as the condition of the wood would allow. The smell of seaweed and dead birds, which had greeted them on their first visit, was now replaced by the smell of polish, which had been slapped down thick on every surface. The interior gleamed, which, as Joe had hopefully pointed out, should be good for sound. The facilities were still primitive, but another member of Voces Civitatis, Bob Parsons, was on the board of inspectors responsible for awarding certificates to enterprises like this, and he was able to encourage agreement that, with proper plumbing and wiring, plans for public performances could be laid. What had finally swung their vote was the obvious trouble and expense that had gone into ensuring that this highly flammable structure would be safe from burning down.

An opportunity had also been identified for the substantial loft area. It had been decided that this space, where originally the grain had been stored, should be reserved as a changing room for the artists, there being no other. To make this possible the floor had had to be made secure and a stairway built. The finishing touch was to install the most robust sprinkler system on the market, on the assumption that if a fire were to start anywhere in the building, dropping water on it from above would be the best way to put it out. This piece of reasoning had found general acceptance, resulting in a specially enhanced link to the water mains. Bob could assure his fellow inspectors that people might drown in Marlowe Wharf, but they were unlikely to be burnt to death.

Once the good offices of the same water mains had been extended to newly-installed bathrooms both in the old pub and in the wharf itself, a certificate for public use had been issued. Plans for performances immediately started to be made. Since the building was not known to the concert-going public as a regular venue, Martin Clark had suggested to Steve that something properly eye-catching should be on the programme. Steve thought of *Spem in alium*, and then thought of Anton. Anton thought of *Spem in alium* and the Allegri. Around those two pieces, and with their two ensembles heading the bill of fare, Steve and Anton had had no trouble putting together a blueprint for a concert which, as it turned out, was to be the opening event in the newly furbished hall.

ONE OF THE MANY THINGS that was remembered about the way this day unfolded, and was talked about for years to come, was how, at the appointed start time of 3pm, only about 25 of the approximately 150 singers who were meant to be there, were actually there. And this was despite the severest penalties having been promised for any latecomer: the severest reserved for members of The Whyte Chorale; very severe for members of Voces Civitatis; and a gentle reminder for the professionals. This sliding scale came about quite naturally, the result of what those responsible for these organisations thought of their personnel. In one way they were right: none of The Whyte Chorale was there, about a quarter of Voces Civitatis had made it on time, as had all of The Gamut Range. On subsequent enquiry it became apparent that the remoteness of Marlowe Wharf was behind all the stories of mishap. Taxi drivers had never heard of it; GPS didn't list it, leaving uber drivers clueless; and Deptford overground station, which boasts a direct service from London Bridge, was apparently biblical distances away on foot. By 3.30 the crowd had thickened sufficiently for Christy to start imagining where everyone would stand for *Spem*, while Anton and The Gamut Range were getting ahead on the 'stage', putting the time to good use, rehearsing what they had to do.

By 4pm the floor panels of the loft overheard were resonating with the tread of many feet, and its walls were covered in coat-hangers. Martin Clark looked anxiously at the ceiling of the hall itself, knowing how weak those timbers had recently been, and hoping the contractor had not cut corners in strengthening them. He was also alert enough to take responsibility for a member of The Whyte Chorale who, on entering the hall and crying out in distress, was noisily sick. A mixture of special pills for multiple health troubles, combined with the smell of polish and disinfectant, had proved too much. A general concern for the wellbeing of the audience was triggered off by these various difficulties. Perhaps they also would never find their way. Perhaps they also would be taken ill. Perhaps the heavens would open and discourage them from leaving home in the first place.

Martin Clark and Bob Parsons had de facto taken on the management of this concert, willingly enough for this first outing, though they were not anticipating making a habit of it. If this was a success, then they would be able to hand it over to 'the team'.

But for now they were prepared to front it up, not least in printing a programme and handing copies round to the participants. This was the first time anyone, including Anton and Steve, had seen the running order. It went like this:

Tallis: *Gaude gloriosa* (The Gamut Range)
Regis: *Salve sponsa* (The Regis Quartet)
Tallis and Byrd: English anthems (The Regis Quartet)
Byrd: *Ave verum* (Voces Civitatis)
Byrd: *Laudibus in sanctis* (Voces Civitatis)

INTERVAL

Allegri: *Miserere* (The Gamut Range, soloist: Caduta Massi)
Anon: *Greensleeves* and other folk songs (The Whyte Chorale)
Tallis: *Suscipe quaeso* (Voces Civitatis)
Tallis: *Spem in alium* (The Gamut Range, Voces Civitatis, The Whyte Chorale)

'I don't think we've missed anything off', said Martin to Anton, who had finished rehearsing his contribution.

'Bit of a dog's dinner,' replied Anton, eyeing the copy with disapproval. 'I don't know why you simply didn't ask us to do the whole show in the first place.'

'Well, we did want to appeal to as large an audience as possible,' said Martin emolliently, 'and all the groups are bringing their camp followers. The Whyte Chorale alone has spawned a hundred requests for tickets, and the place only holds 250. We'd have been happy to get 200 total.'

'So the audience may be a bit of a dog's dinner too?' said Anton, smiling. 'This is acquiring the characteristics of an end of year school concert. I hope they all like Tallis.'

Martin smiled too. 'Half will come to see their friends, another quarter will come for *Spem* and the Allegri, and a quarter will come to hear The Gamut Range do their thing with whatever. I don't see why anyone should not have a wonderful evening out.'

'All right. Let's get a move on,' interrupted Steve. 'We can rehearse *Spem* now. Just about everyone is here, and I think the two keyboards are in place.'

These keyboards had, predictably enough, caused a large administrative headache. They had had to be acquired from somewhere, and then they had to be transported to the Wharf. The management at The Bunker had proved uncooperative in helping with this, since they had other bookings for the afternoon, which had obliged Christy to start asking favours. She knew Jerry had a piano and, following her enquiry, said he would be able to get it there. For the second instrument she had had to cut corners and agree to an electronic keyboard. This had the advantage of being light, with removable legs, which she could fit into the back of her car. All it needed was a reliable supply of electricity. Everyone was impressed that Jerry's piano had arrived in an ambulance, carried into position by four sturdy paramedics. Martin seemed somehow to have pulled off a fast one here, with Jerry's collusion, since the ambulance and the medics then stayed for the performance, fulfilling government guidelines about First Aid on site at public events.

Whatever Marlowe Wharf had been used for over the centuries – storing grain; selling grain; transporting grain to other warehouses; legal and illegal trading in other desirables; illicit drinking before the days of the tavern; murdering those who had fallen out of favour – it had surely never witnessed anything like what transpired in the next half an hour. Of course there wasn't room for all the participants to stand comfortably in the space reserved for them at the far end of the structure, while having to accommodate two keyboards as well. Nor was there the remotest likelihood of everyone being able to see Anton's beat, since he and they were standing flat on the floor, no raking or podiums being available. The shorter men positioned at the back of their choirs stood the least chance. Everyone felt disadvantaged, and for what seemed like an eternity the room was filled with complaint and objection. The intended space was swiftly used up, forcing the singers on both ends further down the side walls and into the public seating. Christy realised that for once the situation was beyond her control.

This hubbub was abruptly silenced by the sound of the opening notes from Choir 1. Anton, losing patience, had simply started to conduct, and his colleagues were quick to follow him. In a split second everyone had forgotten their discomforts, concentrating at last on what they had to do to get to the end of a gigantic piece of music. Fortunately in a way, the natural sound in the building was found to be so painfully dry that, despite the bright surfaces created by the polish, there was relatively little audible delay to the notes coming from the other choirs, giving everyone their leads. Although Anton disdained to notice the existence of the electric keyboard – he had originally had trouble with the idea of a piano – he was the first to acknowledge that its contribution helped to hold the show together. It was with a sense of achievement that everyone finally fetched up at the final chord, the first time. A smile broke out, as wide as the ensemble, and as deep. It was a good feeling. Those who knew they knew nothing about how this music should go were happy; and those who thought they knew precisely how it should go were also happy, able to shelve their prejudices as, to their great surprise, the power of communal singing overwhelmed them.

When it was clear that Tallis's music would not actually stop mid-piece, and that there were no further improvements to be made to the interpretation, Anton called a halt and read out a timetable for when the other groups might rehearse. Since all The

Whyte Chorale were there, he decided they should go next, then Voces Civitatis, then The Regis Quartet. These separate rehearsals would take until 6pm.

Anyone who has staged a concert will know the minutes of anxiety which make up the hour before the start. How many people will come? How depressing will the seating look when everyone who wants to be there is there? How much money will be lost? The young people selling tickets sit at makeshift desks and fiddle with their paper-work, those selling programmes stand around the venue, smartly dressed, throwing uneasy glances at each other, longing to talk to someone. An hour out and all the helpers are in place, though the seating is empty. Forty-five minutes out, and still there is no one: the organisers are putting on brave faces. Thirty-five minutes, and the first people arrive, looking about uncertainly and talking loudly.

In fact the seating was destined to be filled, but not by 7.30, when the concert was due to begin. The problems which the singers had experienced in finding the wharf were also experienced by the public. At precisely 7.30 those who had managed to get there on time had distributed themselves randomly among the available chairs, leaving a large empty block in the centre for the Highbury's booking. Since Martin knew that they were due – he had been informed they were coming on from a drinks party, specially thrown for those attending the concert – he decided to wait for them and announced to the public that there would be a delay, caused by those very difficulties they had all just experienced. There was a buzz of understanding.

At 7.50 the sound of two coaches arriving was heard from outside, followed by many raised voices. A happy gathering of middle-management executives and their partners, led by Darren and Penny, blinked their way into the hall, exclaiming and laughing. They were shown to the general area of empty chairs set aside for them, where they eventually sat in combinations agreeable to themselves. Once settled they giggled at the programme, which was handed to them; at the Latin titles; at the cheaply reproduced mug-shots of the conductors; and if they hadn't been in such a good mood they would have found and giggled at the numerous misprints. They noticed the prominent mention of Highbury's with noisy approval. Thumbs-up were flashed around. They craned their necks to catch sight of the beautiful woman from the publicity. Failing to find her, they resorted to ostentatiously fanning themselves against the stifling heat of the evening. They were unprepared for the first item in the entertainment – Tallis's *Gaude gloriosa*, 20 minutes of mind-bending, unhilarious, mid-Tudor polyphony.

Gaude gloriosa is massive, like *Spem in alium*, but in a different direction: length rather than height. The score for *Spem*, with 40 voices piled on top of each other, is so tall that most music stands cannot hold it, as Anton kept discovering. The score for *Gaude gloriosa* is a thick book. Its music is divided into nine continuous sections of varied scoring – every third section bringing all the voices together. The natural ebb and flow within such a plan can rivet the attention of sober music-lovers of every hue; unfortunately the invited section of this crowd was neither sober nor experienced in the ways of classical music, let alone choral polyphony. At the last moment Caduta had decided to yield her place in this piece for the returning Angela, thereby depriving this part of the audience of its one sure pleasure. As Tallis's exquisite melodies slowly revealed themselves, with all the time in the world to interact and converse, other sounds could be heard in the hall: the rustling of sweet wrappers, the opening of crisp packets, the crossing and uncrossing of bladder-sensitive legs. By the third quarter of the piece a division had made itself apparent between Highbury's guests and the rest of the audience, who increasingly looked at them with regret and admonition. By the end of this first item there was already a steady exodus to the lavatories situated both in the old Tavern and backstage.

The Regis Quartet were on a hiding to very little, as they took over the performing space for Tom's upside-down reworking of Regis's *Salve sponsa*. The end result was not much to the liking even of the cognoscenti; and the docile English anthems which followed were gone in a flash, similarly leaving little impression. The arrival of Voces Civitatis for their two pieces by William Byrd briefly stemmed the exodus, since the increase in numbers had led some of the Highbury's contingent to think that this was their home-grown ensemble. During Byrd's *Ave verum* they listened attentively for the first time, at last quietened by the mood of the music. The second item, *Laudibus in sanctis* – six minutes of abandoned self-expression from the increasingly confident amateurs – also came close to entertaining everybody present; and the organisers could go into the interval feeling that the occasion was going in the right direction, with all the crowd pleasers still to come.

'Tell me,' said Francis Quirk, who had been watching the concert unfold with amusement and now found himself rubbing shoulders with Steve Taylor as they made for the hospitality, 'how much money is Highbury's actually giving to this event?' He reflected that their involvement had given him something of a rhetorical gift, as he fashioned phrases to use in his review, and was as grateful as he was surprised. Not that it mattered to him whether they were going to hand over some cash or not. The important thing was that they were there, and he could use them. Waiting for Steve to reply, he began to chisel and shape. 'This is not quite the usual crowd. Nor is this quite the usual venue,' he mused.

SUPERMARKET BRINGS NEW LIFE TO OLD BOARDS

might be a starting point.' He began to fantasise.

'FROM GRAIN TO POLYPHONY:
SUPERMARKET SHOWS THE WAY.

No, not quite.

PILE IT HIGH:
TALLIS'S SPEM IN ALIUM.

Not bad.

HOW TO MANAGE A MURDER:
MARLOWE WHARF AND HIGHBURY'S.

That one could be saved up for a disastrous second half. 'Do you know how much?' he asked Steve again.

'Well, mate, not exactly', replied Steve, trying to remember how much he had promised to whom, aware that his reputation as someone to be trusted might soon be up for grabs.

The interval passed by to everyone's satisfaction. Large quantities of alcohol, provided by Highbury's, was consumed by the majority of the audience, while some of the performers ostentatiously mingled with glasses of designer water in their hands. Upstairs private supplies of beer were also broached. Everyone felt positive as they went into the second half.

This started with Allegri's *Miserere*, the piece which, if any, the audience had come to hear. *Spem* was famous for its numbers; the Allegri was famous for its notes, especially the very high, coloratura ones. It was also loved for the Mozart story of course, which Tom Morris had felt obliged to repeat for the umpteenth time in his programme note to the event. Rather more willingly he had also mentioned that that high soprano C would originally have been sung by a castrato. Not many members of this audience had the concentration to read this kind of small detail, but the few that did found the subsequent spotlighting of Caduta in the role all the more laden with frisson and ambiguity. From castrato, to choirboy, to Caduta. A pleasing progression.

The effect of that C, sung five times as the liturgy requires, has mesmerised modern listeners to the point where those few seconds may be all they remember from a concert running two hours. In the English cathedrals, sung as part of a church service, it is the idea of a boy sounding angelic that brings on the emotion: purity mixed with otherwordliness. On stage, during a concert, the sight of a beautiful woman singing those notes can bring on a more complicated reaction, the sacred jostling with the profane. The secular trappings of a concert-hall encourage one line of thought, the music another.

The last thing Caduta wanted to provoke was complicated emotions. She was a professional in the mould of those who love to sing as well as they can, with the hope of inspiring feelings that come out of and stay related to the music in question. But the power of the solo soprano line in the Allegri goes beyond the appeal even of a heart-on-sleeve romantic aria by Verdi. Its otherworldly resonances, so understated that they slip into the bloodstream almost undetected, appeal at a level of feeling which most art cannot access. In its depth of communication it is unique.

It was Anton's practice to put the solo quartet, which Caduta would lead, somewhere out of sight. This was supposed to be a re-enactment of the positioning of the choir gallery in the Sistine Chapel itself, where an urban myth decreed the solo quartet of old used to stand, to generate special atmosphere. In English cathedrals there are almost unlimited places for this hidden group to go, the favourite choice being by or behind the high altar, thereby giving greater distance from the audience sitting in the nave. In Marlowe Wharf there were no hidden places. The only possibility was the lavatories, currently in constant use. For this reason Caduta's performance was for once in full view of the audience.

The Highbury's invitees had sat down for the second half in restive mood. A further drinks reception had been promised for after the event, back at their Finsbury headquarters, where dancing would be encouraged. They wanted to cheer on the home team as soon as possible, and then go. Football matches might run the same 90 minutes that this concert was running, but at least with them the object of one's ardent support is constantly in view: the concert had already wandered through a succession of incomprehensible noises allied to boring and unattractive stage presences. Then The Gamut Range walked on, and silence fell.

One of the further many things that were talked about in the weeks to come, was how this British public had reacted differently from the Italian one of two nights earlier, when Caduta was also singing solo. True, what she had sung in Cremona did not involve the exotic embellishments of the Allegri, but even so the response had exceeded everyone's experience. Those who had heard the story of the Cremona reception, most particularly Francis Quirk, waited with pencil poised to see what would happen this time.

Initially, since Caduta's solo part wouldn't be heard for a few minutes, the listeners drank in her appearance. As this was a secular venue she had decided to dress more flamboyantly than usual for a Gamut Range concert – a figure-hugging black silk sheath with burgundy accents, tumbling from exposed shoulders to the floor. To this Little Black Dress formula of stage and screen she dared to add a tight-fitting jacket of gold organza voile. Whatever effect this costume had had on her listeners, after the first of her five solo verses, instead of the silence giving way to audible exclamations as might happen in Italy, here it merely deepened. Her efforts were greeted with voiceless stares of incredulity. By the time all the solo verses had been sung, and it became apparent that the piece was finished, so intensely was everyone wrapped into their inner thoughts that for some time there was no applause. When it came it was reluctant, leaving the performers to wonder if they had made a mess of it. It took fully half a minute to get going, and then never went wild. It just wouldn't stop.

'I've never heard anything so beautiful', sobbed one female invitee, clapping limply.

'My life will never be the same after this', maintained another.

But no one, neither the star-struck women nor the conflicted men, felt inclined to approach Caduta as the Cremonese had. She had become a mythical creature, not flesh and blood. Deprived of the cult of the Virgin Mary since the early 16th century, these English people wanted to put Caduta on a pedestal and worship her from afar.

Unfortunately the impact of this music proved to be superficial, the mood of mystical adoration soon permanently dispelled by the appearance of The Whyte Chorale. In a split second the crowd changed from tearful self-analysts to cheering and waving friends and relatives. Everyone in the reserved seating knew someone in the Chorale, and were keen to show that they had made the effort to come along and support them. Some stood up to wave, others pointed and waved from their seats. Those about to sing were more circumspect, aware that they had to do their best. In that moment, before their performance started, they were as professional as anyone else in the building. What they did next passionately mattered to them.

What happened next also went straight into the gossip mill. Not everyone in the room knew the tune to *Greensleeves*, at least not so it would be recognised, but after the first verse had been sung, and the existence of a moody refrain made apparent, the invited members of the audience quickly decided to join in. The words had been printed in their programmes, along with the texts of all the pieces in the concert, so there was a solid core to the pitchless fog that found its way into every nook and cranny. By the time the singing had reached the eighth and last verse, people were standing and swaying like a football crowd. Steve, who was conducting, soon realised there was nothing he could do to preserve the decorum generally considered appropriate at a classical music concert, and turned to encourage the inevitable. He felt sorry for the people who had bought tickets in good faith, conducting with a guilty smile on his face. He felt even sorrier two days later when he read Francis Quirk's review, and finally realised Highbury's was not going to donate any money at all. For now he decided to move on to *Strawberry Fair*, in the hope it might prove less emotive. But he was to be disappointed in this too. The swaying part of the audience had learnt how to do it, and tucked in – with confused references to the Beatles' *Strawberry Fields* – verse after verse, refrain after refrain. Once this was done, Steve was indicating that the Chorale should leave, when he heard their supporters tip into *Abide with me*. At this he indicated more firmly that the Chorale should leave, which they did, tired but triumphant, to cat-calls of delight.

And so the final act began to unfold. The Highbury's people were just as tired as their singers but rather drunker, which made them sleepy. They lazily reviewed what was left to separate them from the smooth running of what remained of their evening. A few more minutes of music by this man Tallis didn't seem to present much of a threat; so they hunkered down and put their minds into neutral. Switched off, yet as always relentlessly pestered by their daily earthly concerns, there was little in Voces Civitatis's rendition of *Suscipe quaeso* which could reach them. This was a pity, since there was a suggestion in Tom's programme note that *Suscipe quaeso* was one of the most beautiful pieces of music ever written and, even if the performance was not of the first rank, the members of the choir had rehearsed it just often enough to have got the hang of it. They were now able to sing it with an understanding which surprised them, and thrillingly drove them forward. By the end they felt they had achieved something as fulfilling as anybody else on the bill of fare that evening.

This was not lost on those members of the audience who had paid for their tickets. The performance was followed by sustained applause from a part of the seating which had so far kept a relatively low profile. The Highbury's invitees briefly became interested in these other members of the audience, turning to observe them for the first time, immediately losing interest again as huge numbers of performers stumbled into view. They looked for their friends once more, but by now the moment of rapport with the members of The Whyte Chorale had exhausted itself, and anyway the impact was diluted by all these other unknown people.

Spem in alium started out exactly as the composer had indicated it should – a slow, majestic crescendo of sound, sweeping all before it as the first 40-part passage comes into view. The choirs being sung by Voces Civitatis were now able to contribute effectively to this build-up, as the members strained every muscle to be heard. Jerry, standing by his piano, relayed Anton's beat both to Johnny, the accompanist, and to the singers standing nearby. The combined effect was forceful, if not particularly elegant, and it did the job. Then Choir 8, fired by Joe's electronic keyboard, joined the fray just where they needed to, and everyone hit the 40-part tutti right between the eyes.

So the music marched on, sometimes beautiful, sometimes hesitant, but never in serious trouble, until they all arrived at bar 108. Anton had prepared himself carefully for this moment. He had decided that whatever was going on around him, he would block his ears to it and relentlessly count out the beats in this bar, and the ones leading up to it. In this way he supposed the keyboard players would follow him, so that there would be no doubt, at least between the bridge and the engine room, of where everyone should be. In this way the memory of that extra beat in Germany would be finally erased.

As it happened there were no serious casualties in the approaches to bar 108. Without having to fight anybody, or go temporarily deaf, Anton realised that the entire ensemble was with him. He smiled a huge smile as, with unrestrained joy, he indicated the first two beats of the bar, shading those singing there into a rounded cadence. He gave the silent third beat with exquisite care, in obvious preparation for the big chord on the fourth beat. His hand went decisively to the right and then, gripping the air with his fist, he thrust it upwards.

Everyone came in just as planned, but the sound that followed was not just of voices. On the very top of the attack, and showing uncanny synchronicity with the voices, a crack of awe-inspiring magnitude could be heard from above, as if the Almighty had sent a thunder-bolt of encouragement. The building shook to its ancient foundations, and everyone inside it cried out in spontaneous horror. For a split-second Anton thought it must be the long-awaited storm breaking, but it turned out to be more complicated than that. He felt a drop of water on his head, and looked up. The drop turned into a trickle, for a moment blinding him. Then the unthinkable happened. The ceiling came crashing down, as it unleashed an unstoppable torrent of water onto him and everywhere around him.

The new sprinkler system had been set off in the loft. Functioning superbly and instantaneously, it released enough water to quench a fire in a skyscraper. Thousands upon thousands of gallons hit the floor of the loft, and in a single second of unrestrained madness smashed through the boards onto the plasterwork of the ceiling beneath. Whether this plaster was of industrial strength was much debated afterwards when insurance claims were all that was left to Martin Clark and his board, but the reality was that no plaster could have resisted the flood that followed. Solid sheets of water landed on the heads of those in the hall, with such speed that the shock was total. The heads felt the water first, and then the pieces of plaster that came down with it. The lights flashed and fused. Confusion and panic gripped every person present, as they assumed the building was on the verge of collapse.

Instantly soaked through, several hundred terrified people crammed the exits, slipping and sliding as they desperately tried to get out, on all fours if necessary. Few distinguished themselves in this crisis. Everyone ran about trying to protect themselves from a deluge which had an unknown source and wouldn't stop. Clothes were ruined in a few seconds; those wearing thin cotton found themselves on view as if they had entered an X-ray machine. Phones, wallets, credit cards, jewellery were swept up and away, as a river formed within, rushing to the Thames without. How to turn the flood off was a piece of information no one had thought to divulge.

The only person to pass a single second thinking about someone other than himself was Anton, who noticed, as the first sheet fell, that Brian Wiggins had made no effort to protect himself, or show any signs of being alive to what was going on around him. Why Anton was looking at Brian at all, as the world fell about his ears, could not be later explained, but some sixth sense had directed his attention Brian's way. As the general shouts of distress mounted, Anton put out the arm which had just indicated the fourth beat of bar 108, to shake Brian into wakefulness. As he did so an exceptionally large piece of plaster landed on his head and knocked him to the ground, where he lay stunned. Seeing this Brian, and then Christy and Jerry, snapped to. Pulling him towards an exit they bellowed their way through a crowd of moaning, bedraggled people.

'You come with me, young Anton', commanded Jerry as Anton slowly came to his senses. This was said in a tone of voice of such unfamiliar and sober authority that Anton immediately assumed the accident had impaired his reasoning. He was so surprised that he briefly forgot his throbbing head and looked up at Christy in disbelief: 'Jerry?'

'You should do what he says,' said Christy, smiling through the tears she had just collected. 'Sir Jeremy Cartwright is the Chief Medical Officer to the government and senior consulting physician at UCLH. He'll see you right.'

Anton sat up. 'Good God,' he said, continuing to feel light-headed. 'Well,' he added slowly, rubbing his pate, 'drenched as I am, and slightly concussed, all I really need is transport to Ahmed's.'

'Be my guest,' said Sir Jeremy. 'I am going there too. My piano, or what's left of it, on the other hand is staying here, which creates some extra space in the ambulance. You come too', he indicated to Brian.

Hours later, after the fire brigade had finally managed to stem the flow and winch themselves into the loft to make a preliminary inspection, word came to those partying at Ahmed's that the offending sprinkler had been set off by a coat-hanger and suit hanging on its ring. The story, as it became embroidered, was that someone, having missed the earlier items in the concert on account of losing their way to the Wharf, and unable to find anywhere to put their clothes, had mindlessly chosen this handy convenience, changed into their concert suit just before going on for *Spem*, and substituted their daytime and heavier clothes on the hanger. The firemen were adamant that although what they had mostly found later were random piles of formless rags collected against the walls, the metal coat-hanger was still clinging to its ring.

THE MANY AND VARIOUS WAYS by which the performers and audience left Marlowe Wharf cannot quickly be told. The Highbury's crowd, with the members of the Whyte Chorale, dripped into their coaches, now increased in number, and were taken back to base. Utterly deflated, Darren and Penny assumed that no one wanted to go to a party in sopping wet clothes, and so called the event off. This turned out to be a misjudgement. Half an hour after they had all been deposited at headquarters, 20 of the more enterprising trainees decided that this Saturday night should be made one to remember, and blow the expense. With the antennae of homing pigeons they soon found their way back to Ahmed's.

They entered the restaurant with a confidence which took those already established there by surprise. So far they had not done much to draw attention to themselves. The singing had been a test, which they felt had been memorably passed. What was on offer at Ahmed's was the easy part, and they felt they had earned it. They espied Brian leaning against the kitchen partition at the far end of the room, dousing his newly acquired sensibilities with drink.

'Hello Brian.'

'What a laugh!'

'We thought we'd better come and see if you were OK.'

'What've you got in there?', and they formed a group round him.

'Beer from a bottle,' said Brian, 'very tasty. And it's all paid for', he added, indicating with a thick thumb the back of Jerry, holding court at the street end of the room.

'Like, wow!' said a young voice from among them. 'Is the tap going to be turned off any time soon, do you think?'

But Brian wasn't listening. He knew he wasn't looking his best. The deluge had further reduced clothes which had been no more than unassuming at the start of the evening. But he felt an urgent desire to speak to a shy woman of his age named Polly, whom he had noticed at work some days before. She had come up from headquarters with the others, wondering whether she would find Brian there, and wondering how to deal with him.

'Hello,' said Brian, stepping back and sideways with a nimbleness no one would have previously credited him with, to be beside her. 'Can I get you something?'

'Well, a beer?' said Polly, keen not to lose contact with what the general crowd were saying.

'My friend Ahmed will provide,' said Brian with a wink, sweeping a bottle up from a table nearby, already stocked. The drink already inside him encouraged him to take a risk. 'Maybe we could step outside in a moment and cool down a bit?'

Polly looked at him. 'Oh no, I don't think so', she said, and turned back to her colleagues. Brian decided to take this rebuff philosophically, and bide his time. With the same nimbleness as before he repositioned himself inside the group.

The Highbury's contingent had been by no means the first to arrive at Ahmed's, since, apart from Jerry and his ambulance, flashing blue, the surest and most drying way to travel back from the Wharf was by bicycle. Several of the professionals made a daily habit of using one for work, always aware of saving on the cost of public transport. Chrissy, Joe, Francis, Tom and Steve set off from Deptford in convoy. When Ahmed heard their tale he assumed everyone would need cheering up, immediately putting out further *mezze* plates, to add to the ones he had already displayed. Between them there was *baba ghanouj* and humous, *falafel* and *ful medames*, *tabbouleh* and *fattoush*, *khubz* and *ka'ak* bread, *manakish* in all the variations Ahmed could conceive and, as a special treat, the intensely garlicky *labneh bi toum*. As well as bottles of Lebanese wine, western beer and a dwindling supply of *arancello*, Ahmed had taken a risk with a consignment of *arak*, known to be capable of touching 50% when the wind was in the right direction, which a 'cousin' had sent him some time ago from the Bekaa valley. Those holding the purse strings of The Gamut Range and Voces Civitatis had given him a budget to make this party a success, which caused him no problem. These were all ordinary fare in the Middle East.

To his surprise, however, there was an almost unanimous atmosphere of gung-ho defiance about his guests, as they arrived in their separate groups. They seemed buoyed by having survived a catastrophe, and exhilarated by the uncomplicated experience of having got soaked. Everyone was in the same mess: there was no point caring about one's hairdo, or the state of the concert clothes one had no choice but still to be wearing, since any less formal garments left in the loft were by now either on their way to the Thames Barrier, or awaiting the attentions of the local seagulls. The mood was one of liberation and camaraderie.

Those who had summoned ubers, or looked for taxis, or risked public transport, eventually arrived to whoops of ever noisier delight. Since the groups had been separated, and many delayed by having to borrow small change where they could, no one knew whether the general reaction would be to go home first to find fresh clothing, go home and call it a day, or head straight for the party. Something in the way the concert had been trashed, first by the audience and then by the deluge, when everyone had wanted to do their best, led to a collective disappointment which demanded a collective response. Anton reflected that twice that week he had failed to finish a piece by Tallis as a result of outside interference. He had been frustrated as a performer and now his head hurt. Ahmed's hospitality would numb the pain, before it made it much worse.

By the time the last stragglers had found their way to The Blue French – these were Martin Clark and Bob Parsons, who had stayed behind to speak to the firemen – the singing had already started. It had been generated as usual by Jerry and his followers, inaugurated with a stirring rendition of Stainer's *I saw the Lord,* the piece they had been obliged to curtail on the previous evening, when Ahmed had insisted it was time to close. There were no such strictures on this occasion. There was space and energy to do justice to every bar, the organ part represented by a cohort of men exercising their fingers in mid-space, yelling out the missing notes in generous approximations, while young men and women alike dispatched the vocal parts at full volume. For once no one felt this was beneath them, either vocally or morally, and soon there was such a noise that anyone who wanted cover to pursue more private interests, could have it. Until dawn.

The first to take advantage was Eugene. He had started drinking much earlier than everyone else, having stayed in the restaurant during the concert, and his eyes were now filled with alcohol. He found Robin sitting with a group of her colleagues at a table a little way from the singing. Oblivious of the embarrassment his actions were about to cause his beloved who, like every professional singer after a gig and in company with her fellows, wants to remain as anonymous (and carefree) as possible, he knelt at the side of the table and took her hand.

'Ah, Robin', he said in a dream-like trance, staring into her beautiful big eyes and marvelling at how they seemed to open yet wider as he spoke.

'Oh, hello, Eugene', she replied, aware that conversation around the table had ceased. She gently removed her hand and carelessly readjusted her position in her chair, as if nothing was happening.

'You are very beautiful', Eugene resumed, ignoring the pain in his leg muscles. Conversation of a self-conscious kind now started up around the table, but the scene playing out beside them had a fascination which was to prove unmissable. Where Robin's beauty was well-attested, if rarely paraded, everything about Eugene was taken for granted. Until this moment he had been routinely overlooked. Now, as he knelt there, his blue eyes glistening, he presented the very image of a romantic lead. Even the Stainer faltered as everyone took in the sight, before its unEnglish nature caused the singers to pretend they had seen nothing and redouble their efforts.

Robin herself was impressed. She had been known to cause young men heartache, but her conquests were of limited impact, restricted to people like herself, who prized modesty and blushed fetchingly. This apparition on his knee was of a quite different order; and she would have panicked if something in her, an iron something inside, that had taken her to the top of the singing tree against the odds, hadn't persuaded her to ignore everyone else, and concentrate on it.

'Where do you come from?' she asked in a tone of voice which implied more than just polite enquiry.

'I don't really know"' he thrillingly began, finding it hard to speak. 'My parents were Romani...' but mention of his parents caused him to swallow the last syllable of his sentence, unable to go on.

'Oh, you're a gypsy,' said Robin too loudly and too quickly, amazed. 'But I thought they all had dark hair.'

'I had dark hair once. My hair went white at a young age. Suddenly and completely white.' And he ran his fingers through his wavy locks, the only locks in the restaurant, apart from Ahmed's scrub, that looked as the owner had intended them to look when they left home that afternoon.

'Were you brought up in a painted caravan?' asked Robin, feebly extending her display of racial stereotypes and giggling in confusion. Her conscious mind was in disarray.

'No, no,' said Eugene, aware that the story was beginning to go his way, and hoping not to disappoint. 'My parents were Romanian. Diplomats. They were killed. I don't know where I come from, or belong', he added, hoping whatever sympathetic instincts Robin might have, would be awakened.

Robin felt herself slipping away. She wanted to know more, but found it difficult to ask the right questions. She knew she didn't want to offend him – her training in life was still strong enough to make that instinct clear to her – but that simple check-and-balance, so often all that conversations with strangers ever consisted of, was getting drowned in much less familiar reactions.

'Killed?'

'Yes, in an air crash, ten years ago. I became an orphan overnight. Ahmed has looked after me ever since.' But he wasn't interested in talking about himself, once the initial appeal of his story had registered. 'Where do you come from?'

'Basingstoke', said Robin, and became self-conscious again.

'Are your parents in Basingstoke? Why did you come to London?'

'My parents will always be in Basingstoke. I came here for the singing.' A moment of decision had been reached. Mundane information, when eyes can no longer do the whole job, was hard to communicate against a backdrop of Stanford in B♭.

'Would you like to walk about outside for a bit?' said Eugene, the master of nonchalance when at work, found he couldn't manage it so well when in love.

Robin allowed herself to be carried along. All she ever wanted to do was sing, it was true, and everything was subordinated to that. But she had noticed how this single-mindedness could drain the flair out of her colleagues, or so it could seem. The rest of their lives often came over as dull, colourless, their imaginative powers entirely wrapped up in what they did on stage. She was even prepared to go along with this stereotype, and wouldn't have been unhappy if that had been all there was, since she was singing at a level which fulfilled her; yet this modesty made her all the more susceptible to someone of Eugene's passionate address. 'Yes', she said, and they slowly and uncertainly walked through the crowd gathered at the door, out into the evening air.

Of course everyone watched them go. And it seemed to come as a natural sequitur that Ahmed should now offer some sort of explanation of Eugene who, for years, had been a source of wonder and speculation. Yet no one had thought it polite to ask. Ahmed saw that the moment had come.

Tom saw it too, and decided to help Ahmed along. 'Come and sit with us', he said to Ahmed, and found a table as far from the songsters as the room could manage. With them went Steve, Joe, Lotte and Anton. Between them they commandeered bottles of Musar red and white. A healthy selection of *mezze* plates was already on the table. They made Ahmed sit down, and joined him.

Ahmed looked at Tom, and then at Anton, as if for advice. They both nodded encouragingly. Ahmed half-smiled back, grateful.

'I have wanted to speak this story for years. It would have been relief. Eugene's life has been difficult one', and he hesitated.

'How long have you known him?' said Lotte.

'Since before he was born,' said Ahmed deliberately. 'I met his parents in difficult situation. You see I'm not Lebanese, I'm Palestinian. I was born in East Jerusalem in 1975, just as the Israelis started to fuss the Palestinian Liberation Organization.'

He looked round the room, wondering how far he could go with these people, almost friends.

'My family home was beautiful place, where good cooking was normal, where my family had lived for years and years. But such ordinary was not part of the life of the Israelis. One night the whole area was cleared for illegal occupation, and we, along with many innocent families, were sent to refugee camp. This killed my grandmother quickly. I remember the last thing she said to me: "Take this cooking round the world. It will interest them".' He paused, and took a mouthful of wine.

'So you had to rely on the PLO for protection – and for somewhere to live?' said Lotte.

'The PLO, responsible for us, moved us around, but they had tiny resources so that all the camps were very bad. Healthy people died in these places like insects. Eventually we were moved to the Shatila camp in Beirut. There, for three days in September 1982, a political right Christian militia carried out a famous massacre which killed unbelievable number of unarmed, innocent people. My parents were killed in this massacre.' He paused again, unable to continue. He pretended to arrange the cutlery on the table.

'Were these the Phalangists?' asked Tom, to give Ahmed time to recover.

He nodded. 'They said it was to fight assassination of elected Lebanese president Bachir Gemayel, leader of the Kataeb Party that Israel loved. Later they found that PLO had nothing to do with this assassination, but anyway the massacre took place, agreed before by Israeli government, as part of a plan to kill PLO for all time. So they invaded Lebanon in June 1982; by September Shatila was doomed. Because the Israelis were cowardly, they employed friendly local militias, telling their own troops to do nothing as massacre went ahead, but putting them at all exits to stop any escape. Their reward was Arafat, the leader of PLO, moved to Tunis, meaning survival of PLO; and Ariel Sharon, Israeli Defence Minister, resigned once real story was out.'

He looked up and nodded some more. 'Yes, my parents were murdered by Christians', and he stopped again.

There was a long pause. 'How did you escape?' Lotte finally managed to ask.

'After three days of shooting and hiding and shooting and hiding, Israeli soldiers finally said stop. Blood was quickly washed away, and selected diplomats were allowed to enter the camp, so to prove rumours they had heard was exaggerated. This did the Israelis no good, but the important point for me, and some children who were small enough to hide, was that these ambassadors were chosen from countries which the Israelis, in their small world, thought most likely to understand the situation: people used to state violence, and not upset by some blood on ground. So, naturally, they chose people from Eastern European countries – Russians, Poles, Bulgarians, Romanians. A crowd of smart foreigners appeared from nowhere. Israeli military authorities could not do enough for them.'

'How on earth did you, you know, get to meet these people?' asked Tom, making signs to Chrissie, who he saw listening from a nearby table, that this was not the moment to come over. She smiled back, intrigued.

'That was not difficult. It was clear that Israeli authorities would be happy if a few children playing in the blood and dust disappear, and that was what happened to me and a number of my friends. It was the best fortune that I happened to catch the eye of Mr Mihalache. I still don't know quite how it happened. I was seven, hungry and thirsty and in deep shock at seeing my parents being shot in front of me – so I suppose I just stood there and stared at him in complete agony, understanding nothing. Being a most sensitive youthful man, he took my hand just like that and didn't let go until we were safely in his official car outside the gates.'

'Did they say anything? What happened next?'

'He and his wife, Eliana, took me to their house, in silence. But no one followed. I think they must have had difficult job dealing with me in the next few months. They had no children of their own, and though they had some help in their house, because diplomats, I was a bad mess. And it had all happened so quickly. Perhaps that is the best way to make big decisions, but you must have character to last. My new parents certainly did. And so, with diplomatic protection, I disappeared from the record. Well, there were no records of who was in those refugee camps, but it was as if I had never been born. They helped me to be born afresh, and eventually to grow up as their almost son.'

A glance expressing incredulity went round the table. Anton broke the silence. 'So where does Eugene fit into this story?'

'Baba, that is Mr Mihalache, was too young to be an ambassador in 1982, but he was promising enough for the real ambassador to send him out on unfortunate missions. He and Eliana soon were promoted. By 1990 he was second in the London embassy, in 1998 he went as Romanian ambassador to Portugal, and then became ambassador to Poland in 2005. And in 1992, after many doctors and disappointments – they were now late 30s – and having recently moved to London, Eliana gave birth to Eugene.'

Another pause, another drink, and another long silence. One of the kitchen staff, seeing that no one was talking, sauntered up to ask whether they should continue preparing the *mezze* plates. Ahmed looked straight through him.

'So, Eugene is your brother, and he was born in England', prompted Lotte.

'Yes. In fact Eugene has never left England, though maybe that is surprise. He doesn't speak English with confidence, and his

Romanian stopped when Baba went to work in Portugal. He was six then. They had made decision stop in England, and treat work abroad as necessary. They bought a house in London, which Eliana, Eugene and I lived in while Baba was away. We spoke English there, partly to help Eugene with schooling. It was the happiest time we knew as a family. Baba was never away for long times; I had got over the traumas I could easiest to remember; and Eugene was something of a miracle to his mother, which she was happy to show him, while never forgetting me. He was spoilt, but I don't think that was what made him the careless young man he seems now.'

'So where are these parents that you share? I never see them here – at least I don't think I do', said Lotte, who hadn't heard Eugene's explanation to Robin.

Ahmed looked round the table once more. He took a deep breath. 'Yes, there is one more thing to say. A very difficult and bad thing.'

'In 2005 Baba became ambassador to Poland. Eugene was now thirteen, right in the middle of his school, which had been entirely in English private ones. For some time I had been looking for my own place to work, determined to obey my grandmother's words. In 2008 The Blue French was in need of a manager, and as you know I have been here since. In 2010 I was able to buy, and live upstairs in my apartment. Before I could do that, it had been decided to maintain the system of living and working that we had been running for all these years, so Baba went to Warsaw, and we stayed behind, leading our lives as usual.'

'Occasionally there were diplomatic events which required the show of family. This was especially true in Catholic Poland. In April 2010 there was to be a grand memory of the 70th year of the Katyn massacre. An official flight, carrying the President of Poland, Lech Kaczyński, with also senior members of Polish clergy, relatives of victims and other important peoples was fixed.

It also included senior diplomats and their wives, also those from the earlier Warsaw Pact countries. In case you wonder my father's career didn't suffer from his association with Soviet system. The new people needed experienced diplomats, and assuming they didn't do bad things, they carried on as if nothing had happened. And on that day it really seemed as if nothing had changed.'

'The plane, nearing the past military airport at Smolensk, ran into very bad weather. Planes before them had given up trying to land that morning, requesting permission to land at another place. But the pilots of this plane had unusual pressures. The President of the Republic was on board, not wanting any rearrangements on protocol of the day, and the Commander-in-Chief of the Air Force was actually in the cockpit during the final moments. The plane crashed into trees on the approach, and all 96 people on board were killed.' Ahmed fiddled some more with the cutlery, in his distress knocking a knife onto the floor. He looked down, distraught.

'Yes, I remember this,' said Tom gently. 'Of course there have been endless conspiracy theories ever since, most of them directed at the Kremlin.'

Ahmed, still staring at the floor, hadn't heard him. 'Since then there have been many guilt theories. It's been too easy. Katyn, the site of a series of mass executions by Stalin of the Polish military in 1940, is near Smolensk. That was why the President didn't want flight diverted. Putin has been blamed for the catastrophe by all manner of people, although there is no evidence that the Russians did dangerous things. Wars like this never end, but I am sure this crash was a result of avoidable pilot error. Whether this fact made it any easier for Eugene and me to come to terms with the news is our problem.'

Bending down to rescue the knife, Ahmed forced himself to finish. 'Of course I had been through it all before. Despite the beautiful view which Baba and Eliana had given me, I never forgot the other view which had come first. I knew I was on my own, and accepted it. But for Eugene it was different. He was 18. He had had happy and proper upbringing, from loving parents. I was an amusing and not completely understandable extra. We got on well, but there was no doubt we were not of the same background, if you see what I mean. The same family blood may count for little most of the time, but ultimately, when the pressure is really on, it is this blood that counts, for better or worse. I know families who hate each other but are not strangers. In our case we loved each other, but were strangers at the same time. There was nothing I could do to get over that with him – or he with me, the same.'

'So we were left alone, now just the two of us. Kindness was what we were used to at home, and it has carried on without trouble to right now. But as you see, Eugene never recovered from the shock. His hair went white before the next day. He became silent, a sensitive, intelligent boy in silent agony, working with me here in an endless not proper job, which he doesn't enjoy and isn't good at. He inherited some money, as I did, and the house; but he needs more than money. Robin looks a little like his mother. The same big eyes, the same gentleness; and I've never seen him like this before. Suddenly there is no guard in him. The danger is that he will be disappointed and his emotions even worse.'

This time Ahmed stopped finally, the story told. The group round the table were slow to speak, any awkwardness covered by the communal singing at the end of the room. Eventually Lotte, unable to address the larger tragedy, remarked 'Yes, I hope young Robin is up to this. She would be inheriting a casualty, one she may not have the personal resources to heal. And someone like Eugene is well outside her normal experience of people.'

'You never know,' said Ahmed. 'Baba and Eliana gained a casualty, and they were young and idealistic like maybe Robin.

You never know when that single glance of understanding and sympathy may come, or if you will meet its meaning when it does.' He smiled at last. 'Inshallah.' The word passed round the table.

FOR SOME HOURS MORE Ahmed and his guests instinctively watched the door to the street. Even when they drifted away to join other groups, the door remained their sixth sense. Chrissy saw Ahmed, Steve and Joe in turn get up, which left Anton and Lotte alone together. She felt that she could finally intrude. 'Was that interesting?' she asked, indicating the retreating figure of Ahmed. 'You don't need to answer that. I could tell from your expressions that the conversation was not trivial. Now someone is going to have to relay it to me, and I suppose it won't be Ahmed. So you'd better get it right' and she grinned.

'Romanian,' said Tom Morris to Steve, as they joined adjacent tables hosting Gamut Range singers. 'You know, that explains something I didn't understand about Eugene's behaviour. Whenever he hears Italian spoken he gets, you know, close to it, a kind of instinctive closeness, as he did with Robin. He heard in it, and saw in her, something he recognised but couldn't immediately place. Romanian is a lost language in the West, you know, but in fact it is as close to vulgar Latin as Italian is. Of course it has many Slavic loanwords now,' he continued, expanding. 'But in essence it is another central romance language, just pronounced outside the usual stable. From what I gathered Eugene wouldn't have heard much Romanian spoken at home, not least because, you know, Ahmed himself couldn't speak it; but something went in with Eliana's milk, and now he's half hearing it. I reckon he's been living a shadow existence for years now, poor fellow, self-absorbed and lost. My heart really goes out to him.' Steve mumbled something sympathetic, which Tom couldn't catch, on account of a super-charged wall of sound that suddenly enveloped them.

At this moment, for complicated emotional reasons, the songsters briefly abandoned their exploration of Anglican service music and started out on the choruses of Haydn's *Creation*. Some of them had been part of a performance earlier in the season and it only took one of them to begin 'The heavens are telling' for all hell to break loose. Dah, dah, DAH – dah, dah DAH – dah, dah DAAAHHHH – the fists pumped the air, the orchestral fingers waggled, heads were thrown back, bottles of Timmy Taylor's Landlord disappeared down open throats.

However even they were destined to be interrupted. Even their decibel level was not sufficient to drown out an all-enveloping Russian voice, projected from the edge of the group. 'Why not we sing some Bortniansky? He more genius than Sir Stanford any day, my God.' With remarkable persistence Leonid Moudrich had not only picked himself up from the chair Joe had dumped him on some hours earlier, but sobered up sufficiently to follow everyone down to the Wharf for the concert. In doing so he had befriended Judith Brook, one of The Gamut Range altos, as she passed by his table outside. She had reacted positively to his questions about where they were all going and whether she could help him get there, offering to share an uber with him and Nancy Silver, her closest colleague. Leonid, in turn, had reacted positively to the kindly treatment, the concert and the drenching, which had freshened him up no end. It hadn't mattered that he had found the concert vapid and inconsequential, and the drenching the best fun he'd had since his family's dacha had burnt to the ground, his good humour pleased Judith. She was attracted to his deep-pitched speaking voice, replete with rattling phlegm, and decided, as Robin had done, to go out on a limb. Eventually the two of them travelled back to Ahmed's from the concert together, Nancy deciding to go back with other colleagues.

So it was that, with Judith on his arm, Leonid finally achieved his ambition of singing with these famous London professionals. By good fortune he had found himself allied to another low-note person – Judith specialised in the lowest part of a woman's register, a genuine contralto, just as Leonid did for a man's. Having made his pitch for Bortniansky, he decided to lead Judith into a little friendly sparring. With increasing commitment they descended the alphabet. Judith started with a low G, which Leonid countered, an octave lower, with an F. Judith hit an E♭, at which Leonid sang a D. By the time Leonid had roared out his longed-for, career-defining bottom counter-G, projected into the building as if its walls were on the other side of the street, Judith was ready to take her social experiment a stage further.

'Do you have any fags on you?' she ventured, looking him straight in the eye.

'What are these things? Fags?'

'Oh sorry, cigarettes', she said.

'Да. Мы могли выйти на улицу?' with which he took her hand and marched her outside, ignoring the songsters in their path who, to be fair, had ignored them after the initial distraction, continuing their Haydn through the display of chromatic rivalry, disinclined to be impressed by someone so obviously from a different singing tradition.

It was heading towards 3am. As the cacophony intensified Ahmed spared a thought for the neighbours. In fact he had never had any trouble from them, either because they were never at home, he assumed, or because they were in his restaurant already. He glanced round to find elderly Mrs Pritchard, who lived two doors away, singing along like a teenager, Becky Cavanagh singing along as a teenager, Mr Cavanagh holding his stomach for laughter, Mrs Cavanagh singing softly and Becky's 13-year-old brother outside smoking. At this moment the very last arrival of the evening walked through the door. It was Araminta Flatt with her dog. She had gone home after the concert to steady her nerves, decided to spruce herself up, and gave her toy poodle a bath and a careful combing of its elaborate topknot. They ventured forth, Araminta clicking along in high-heels, the dog adopting a similar gait, the two of them radiating polished style.

'Hello, Araminta,' said Jerry. 'That is a very smart dog. You look very smart too. Rather smarter than the rest of us.' His professional eye skirted the rear of the dog, followed by its underneath. 'What is her name?'

'Natural', said Araminta.

'That IS an unusual name,' he carried on, as if speaking to a child. 'Why did you call her that?' The moment these words were out of his mouth, he knew he was going to regret them.

'Well, you know, years ago, I used to work for the people at Cecil Sharp House. Such a lovely atmosphere. They asked me, as an up-and-coming soprano, to sing some of those wonderful old folk songs Cecil had collected, so their students could dance to them. I spent hours every day singing modal music. Can you imagine? Not the best preparation for Bach. But there was no getting round it. Not everybody knows that Cecil's primary inspiration was dance, followed by the music that traditionally went with it. He actually single-handedly revived the corpse of English country dance, to the inestimable benefit of the generations who have followed him. He particularly encouraged an interest in Morris Dancing, which is now so loved...'

'Wasn't it Thomas Beecham who said he would try anything once except incest and Morris Dancing?' said Jerry, hoping for an exit.

'No. It was Arnold Bax, in his Autobiography,' sniffed Araminta, now derailed. Her mind whirred like a gyroscope. 'Do you know I met Sir Arnold? I was seven or eight. He came to our school to talk about Tintagel and Celtic culture. He was fascinated by Ireland, even writing fiction under a Celtic pseudonym. He was rather old and used-up by the time I met him, but not so gaga or grand as to disdain encouraging a very enthusiastic young soprano. I sang him all my best...'

'When I was training I went to Moscow to attend a medical conference,' said Jerry firmly, not averse to playing Araminta at her own game. At the sound of his enhanced voice, the circle standing just in earshot moved closer and became more numerous. 'There were many posters up for concerts – the Russians are mad for classical music, as you know – many of them advertising the music of Bax. I couldn't understand it. He wasn't THAT well-known here, let alone abroad. And his name kept appearing alongside baroque composers, especially Vivaldi. My English friends and I couldn't help wondering where he would have spent all his non-transferrable royalties. I'd not heard of him passing his declining years on the Black Sea. It made no sense, until one day, when I was trying to decipher an advertisement for toothpaste...'

'Oh yes. Absolutely. That's very good. Hahaha', went Araminta, not getting it.

'Hahaha', went the circle, equally in the dark.

Jerry turned away to sing, accidentally treading on Natural as he did so.

At another table, as far removed from the mêlée as Jonathan could make it, he and Caduta sat uncomfortably together. No one disturbed them. Caduta's Little Black Dress had rearranged its curves in unconventional places, but she had the figure of someone who would look good in absolutely anything. Jonathan had clocked this, of course, which seemed to him to beg the question as to why she felt it necessary to spend money on fancy outfits, when all she needed was a basic minimum. Everyone would notice her. Although in his cups he decided not to mention this.

'I don't understand you, Caduta,' he moaned. 'You have the world at your feet, and yet you are unattached and aloof. You are friendly, but remote. Don't you have it in you to try something fun with someone – with me? When we sang that duet together the other night I thought we were made for each other. Didn't you think so? You seemed to be loving it.'

Caduta noted again the pleading expression in Jonathan's eyes, the sort of look Italians do extremely well. They tend to have round, brown, cow-like eyes, Jonathan had round, blue, dog-like eyes, but the effect was the same, and met the same response. 'Is there something the matter with me?' she mused silently. 'I'm sure sex will come one day, and when it does I shall enjoy it. What these young men don't understand is that just because they think I look sexy, it doesn't mean I'm gagging for it 24/7. Or, as a matter of fact, at all.' She paused in her thought and then added: 'at least not with them. How do I make love to boys who one minute treat me like a doll, and the next like their mother?'

Out loud she said 'I did love it. I loved the music, I loved the singing, and I am very fond of you. But I am exactly as fond of you as I am of all these wonderful colleagues we have. You and they are fantastic people, and I can't believe my luck in finding you all.' As earlier in the evening, she spread her palms on the smooth surface of the table, this time not so much to find solace, as to have something to look at, private to her.

'But I came here to sing. Clever people on their death beds often say they are glad they lived for the one really important thing in the world – human relationships – and then, just in case it is remembered what a selfish mess they made of it, they mention their abiding and uniquely powerful interest in The Arts. This is eyewash, for people who never really got their hands dirty. All I ever wanted to do was get in amongst singers, and sing, sing, sing.

The London scene has given me a unique opportunity. But unlike some of you bizarre British people I don't equate music with sex. When I get off stage the first thing I want to do is revel in what has just happened. I do not want that memory to be overlaid with something which may prove more temporary than the impact of the performance we've just given. And I don't want to be with one person when we've all just performed as a group. I want to lose myself in the group', and she stared hard at her splayed fingers.

'Is singing really everything?', asked Jonathan, who could follow quite a lot of what she had said, but would never voluntarily eliminate sex from his to-do list, just to enjoy the singing a little more. In this context Caduta's next remark was inexplicable.

'Just in case you think I'm not interested in you, but have a secret lover hidden away somewhere, possibly in Sicily, I am a virgin.'

Jonathan's mind began to race. He thought of how her first time could be – with him. How he would make it wonderful for her. How they would sing all the better afterwards. How this exquisite person, now suddenly so vulnerable, would dote on him, her one true love.

Caduta watched him, reading his mind like an open book. Although she wasn't in the habit of revealing what she had just revealed, she knew the reaction was going to be no more than a hyped-up version of all the more standard reactions. She looked cold at this moment, depressed that her charms meant these people couldn't deal with her, and would never be able to deal with her. She envied her colleagues the ability just to give and take, to be treated as ordinary, to sleep around and have fun without inventing a form of modern worship. English as her voice might sound, she knew she didn't fit. She was too good to be true. Depression turned into a taunting unhappiness.

By some sixth sense, Jonathan realised he needed to say something unexpected. He surprised both of them. 'Did you always want to be a boy?'

'Of course not. What makes you think that?'

'Well, you sound like one, and... well.' He hadn't meant to be unpleasant, he was just maudlin and rather lost.

'The old adage that women singing without vibrato automatically sound like boys, is one off the rubbish tip of history. That's something I've learnt here. Surely we got over that one decades ago', said Caduta, aware that not so long ago she had been worried by this very topic. She was equal to it now, reflecting that this piece of clichéd thinking was bad enough coming from the public – and she had suffered from it – but coming from a fellow pro it was maddening. It was equally maddening when some members of the public, having made the comparison, would then meet her and elaborately acknowledge their mistake. Her sense of dislocation deepened.

'Maybe you should start singing very obviously female roles from now on, just to balance things up', said Jonathan, his bitterness intensifying.

'Maybe it is time for me to go back to Italy, and start again,' snapped Caduta, projecting every syllable right between his eyes. 'Maybe I should deliver on what I always said I would do, and show talented singers in Italy that there is a life and a career outside the stifling operatic tradition', and her body stiffened with a consuming sense of outrage.

'Oh,' said Jonathan, collapsing in a heap. 'Don't do that.'

'I think I must. Yes, I shall go soon. Time to start a new life and a new career. This one only half fits', and at this her eyes softened.

She looked at him again, with something approaching affection, or at least an acknowledgement that she had put him through it and he was still there.

He began to let go.

FRANCIS QUIRK'S APPEARANCE had not been helped by the deluge. His baseball cap had vanished in the first impact, revealing untidy, thinning hair and intensifying his pathological fear that if he had no cap to prevent it his mind would empty. His tee shirt had been torn in the scramble to get out of the wharf, which left his lower-half Oxford-based accessories intact, to carry him and the day. His note-pad and pencil had also perished early, leaving him desperately to conjure phrases in his head, which he would now have to remember. He turned to Christy Benningham, who he found next to him and yelled (they had been slow to find a table away from the singing) 'how would you describe Caduta's Allegri tonight?'

Christy paused, aware that her words might find their way into one of the country's most respected broadsheets. 'Lovely', she finally managed. Another pause, as Francis waited, politely. After a while he said 'Well, do you think she sounds like a boy?'

'No', said Joe Farrant, who had left his earlier companions in order to pursue interests of his own. Becky Cavanagh hadn't yet quite made up her mind to leave the singing circle and her parents, but Joe could see that her mind was working on it. She saw where Joe had gone to sit, and with whom. He decided to make a spectacle of himself.

'Of course she doesn't sound like a boy. Boys don't sound like mature sopranos. They sound like children.' He gesticulated, speaking loudly against the continuing Haydn. 'How could a child be expected to rival one of the most accomplished singers in the English choral tradition you will ever hear? A boy might just conceivably manage to approximate to what she did this evening, but he will always sound breathier, more fragile, more abstract. Caduta's genius is to sound absolutely assured, while producing a tone quality on a top C which is so beautiful it could change people's lives. We call that tone quality English, which is a neat parochialism really. Why shouldn't an Italian soprano be able to do this? We just don't expect it – yet. But the time will come when there will be Caduta Massi clones dotted all over the globe, just as there are Gamut Range clones; and the world will be a richer place for them. It's just that none of this has anything to do with boys.'

Francis was aware that part of his readership still hoped the Anglican cathedral tradition was an all-male one, as it had been from time immemorial. He realised that to make Caduta's performance of interest to many who weren't there, he would require some very adept use of adjectives. Joe was helping, if he could only remember the best words. 'Absolutely assured.' Good. 'Change people's lives.' Excellent. 'Could I imply that she is a kind of super-treble?' he asked.

'You mean she sings like a boy, only more so?' asked Joe.

'That would be ideal', said Francis.

'No. Just say she is an Italian soprano from Caltanisetta, who sings the Allegri better than anyone has ever heard it: a proper professional singer, in a quite different league from any boy treble. This is music-making outside the little box of daily Anglican choral singing. Jesus Christ', said Joe with a concluding flourish, aware he was being watched.

'Outside the box', repeated Francis, reaching to cram down his non-existent cap, hoping all this would stick.

BY 4.30AM THE SONGSTERS had finally had enough. Dawn was approaching. The last few suggestions, introduced with the usual bravura, had started promisingly, but after a few minutes of the expected welly, attention had wandered. This led to other hopefuls beginning a new hit before the previous one had ended, a recipe for decline. When Malcolm Sargent tried once again to light a fire with Murrill in E, he was greeted with exhaustion. 'We did that one already,' said Dave Acolyte, 'hours ago.' The time had come to eat and drink some more, without exertion. Ahmed had seen this coming and, with consummate professionalism, brought out some plates he had been keeping in reserve: *bakhlava* and *meghli'*, and *knafeh* and *shanklish* for the first time that night. The supply of *arak* was reinforced. Tired people sat heavily down on nearby chairs.

One or two quickly took advantage of the relative silence. The group of Highbury's trainees thought it was time they met their benefactor. Peeling themselves off the kitchen partition, where they had happily spent the best part of five hours, they advanced through the room to find him, Brian bringing up the rear with Polly a pace or two in front of him.

They identified Jerry, which wasn't hard. A forthright middle-aged woman went up to him and said 'Were you the gentleman who provided the drink these last five hours?'

'Yes, I was. You looked thirsty, on arrival.'

'Well thanks to you, that's no longer a problem', and they all murmured their appreciation.

'Did you enjoy the concert?'

The group looked at itself, in such a way as to suggest they had been considering this question, at some length. They didn't know how far Jerry had been responsible for it.

Eventually the forthright one said 'Not much.'

Jerry looked more carefully. 'Oh dear, wasn't it what you were expecting?'

'Apart from the flood it was what we were expecting, but not what we wanted', came back a steady reply.

Jerry looked harder. 'What did you want?'

'We wanted a higher standard – from what we were doing, I mean. It became apparent early on we were a colossal embarrassment. But we didn't know any better. None of us had ever heard anything like what The Gamut Range was doing. It was from another world, another planet, another galaxy. When I first heard them, I just wanted to shrivel up and die. Later I had a more useful thought – maybe I could start to sing like that myself. We all think like that, don't we Brian?' the forthright one added, calling across the group.

Brian nodded, vigorously rubbing his cheek. Some hours earlier he had decided that the beauty of sound which had just come into his life, need not be merely the pure and innocent thing it seemed at first encounter to be. To worship it day and night was the way to madness; and if his multiple attempts at employment had taught him one thing, it was that he wasn't impressed by people who seemed mad. He realised he had to pin this new enthusiasm down and make it practical. He giggled to himself as he took another swig from the bottle he was carrying and readjusted his cloth cap, now back in place. 'Yes, we do... We want to sing like those...' he swayed as his hand swept the whole room into consideration '... angels.' His arm came nonchalantly to rest around Polly's waist.

Suddenly everyone had sprung to life and was in motion.

'What would it take for you to realise this dream?' said Jerry.

'Money, natch,' said Steve, who had come up to see what was being discussed, quick to assume it might concern him. 'Not very much. Seed money really. To buy scores, hire a rehearsal room, ensure independence from the publicity department at Highbury's, and pay me enough to make me want to continue with the project, which will take time. If all this were to fall into place, this is exactly the kind of thing which I feel I've been put on this planet to make work.'

'Well, let's see,' said Jerry. 'Let's do something worth doing. I'll be back in a tick,' and he headed for the Maserati, parked outside, to return with several copies of *The English Hymnal*. 'Now we are going to sing something from this together.'

Alarm seized the group. 'But I can't read music', wailed the forthright one.

'It's dead easy,' said Jerry. 'I give you the starting note, and you go up or down as the notation tells you. Where the notes are not moving by step you'll have to guess. We'll do one part first, as you did earlier, and then slowly add others. Here's the first note to a beautiful tune by Orlando Gibbons', and off they went, Jerry leading and Steve encouraging. It was remarkable, and inspiring, how quickly in this situation they picked up the basics. In fact it was remarkable how well they could sing, once the clutter had been cleared from their minds. And they were loving it, as much as they had loved *Greensleeves*, but in a more rewarding way. After twenty minutes they couldn't believe what they'd achieved. Jerry said he would put together a small committee of well-wishers to ensure the future of whatever they decided to do.

Steve reflected that everyone can sing – the tone deaf as well as those with perfect pitch – but not in every forum. Not when they are self-conscious, or culturally alienated from the material. One step up from rock bottom could be a big step, but then no one needs to be at rock bottom. His job was to make sure that all the people who came to him to sing did not think they were rock bottom material. Everyone can sing, and every vocal timbre has colours in it which has something to say. And then there is the sheer physical joy of doing it. He wouldn't give up his calling for Anton's for the world.

Anton, Lotte and Chrissy, still sitting at a table together, bottle of Musar to hand, were listening to the students. Coincidentally

Anton was thinking in parallel with Steve, only from the other side. He saw the happiness and achievement, but wanted nothing of it. Nothing excited him less than the prospect of dragging idealistic people through small and easy masterpieces of a cappella art. He even found their enthusiasm off-putting. As so often before he wondered why he was in this profession. Was it just as an aesthete? Didn't he get any satisfaction from interacting with his colleagues? Did it always have to be disciplined perfection? Why not give simple, powerful pleasure, as Steve was doing now?

Restless with this thought, he looked at Lotte, who knew that look. 'You don't want to do that sort of work,' she said. 'You're no good at it, and having a social conscience won't make you any better. You'll come over as condescending, which you do anyway quite easily. Your niche is a rather unusual one, and it is too late to change it.'

Anton sighed, noticing that his head still hurt from the plaster that had struck him. He suddenly felt cross. 'Is it really enough to live the life of those orchestral conductors who dot from highly professional group to highly professional group, claiming to give classic performances of music the general public takes for granted but still pays for? Where does Tallis come when Beethoven is in question? If I'd wanted to be a classic performances conductor, with good funding from both the public and private sectors, I should've stuck to Mozart. Or at least Bach. For some reason I got stuck on what people still insist on calling Early Music – a belittling term', and he looked as though his career had been hell from start to finish. The only recourse to hand was the bottle of Chateau Musar, which he poured liberally into his glass, making the mental note that he would suffer for it.

Chrissy intervened. 'Come off it, Anton, you specialise in little old Tallis because you take his music more seriously than you take Mozart's, or even Bach's. What was it you said about the relentless progress of Bach in recent years? "He has become like Shakespeare. He can do no wrong. Shakespeare did plenty wrong, and so did Bach. The mindless adoration of Bach these days is distorting and otiose." Now where did you say that? It must have been somewhere posh. Never mind. You would never say that about Tallis or Palestrina. You love their music too much. You respect it.' Noticing that the bottle was finished, she turned to find Ahmed, waving the empty in the air.

'How do you know?' said Anton defiantly.

'I see it in your eyes when you're conducting. It doesn't have to be the big Amen, the culmination of a vast edifice; it could be the simplest four-part setting by a minor figure. But something in the make-up of these things – the lack of instruments, the way the voices interweave, the cultural context, the abstract nature of the writing, the way the words retreat into the background, something, appeals to you at a level that later music does not. This surprises me because symphonies are even more abstract than votive antiphons – and you really do like abstract.'

'I love symphonies. The bigger, the noisier, the better.'

'Yes, I realise you react passionately to good music of any kind,' she said indulgently, 'but there is no need for you to conduct it all.'

'Conducting a Bruckner symphony is top of my bucket list', smiled Anton, readily accepting the new bottle from Ahmed, already opened. He indicated to Ahmed that he would pay for it when the time came.

'I don't suggest you try,' said Lotte. 'You don't have the technique for it, and you certainly don't have the money or the experience. You have the technique, the money and the experience for doing precisely what you do, and nothing more. Just be happy with that.'

Chrissy felt caught. Anton certainly had his limitations as a conductor – and Lotte was adept at pinpointing them – but what had made him so renowned? She knew he deserved his fame, but it was hard to quantify. 'For Christ's sake. You don't need to conduct Bruckner to justify your existence. Nor do you need to start doing masterclasses with musical illiterates, however beautiful that might turn out to be in human terms.

Look. I'll give you an example of what you need to do, or keep doing. Towards the end of *Gaude gloriosa* this evening there was a moment of the purest genius.' At this Anton embarked on the routine which Englishmen standardly follow when they are being praised. The first stage is to look down, confused.

'By then we'd been rumbling along, slipping and sliding for at least 16 minutes. We had entered the final straight, the last lap, exhausted but determined if possible to make it to the end without any hint of flaking. Just before the Amen is a phrase, to the words 'adesse caelorum regnum', which no one who has sung it can forget. You had that look in your eyes. No one was to be spared, however sung out. You were going to lead us into battle, just where the music most needed it, not caring if people expired in the sodding attempt.' At this Anton, who had been shifting uneasily in his chair, careful not to catch anyone's eye, felt his cheeks begin to burn.

'Almost nobody else on the planet knows that this is what is needed right there. How can a conductor specialising in Beethoven or Bruckner possibly know this? It takes specialist knowledge. And then it takes something extra. Something abandoned. Something wild. Something that only a frankly great conductor can provide. One day the general public will see that *Gaude gloriosa*, or *Spem in alium* for that matter, is every bit as worthwhile as a romantic symphony, and then there will suddenly be hundreds of you. But for now, you're unique.' Finally Anton looked up, trying to seem grateful while fumbling for something ironic to say. He needn't have worried. Chrissy was already onto the next thing.

Just as she was reaching her climax, and feeling as though she could sweep the world with it, she noticed Christy walking by. She got up.

'Are you still here?' she asked Christy. 'You've done well.'

'Ah, I was just on my way back to the clapped-out songsters commune over there,' Christy said, looking at once embarrassed and guilty. 'They probably need a bit more nannying.' She shrugged her shoulders, trying for a smile.

'Oh for heaven's sake, come on, don't rush away just yet,' said Chrissy. 'Let's sit here and talk about things. Ahmed,' she called over, 'are there any more plates to be grazed upon? And a bottle of Ksara?'

'Goodness, I really shouldn't drink any more. I'm relying on my bike to get home, and I'm unsteady at the best of times. Anyway it's so terribly late. I ought to have... hours ago...'

'For Christ's sake do be quiet!' said Chrissy, tired of the meek and mild housewife act, at least when it was wheeled out against her. 'Bloody well sit down, and tell me what really makes you excited in life. How was the concert for you?' Ahmed brought the requested wine, and some *mezze* plates. They found they needed both. Christy began to relax again.

'It was awful really' said Christy, after several mouthfuls. 'I mean who were those people? They were so hopeless. The whole concert was hijacked even before it was completely written off. I felt so sorry for all the organisers, not least Steve, who had put so much careful preparation into it, I helped him plan everything, all the staging, making sure everyone knew what to do and where to go, what to wear, where to hang up their clothes...' Her voice faltered. Chrissy drew closer. 'It was a disaster for everyone except you lot, who just seem to swan through everything without a care in the world. We were terribly exposed, we sang badly, there was nothing I could do...' and she started sobbing.

'Honestly, don't be silly, you can't blame yourself for all these shortcomings. We swan through not because we don't care, but because we know when to back off. We know when it's our responsibility, and when it's someone else's. That's one definition of professional. We sang OK, and cleared off, as best we could. You're not obliged to take on all the woes of your hobby. You have full-time concerns.'

'Yes,' she sobbed some more. 'But those are routine, home-based concerns. Everyone has those. They are wonderful and necessary, but Voces Civitatis is unique. Everyone has babies and a husband who is doing something else – being professional you would call it. But for me, the special thing is to get Voces Civitatis right. And then, having got everyone there in good order, and made Steve's life easier, to sing as well as I can. In the concert little of this happened. The staging in *Spem* was a complete shambles – there was nothing I could do; and I was so strung up I couldn't sing properly. I'll never forget my first note in *Spem*. It stopped in my throat. I COULDN'T SING...' and, unable to go on, she gripped the table.

'Listen,' said Chrissy, putting her hand on Christy's. 'This is no way to live. You spend your time trying to make sure everyone else's life is functioning smoothly, with no thought for yourself. Has it occurred to you that if you go on like this, you'll be of no use to anyone? You'll burn yourself out, and everyone will quickly say "what a nuisance".' Christy felt the hand and saw the sympathy. Something stirred in her she didn't recognise.

'One thing we professionals learn very quickly is that if we don't say "fuck off" periodically, no one respects us. In the amateur world I've noticed that if you go all supine and say "I'll do that for you because I so love what you do", you'll soon be taken for granted. And then if you do say "fuck off", because no one expects you to, you'll quietly be dropped because actually you were being kept on not because you were singing well, but because you were being useful, probably inexpensively, behind the scenes. That is a major difference and you have fallen into the trap.' She gently prised Christy's hand up from the table's edge.

'But I sing really quite well.'

'Do you? I've no idea, but I suspect you could be replaced in the twinkling of an eye, if you put it to the test. I'm repeatedly told I could be, if that makes it feel any better', and she gave the hand a scarcely perceptible squeeze.

During this trial Christy had found it soothing to drink Ahmed's lovely Lebanese wine quite quickly. Her sobs needed irrigation, and Chrissy saw that she was becoming more relaxed, prepared to step outside her habitually constraining box, and imagine new possibilities. This did nothing to dissuade Chrissy from repeatedly filling her glass. Or her own; but she had been in this situation before.

'I'm sorry – listen, you probably sing really well. So your daily horizons are made up of children, husband, house-hold concerns, and Voces Civitatis. Right?'

'You make it sound terribly banal,' said Christy, putting her hand back in her lap, avoiding further embarrassing contact with Chrissy's. 'Actually it isn't such a bad life at all. You haven't got everything that I've got, so you wouldn't know.' Chrissy had stung her, right where it hurt.

'Actually,' Chrissy said gently, 'I don't want children, a husband or household concerns. I just want to sing. Then I want to go home and sleep. Then, the next day, I want to sing some more. That's enough for me. I couldn't handle any more.'

'Oh, you are hopeless,' giggled Christy, happily at a loss. She had stopped crying, and begun to expand. She realised she had a new friend, who gave the impression she understood her. She could say anything now, without fear of rebuke. Indeed she could rebuke Chrissy, and was going to enjoy doing it. Years of inhibition were being washed away. She pulled herself together.

'That's a pretty narrow ambition. I can sing. And I've brought four new people into the world as well. What's so grand about your way of doing things? Even your singing isn't as good as some people's. You're just a choral singer really. Real singers – opera singers – earn so much money they can take weeks off when they like. To live real lives. With their partners and children.'

She had meant to draw blood, but Chrissy had the kind of chemistry even mosquitoes instinctively avoid. 'You've done a fantastic job, and people love you for it. You probably sing beautifully – far better than me. My approach has always been uncomplicated, selfish and alone. But I don't regret it. I've done my best with what I was given.' And she poured some more wine.

Christy stared at the brick wall that was the woman opposite her. She had suddenly lost the desire to attack it, aware she had no weapons to attack it with. But she wished she could acquire some of the bricks that made up that wall.

'I didn't mean to doubt you. I wish I hadn't said that. I admire you very much really.' And she slumped in her chair, silenced.

'Christy,' said Chrissy. 'Tell me something,' and she put the hand which had clasped Christy's hand around her shoulders, gently drawing her closer. 'Have you ever gone with a woman?' and she let her hand slide down Christy's arm.

Christy looked up. 'Gone with a... You mean...' There was a long pause. 'I've never thought about it. Not once. I mean I knew it was possible, of course, but not for the kind of people I know...'

'Look here, would you like to try it? With me? Now?' Her hand moved onto Christy's hip and then round her waist, finding the small of her back. 'If you can ride your bike for ten minutes, we can go to my place.' She was suddenly no-nonsense, hard to refuse.

'Well, I would quite', said Christy, happily lost again. She felt Chrissy would smooth out all the wrinkles. She was wonderfully strong. She knew how life should be lived, by artistic people.

Gently Chrissy stood up and helped Christy up too. A ten-minute cycle-ride was not beyond them. They moved towards the door to the street.

Ahmed was there, as ready for action as if it were midday, hands on hips, fingers splayed forwards, his apron still impeccable, half-smiling, alert. He nodded as they passed and watched them fumble with the locks on their bikes. Eventually they peddled away; and as they did so the parties inside, one by one, broke up too.

It was 6am. Ahmed nodded to Araminta and Natural; to Tom and Francis; to Mrs Pritchard and the Gallaghers; to Sir Jeremy, Steve and all those in the rank and file who had sung themselves into tomorrow; to Brian and Polly, now arm in arm; finally to Anton and Lotte who only had to walk up Tippett Avenue to reach their front door. He realised he had missed Joe, and looked around for him. He noticed two bodies pressed together in the shadows, their two heads one. 'You know Becky, don't you?' said Joe, on being noticed. Yes, he did.

As they too walked into the morning light, he saw another couple approaching from a different direction. They were as pale as ghosts, silent and detached. 'Just collecting our things', said

Eugene. Ahmed made to offer them whatever he could, but was immediately deterred by their look of exhausted determination. They stared straight through him, went inside, collected their things, and disappeared again into the night. Ahmed felt a wave of such relief pulse through him that he put out a hand to support himself, struggling for breath.

LEFT TO HIMSELF AT LAST, Ahmed stood in the doorway of his restaurant, looking up Tippett Avenue, cigarette in hand. He had decided to leave the chaos of the tables behind him, covered in dirty plates and glasses as they were, for later in the day, and savour the deeply satisfying memories of the scene it represented a little longer. He allowed the clear light of early morning to refresh him. Nothing that he could see had an unwanted accent, nothing stirred. It would be another hot day. His eye followed the lines of perspective that had so long fascinated him. He had mentioned to Tom that those lines pleased him, and had been told that in art theory the place where they would come together was called the Vanishing Point. This seemed a beautiful concept to Ahmed, articulating a kind of ideal. He thought of his grandmother, his parents, Baba and Eliana, and imagined going there. He wondered what was on the other side.

[Final draft finished on the 7 August 2021, at the Monte dos Outeiros, San Miguel de Machede, Portugal]

Translations

Page 33

'*as-salam ealaykum*' and '*ealaykum as-salam*' – traditional greetings in Arabic meaning 'peace be upon you'.

Page 80

Leonid's speech

Penitential Verses was written by Alfred Schnittke for the 1000th anniversary of the Baptism of Rus, completed in 1987, and first performed by the Ministry's State Chamber Choir under Valery Polyansky in 1988. The texts of the Penitential Verses were taken by the composer from the eighth volume of *The Monuments of Ancient Rus*, edited by D.S. Likhachev, published in 1986. This edition contains the eleven Penitential verses, set to music by Schnittke. In 1986 Schnittke suffered a heart attack. Feeling the nearness of death, he turned to penitential poetry as a source of text for his final choral work. It was preceded by the following works for a cappella choir, also written in collaboration with V. Polansky: *Three Spiritual Choirs* (1984) and the *Concerto for Choir to a Text by Grigor Narekatsi* (1985). The composition of the Penitential Verses is structured in such a way that the eleven 'poems' are followed by a concluding twelfth number, written without words. The composition rushes through this afterword, into silence.

Page 234

Leonid's reply to Judith

'Yes. We could go outside?'